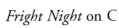 *Fright Night* on C

Fright Night
on Channel 9

*Saturday Night Horror Films on
New York's WOR-TV, 1973–1987*

JAMES ARENA

McFarland & Company, Inc., Publishers

Jefferson, North Carolina, and London

LIBRARY OF CONGRESS ONLINE CATALOG DATA

Arena, James, 1960–
    Fright night on channel 9 : Saturday night horror films on
New York's WOR-TV, 1973–1987 / James Arena.
        p.   cm.
    Includes bibliographical references and index.

    ISBN 978-0-7864-6678-8
    softcover : acid free paper ∞

    1. WOR-TV (Television station : New York, N.Y.)   2. Fright
night (Television program)   3. Television broadcasting of
horror films — New York (State) — New York.   I. Title.

                                            2011048665

BRITISH LIBRARY CATALOGUING DATA ARE AVAILABLE

Cover images © 2012 Shutterstock

Manufactured in the United States of America

McFarland & Company, Inc., Publishers
  Box 611, Jefferson, North Carolina 28640
  www.mcfarlandpub.com

*To my mother and my late father who have blessed
me with their unconditional love and support
every day of my life and without whom
this work would not be possible.*

Table of Contents

Acknowledgments

A very special thank you to cult film legend Sam Sherman for the incredible movie legacy he has given us all, his generosity and his friendship.

Thanks to Rob Craig for his invaluable assistance and constant encouragement with this project.

My deepest gratitude to Larry Casey for sharing his memories of Channel 9 so pleasantly with me, and to all the staff of WOR-TV during those glory days of horror for their unknowing contributions to the wonderful youth so many New Yorkers and I enjoyed.

Lastly, my sincerest posthumous respects and appreciation to Chris Steinbrunner, whose entertainment vision and love for mystery and horror films kept a generation of genre fans in front of the tube and on the edge of their seats.

Preface

"Now, from the world of the gruesome and grotesque, comes your most horrifying meeting with nerve-chilling fear! It's an unbelievably terrifying experience ... but you must see all this for yourself ... if you are brave enough!" So claimed the theatrical trailer for *Beast of Blood* (1970), a drive-in movie smash for Hemisphere Pictures that was eventually broadcast on an independent New York television station called WOR-TV, Channel 9 on the old TV dial. But the trailer might very well have been referring to the Channel 9 program which would feature the film upon its eventual syndication: *Fright Night*. An ultra-modestly produced movie showcase relegated to the late hours of Saturday nights from 1973 to 1987, *Fright Night* was a genre fan's nightmare come true. Dinosaurs, ghosts, madmen, monsters, murderers, vampires, were-wolves, zombies and creatures of all shapes and sizes paraded across the tube for, incredibly, nearly 14 years, influencing and entertaining an entire generation of tri-state kids and adults ... provided you were dedicated enough to stay awake for it (and sometimes *through* it).

WOR-TV / 1440 BROADWAY / NEW YORK, NY 10018 / (212) 764-7000

WOR-TV stationery logo from the mid '70s.

There was no crazy, memorable horror host for *Fright Night*, as had been popular in the past with this type of program, save for the efforts of an off-screen announcer occasionally offering a creative vocal introduction to the movie. The program usually featured just a brief video bumper at the beginning of each installment to herald in the *Fright Night* name ... and sometimes not even that. This was a no-frills station with no budget for extras. But what money WOR had, they spent on film packages whose variety and levels of quality were staggering. From classic horrors from cinema's early days — to incredibly lowbrow and low-budget grinders — to foreign chillers with a flair for shock — to the most modern blood-letters of the day, *Fright Night* delivered them all. The intentions of Channel 9's programmers may simply have been to make money without incurring any grand expenses, but the results of their efforts with this rather innocuous Saturday late night program, especially when broadly viewed in retrospect today, were stupendous.

The show was, albeit quietly in its remote weekend time slot, a living, breathing incarnation of every horror movie magazine, every gruesome comic book and every sleazy thriller paperback that every graced the shelves of newsstands in the '70s and '80s. It was just as fun and exciting as every trip I ever took to a movie theater in town to catch the latest scare flick that had come out, and brought the big screen right into my den. And it was loyal ... *Fright Night* was faithfully broadcast with just a few interruptions for an unheard-of length of time.

This book tells the story of the *Fright Night* and all that encompassed the experience of watching this program. It's the result of countless hours of sifting through old TV guides researching what films were shown, speaking with those who worked for and with Channel 9 during these glory days, and referencing a stream of notes I personally made while watching the movies during the '70s and '80s. The *Fright Night* experience encompasses the reaction and enjoyment of its viewers as well as the motivations and inspirations of its creators and programmers, suppliers and announcers. Interviews were conducted with former WOR-TV announcer Jesse Elin Brown via email in September 2010 and with author Rob Craig in February 2011. Telephone interviews were conducted with Channel 9 programmer Lawrence P. Casey and film producer Samuel M. Sherman during September 2010 and February 2011.

This book also attempts to encompass the experience of actually watching the extraordinary selection of horror, sci-fi, mystery and fantasy movies which *Fright Night* (and its program cousins) uniquely showcased. It is, quite simply, a humble homage to a horror movie show whose merits have gone largely unsung. It's a personal tribute to a television program that never suffered from illusions of grandeur or made claims to be anything more than it was ... just great entertainment on a Saturday night.

Part One: The Story of *Fright Night*

1. The Awakening

My connection to *Fright Night* was a logical and inevitable one and you've certainly heard it all before. I was a kid growing up in the 1970s, attending a highly ... shall we say ... sobering ... Long Island Catholic grammar school. If you were a Catholic school survivor, you likely know what that means. And to make matters worse, I was a bit of a physical runt. As such, I was an easy target and, like other geeks, I lacked great social or sports skills to get myself off that damn freak radar everyone seem to have. I felt very much like an underdog. Any psychologist would probably say these were all factors that made me gravitate towards monsters and madmen, like so many other youngsters across the country suffering the tortures of adolescence. Me, and a million other kids like me, had a bond with monsters. Maybe it was identification with these creatures' inability to fit in with mainstream society or maybe it was their way of "handling" difficult people that we admired so much. Whatever it was, I knew I was intrigued by them ... and I liked them ... a lot!

For me, it started years before *Fright Night* came on the scene with a curious attraction to horror-themed Bugs Bunny cartoons and chance partial viewings of Universal monster movies when I was still in my single digits. There was that painful phase where such things caused nightmares, but I kept coming back for more. Then, as I got a little older, they didn't scare me quite so much. Eventually, fear and entertainment merged and both a taste and hunger for the stuff began to grow. It became a refuge from the annoying realities of adolescent life. Soon to follow was the purchase of my first issue of Warren Publishing's *Famous Monsters of Filmland* magazine, Gothic Castle's infamous *Castle of Frankenstein* magazine and comic books like Eerie Publications' demented *Tales from the Tomb* and *Tales of Voodoo*. And playing with toys like Colorforms' *Monster Putty* and games like Mattel's *Bats in Your Belfry*, Milton Bradley's *Monster Old Maid*, and the *Green Ghost* game from Transogram. Not to mention repeatedly putting together Aurora plastic model kits of the classic Universal monsters and staring at the awesome box artwork. I began to learn what television stations had monster movie shows and started watching them nervously the whole way through. Television was the cement that solidified my passion for horror and the path I was on eventually led me to WOR-TV, Channel 9 ... and *Fright Night*.

There were quite a few horror movie programs being televised during the early '70s in the New York broadcast area. Probably one of the best known was the WPIX-TV (Channel 11) prime time Saturday night telecast *Chiller Theater*, which was introduced early on by a montage of '40s and '50s movie monster clips and later (and most famously) by a Claymation six-fingered hand emerging from a bloody creek and laying out the letters C-H-I-L-L-E-R. The brilliant creator of this legendary bumper still remains unknown. *Chiller* favored a library of American International monster movies like *I Was a Teenage Werewolf* (1957) and *Blood of Dracula* (1957) and a few Euro-thrillers like *Horrible Dr. Hichcock* (1962). Probably the scariest film they ever showed was *The Lodger* (1944), a blood-curdling embellishment of the Jack the Ripper story starring a brilliantly terrifying Laird Cregar. Arguably, *Chiller* and its six-fingered hand remains today the most readily identifiable of the horror movie shows broadcast during this era.

WNEW-TV (Channel 5) offered *Creature Feature*, which had begun in 1969 and was often competing with *Chiller*. This show gave young monster lovers of the era their first exposure to horror movies, showing a wider range of horror flicks that, for a time, included the Universal classics. Later, the program became a frequent showcase for B-pictures like *Horror Hotel* (1960) and *Attack of the Crab Monsters* (1957). The local CBS affiliate had its *Saturday Shocker* that featured a traditional mix of sci-fi and monster movies, from *The War of the Worlds* (1953) to *The Navy vs. the Night Monsters* (1966). For a short time, there was even a local Long Island station that joined the party, WSNL-TV (Channel 67), accessible only if you had a good antenna on your roof or lived nearby as I did. They had a neat little horror flick show called *Shock Theater* ("See it with someone you trust!") at 2 P.M. on Saturdays. The show didn't last long (and neither did the station) but they managed to feature a fairly wide range of scare flicks in their short time on the air. *Jesse James Meets Frankenstein's Daughter* (1966), Mexican "Santo" movies (like *Invasion of the Zombies* [1962]), *Vampire People* (1971) and *Inn of the Frightened People* (1971) from Hemisphere Pictures' import collection, German crime thrillers such as *Carpet of Horror* (1962), and oddities like *The Devil of Paris* (1962) were among their more memorable offerings.

The movies on all these stations were wonderful, but I felt a special kinship and connection with Channel 9. Like me, WOR had a long history of being a bit of an underdog. It was the last of three independent television stations to enter the newly emerging New York broadcast market in 1949 under the ownership of Bamberger Broadcasting. The company sold the New York station and its affiliates in Boston, Memphis, Los Angeles and San Francisco in 1952 to General Tire and Rubber Company. General Tire acquired RKO Radio Pictures a few years later and merged its film and broadcasting divisions under the name RKO General.

Throughout the '60s and '70s, Channel 9 was something of a last choice source for TV entertainment with low-budget local programming like *Bowling for Dollars* and the children's favorite *Romper Room*, old syndicated sitcoms like *The Lucy Show* among others, and even a retro talk show that became something of a New York legend, *The Joe Franklin Show*. But most important to Channel 9's programming were its film shows. The station showed every type of movie imaginable, from Astaire & Rogers classics to dusty John Wayne western spectacles as the core of their programming for many years and they were essential moneymakers for this runt of a station. It was widely considered the lowest, smallest, and least important of the New York stations. Competing against the programming found on the big networks and the better-financed indies was tough. Channel 9 had been seeking revenue from movie programming as the cornerstone of the station's appeal somewhat successfully since the late '50s and '60s.

According to author Rob Craig, entertainer and voice-over artist Claude Kirchner, who gained national fame via his 1954 ABC program Super Circus, moved to New York City in 1956, and headed up several popular children's programs on Channel 9. "*Terrytoons Circus* [1956–1962] and *Merrytoons Circus* [1962–1963] both used a circus motif—likely due to Kirchner's reputation on *Super Circus*—as a backdrop to host old theatrical cartoons," says Craig. "Dressed as a circus ringmaster, Kirchner would introduce the cartoons, give live commercial promotions of products such as Cocoa Marsh chocolate milk mix, and exchange comic banter with his assistant, a wisecracking hand puppet dubbed Clownie. This same format was then applied to Kirchner's longest-running program, *Super Adventure Theater* [1957–1969] where, instead of introducing cartoons, Kirchner and Clownie would offer genre films, primarily of the science fiction, horror and thriller variety, but with the occasional Laurel & Hardy or Three Stooges comedy feature thrown in." Popular films shown numerous times included *Godzilla, King of the Monsters!* (1956), *Rodan, the Flying Monster* (1957) and *The Incredible Shrinking Man* (1957). Craig recalls, "One memorable broadcast in 1965 featured the screening of Monster from Green Hell [1957], with Kirchner rather conspicuously announcing the film as 'Monster from the Green Jungle'—presumably so as to not anger parents by using a blasphemous term on what was ostensibly a children's program." Craig remembers that *Super Adventure Theater* aired on both Saturday and Sunday mornings for almost a decade, and was undoubtedly Kirchner's most popular program. "No one who has seen the show can forget its memorable opening," says Craig, "wherein Clownie burst through the *Super Adventure Theater* logo, introducing the host thusly: 'And now, here's *Skinnybones!!!*'"

However, for young monster movie fans like me in the early '70s, blissfully unaware of what had come before, Channel 9 was just a spunky little station opening up a whole new world of horror with its movie shows. And it was done on the cheap, with bare bones pageantry and with no cash on hand for any hosts, which were now a thing of the past. Horror films were definitely a specialty of WOR. They showed up on nearly every movie program vehicle the station offered during this period, including its legendary *Million Dollar Movie, The Big Preview, Showcase 9, Sunday Night Showcase, Action Theater, The 4 O'Clock Movie,* and *Movie 9* to name a few And in the late '60s and early '70s there were even a few movie shows that specialized in horror such as *Supernatural Theater, Mystery Theater* and the cleverly titled *The Witching Hour.*

Fright Night was arguably its most famous program devoted to the horror genre. Discovering the show and watching it each week, often with a cassette tape recorder set up to preserve at least the audio, I became instantly, hopelessly captivated by it. With its incredibly diverse line-up of classic, rare and obscure horror movie gems, *Fright Night* became a reliable companion of sorts for me, a powerful escape and outlet, and an addiction that endured through my early teens and well into adulthood. It was, in fact, a ritual for me. My personal rite included placing a ceramic skull similar to the one in the show's introductory bumper (purchased on a family trip to Disney World) on top of the television set for every telecast. Yeah, I guess I *was* kind of weird.

The years went by and much of Channel 9's programming, including *Fright Night* save for some "rest" periods, remained virtually unchanged. In the late '80s, WOR-TV relocated its studios from its Broadway-Times Square digs to Secaucus, New Jersey, and endured a long series of FCC issues that forced RKO to put the station up for sale. Just a few months after MCA took control of Channel 9 in 1987 and it became WWOR-TV, the station's programming was completely revamped. Among the casualties was *Fright Night*, which ended a 14-year run on September 26, 1987.

It's been nearly a quarter of a century since the last *Fright Night* movie was telecast, but this amazing little program, its astonishing broadcast run, and its producers haven't been totally forgotten judging by the number of blogs and online discussion boards that still reminisce about the program. I myself have written small articles about the show for wonderful contemporary magazines like *Scary Monsters* and absolutely essential websites like dvddrivein.com, and as I continued to find out new facts and secrets about the program, it's been a dream (or nightmare) to give *Fright Night* the type of recognition and analysis that might be worthy of a book before the program faded from the memories of my generation and disappeared completely into oblivion. In order to accomplish this, I needed to hunt down some of the original folks who played key roles in the program's history. Fortunately, some of the major players from this era were still available to offer their recollections and feelings about WOR-TV and the *Fright Night* experience.

2. The Station That Kong Built

For any discussion of *Fright Night* to be truly complete, the participation of one of the show's creators and most loyal advocates, Lawrence P. Casey, would be essential. Casey still lives a train ride away from the Times Square location where WOR-TV once housed its operations and eagerly recalls how his career began and how the show came to be.

"I knew when I started high school I wanted to go into television," says Casey. He attended the RCA Studios School in New York, which, at the time, was the only place one could get a real education in television broadcasting. After graduating, Casey's first job was with Columbia Pictures on 5th Avenue in, where else, the mail room. "Then I got offered a job at Channel 9 as a summer replacement for a cameraman at Shea Stadium. From there I moved up to apprentice film editor at WOR, where I was the person who took the portions we cut from movies and put them back in." A two-year stint in the Army temporarily put things on hold.

However, Casey's enthusiasm and skill allowed him to climb the ladder when he returned to WOR. He was promoted to film editor, and then, after briefly leaving the station to work in public television, was given an offer to oversee management of Channel 9's film and program services. "My job was to produce the entire weekly schedule and select and procure movies," he says. "I would develop the program folder which consisted of promotional material sent to newspapers and other media outlets which would utilize the information." The material also included the all-important film descriptions, many of which appeared in countless TV guides and are used for some of the plot summaries featured in this book.

Casey is quick to recall the station's location and layout. "Our studios were located at 1481 Broadway, which was right in Times Square directly across from where the ball was dropped from the Allied Chemical Tower on New Year's Eve. We were really at the crossroads of the world. Up on the third floor we had offices which included the film editing department, the master control section, and some production rooms. The fourth floor held more offices and studios and, later on, my office when I was in charge of film programming. We had a main studio there, which was built for the news broadcasts, and behind that studio was the film library. We kept all the films we had under license at Channel 9 on the premises in that room. It was really quite a huge collection. It was very well air-conditioned, because in those days we were using vacuum tubes in much of the television broadcast equipment which would generate quite a bit of heat. You had to have very, very good air conditioning. I believe the film library was kept at 68 or 69 degrees at all times."

Casey says his work there was merely an extension of the station's previous history with film. "Back in those days," he says, "we were owned by RKO Television Broadcasting, a subsidiary of General Tire and Rubber. When General got into TV, they were very forward-thinking. They realized quickly they needed a strong supply of entertaining, affordable product for their stations to show. They were mostly independent stations, which means they had to generate most of their own programming. When RKO Pictures was on shaky ground around 1955, General Tire bought the movie company. They were really ahead of their time in that respect, decades ahead of Ted Turner, for example, who later bought MGM. General only had an interest in handling the movie studio for about a year or so before they shut it down. I believe they sold the studios to Desi Arnaz and they became Desilu, where *I Love Lucy* was filmed. What General really wanted was the vast movie library. Some 600 or so RKO pictures, all available for their television stations to show, including all the Saint and Falcon mystery movies, classic dramas and westerns and, of course the horror films. The stations were already showing whatever odd movies they could get their hands on, but once the RKO package was in place, movies became a focal point and out of that film acquisition the famous *Million Dollar Movie* really kicked off. In the horror movie area, the back catalog included the Val Lewton pictures and of course the three gorilla movies. *Million Dollar Movie* became a primary showcase for these films and a local television icon here in New York and Los Angeles."

Channel 9 is synonymous with the three RKO "gorilla" movies. Casey is proud of his efforts to pioneer the now legendary telecasts of *King Kong* (1933), *The Son of Kong* (1933) and *Mighty Joe Young* (1949) on the Thanksgiving holiday, essentially re-introducing a new audience to what was actually an old movie and holiday tradition. Those who grew up in the tri-state area during the '70s still, to this day, associate these films with the smell of turkey cooking, the cold gray November skies outside and family gatherings. But Casey believes previous generations with good memories may experience some *déjà vu* when it comes to this television tradition. "Channel 9 was truly the station that Kong built!" he says. "The germ of the *Kong* idea I had come from

WOR running a holiday special when I was a teenager called *Christmas with the Kongs*. It was *King Kong* and *The Son of Kong* as a double feature on Christmas Day. It wasn't until much later when I joined Channel 9 and met Chris Steinbrunner, a longtime film programmer at the station, when I found out that Chris was behind the scheduling of that great double-bill. I'm not one hundred percent sure it was entirely his idea, but he was with Channel 9 at the time and was definitely somehow involved in the mechanics of making it happen. I had mentioned it to him when I came to work at Channel 9 and he definitely confirmed he was involved in it. He may also have written the promotional copy for it as well."

"*King Kong* premiered in New York in the late '50s — shortly after General Tire bought the RKO library — and I believe it was first shown on Channel 9's *Million Dollar Movie*. It was shown up to three times a day and ran at least 16 times a week back in those days. The movie was telecast weekdays at 7:30 P.M. and 10 P.M. and three times a day on weekends. It was kind of the forerunner of cable television in some ways. You know ... lots of repeat telecasts

King Kong, star of the 1933 movie, makes his way from the jungle to WOR-TV. Fay Wray too!

in a short space of time. The CUMs [Cumulative Rating Share] back in those early days for the movie were over 100 percent. This meant the entire population of New Yorkers who were surveyed had watched at least one full telecast of Kong and at least a part of another. That was unheard-of! After that, I believe it was Chris who had the idea of showing *King Kong* on Christmas as a regular holiday movie special. I remembered those telecasts when I came on board at Channel 9, and when marketing came looking for some good, revenue-generating programming ideas for Thanksgiving ... something fancy ... it got me thinking."

Casey continues, "Thanksgiving Day was an import event in television because that's the day when advertisers opened up the strongbox, so to speak. The strongbox that contained what we referred to as the 'toy money.' That was all the cash budgeted by the big-shot companies and allocated by advertising agencies to represent their various toy and game manufacturer accounts, like Marx, Remco, Ideal and other big children's industry companies of the time. Every television station would be acting like a trained seal and would be jumping through hoops and snapping to get those dollars. Marketing wanted to know what I could deliver that would get a nice chunk of that cash. I said we could do *King Kong*, *The Son of Kong* and *Mighty Joe Young* as a triple feature and start the show at noon. It would run for six hours or whatever it came out to and that would be all the available commercial time they'd ever need to sell right there. When everyone was sitting around Thanksgiving Day eating turkey, going in and out of the kitchen and living room and watching TV, I was sure they'd tune in for *Kong* and we would get good numbers. They gave the green light to the idea and agreed to try it. The ratings were even better than I had anticipated and the broadcast really became an iconic event in the New York area. We got ratings through the roof with it. I don't know why they don't replicate that today. I am sure there'd still be a sizable audience for it.

"Broadcast of the gorilla movies was easily orchestrated back then as the films were, of course, among the many RKO Studios properties the station owned. Such ownership was really uncommon in the day," he adds. "Probably the only comparable deal I can recall was Channel 11's purchase of *March of the Wooden Soldiers* [1934] starring Laurel and Hardy. And they just had that one film." According to Casey, Los Angeles affiliate station KHJ followed suit and had similar success with the gorilla films. Channel 9 continued the tradition throughout the '80s, expanding the event to include the Friday after Thanksgiving when many people were still off from work and school, and largely devoting the afternoon to Japanese horror movies such as *King Kong vs. Godzilla* (1962), *Godzilla vs. the Sea Monster* (1966), and *King Kong Escapes* (1967).

3. The House of Steinbrunner

The *King Kong* Thanksgiving tradition is probably more memorable to the tri-state general public growing up in that era than *Fright Night*, but for many genre fans emerging in the '70s, the Saturday late night program encompassing so many years of horror movie telecasts is the experience for which Channel 9 will be most revered. *Fright Night* would begin under the watch of Chris Steinbrunner (1934–1993), a Fordham University graduate and Queens, New York, resident, and a longtime friend of Casey's. In addition to the *Kong* broadcasts, Steinbrunner had been responsible for creating many of Channel 9's earlier and lesser known horror movie programs that preceded *Fright Night*. He was an accomplished writer whose books *Cinema of the Fantastic* (with co-author Burt Goldblatt, 1974, Galahad Books) and *Films of Sherlock Holmes* (with co-author Norman Michaels, 1978, Citadel Press), among others, were early essential reading for genre fans. According to Casey, Steinbrunner had also produced the classic *Zacherle at Large* show in 1959 and the '60s. He passed away in 1993 at the relatively young age of 59 following a long illness.

Casey describes Chris Steinbrunner as "a wonderful man! He was a bit rotund in appearance and almost like a character out of one of the movies he loved so much. Chris was a great author and one of the heads of the Mystery Writers of America organization that was based in New York. As a very young man, he wrote several scripts, including a few for the famous radio program *The Shadow*. That was quite an accomplishment for a teenager. He managed to parley that scriptwriting success into a fulltime job at WOR Radio. WOR Radio was the flagship station of the Mutual Radio Network and a major broadcaster at the time. Chris spent his entire life working for one company ... WOR ... in a number of its forms including Channel 9 and most of its predecessors. I recall that his very favorite word was 'melodrama.' Horror, sci-fi, mysteries, serials ... it was all one word to him ... melodrama. Chris was a very friendly and gregarious man. You might say even a bit eccentric. And he was unquestionably a lot of fun to be around. And I can certainly tell you he earned every dime of his paycheck at Channel 9!"

The tradition of Saturday night horror movie telecasts goes way back at

Larry Casey (left) and Chris Steinbrunner at a WOR-TV Christmas party in 1977. The man above Steinbrunner's shoulder is Casey's boss George Snowden, vice-president of programming.

Channel 9. *Mystery Museum*, the brainchild of Steinbrunner and occasionally called *The Late Movie*, had been telecast on Saturday nights in the 11 or 11:30 P.M. time slot. Records show that the program appears to have begun in January of 1971, although it may have been around longer, and lasted through May of that year. Casey vaguely recalls the show's bumper: "The *Mystery Museum* introduction, as I remember it, was just a simple cauldron of bubbling dry ice. The title would just appear to materialize out of the dry ice fog. It had a nice, spooky feel to it." The still traceable lineup of movies that were shown set the stage for what was to come at Channel 9. The program initially focused on mystery thrillers and eventually moved into outright horror. Says Casey, "One of the reasons *Mystery Museum* was created, frankly, was to showcase all that mystery and horror stuff that was lying around in our film library."

MYSTERY MUSEUM
1971

01/22 *The Frozen Ghost* (1945) Lon Chaney, Jr.—a future *Fright Night* feature.

01/30 Looks like *Mystery Museum* was pre-empted for a telethon.

02/06 *Mystery of Edwin Drood* (1935) **Heather Angel**—A early Universal take on a Dickens mystery with Claude Rains giving a strong performance as a man who falls under suspicion of murder.

02/13 *Murders in the Rue Morgue* (1932) **Bela Lugosi**—a future *Fright Night* feature.

02/20 *The Mad Ghoul* (1943) **George Zucco**—a future *Fright Night* feature.

02/27 *The Curse of the Cat People* (1944) **Simone Simon**—a future *Fright Night* feature.

03/06 *Mystery of Marie Roget* (1942) **Maria Montez**—a future *Fright Night* feature.

03/13 *Pillow of Death* (1945) **Lon Chaney, Jr.**—a future *Fright Night* feature.

03/27 *Horror Chamber of Dr. Faustus* (1960—aka *Eyes Without a Face*) **Alida Valli**—a rarely televised horror drama starring Pierre Brasseur as a mad surgeon running amok, grafting the faces of female victims onto his disfigured daughter.

04/03 *Man Made Monster* (1941) **Lon Chaney, Jr.**—a future *Fright Night* feature.

04/10 *Slaughter of the Vampires* (1962—aka *Curse of the Blood Ghouls*) **Dieter Eppler.** Channel 9's description "The Earth is invaded by seemingly indestructible vampires as the human race begins a desperate struggle for survival" was more appropriate for a movie like *The Last Man on Earth*. This turned out to be a fun piece of Italian gothic horror that was actually about a vampire taking up residence in a newlywed couple's chateau. The film would migrate over to Channel 5's *Creature Feature* where it was a staple for years.

04/17 *She-Wolf of London* (1946) **June Lockhart**—a future *Fright Night* feature.

04/24 *House of Horrors* (1946) **Robert Lowery**—a future *Fright Night* feature. In its final installments the show began presenting double-features.

05/01 *The Mummy's Tomb* (1942)/*The Mummy's Ghost* (1944) **Lon Chaney, Jr.**—both were future *Fright Night* features

05/08 *The Ape Man* (1943)/*The Return of the Vampire* (1944) **Bela Lugosi**—these features would wander off to Channel 11's *Chiller Theater* and Channel 5's *Creature Feature* respectively

05/15 *Isle of the Dead* (1945)/*The Raven* (1935) **Boris Karloff**—both future *Fright Night* features.

Tales of Terror, sometimes referred to as *The Midnight Movie* in some television listings on some dates, replaced *Mystery Museum* and kept the focus firmly on traditional horror movies. Another Steinbrunner creation, it featured haunting music and a multitude of cobwebs and melting candles in its opening bumper. The show appears to have debuted on May 22, 1971, with the same *Mystery Museum* time slot and essentially grandfathered in *Fright Night* with a run that lasted until September 29, 1973. It featured an eclectic mix of oldies and newer films, and single and double features from a surprisingly diverse mix of major studio movie packages.

TALES OF TERROR
1971

05/22 *Dead Man's Eyes* (1944)—*Calling Dr. Death* (1943) Lon Chaney, Jr.—future *Fright Night* features.

05/29 *Abbott and Costello Meet Frankenstein* (1948) Lon Chaney, Jr.—*Captive Wild Woman* (1943) John Carradine—*Abbott & Costello Meet Frankenstein* would become a staple at Channel 11's *Sunday Morning Movie* and *Captive* would become a future *Fright Night* feature.

06/05 *Jungle Woman* (1944) Evelyn Ankers—*The Jungle Captive* (1945) Otto Kruger—future *Fright Night* features.

06/12 *Murders in the Rue Morgue* (1932)—*Mystery of Marie Roget* (1942)—future *Fright Night* features.

06/19 *House of Horrors* (1946) Robert Lowery—*Horror Island* (1941) Dick Foran—future *Fright Night* features.

06/26 *Pillow of Death* (1945) Lon Chaney, Jr.—*The Mad Ghoul* (1943) George Zucco—*Pillow* was another in the line of Universal Inner Sanctum films. *Ghoul* would become a future *Fright Night* feature.

07/03 *Tales of Terror* not shown, replaced by a telecast of the film *Mister Roberts* (1955), no doubt to celebrate the Fourth of July holiday.

07/10 *Cat People* (1942)—*The Curse of the Cat People* (1944) Simone Simon—a neat double feature and both future *Fright Night* features.

07/17 *Bedlam* (1946)—*The Lost Patrol* (1934) Boris Karloff—*Bedlam* would become a future *Fright Night* feature. *The Lost Patrol*, though not a horror film, was a solid RKO drama from director John Ford.

07/24 *Stranger on the Third Floor* (1940)—*Island of Doomed Men* (1940) Peter Lorre—a terrific night of Lorre mayhem with *Stranger* becoming a future *Fright Night* feature. *Island* was an adventure drama about a cruel tyrant running an island prison camp.

07/31 *Horror Castle* (1965 aka *Virgin of Nuremberg*) **Rossana Podesta**— This Christopher Lee chiller would become a staple over at Channel 5's *Creature Feature.*

08/07 *Slaughter of the Vampires* (1962)

08/14 Looks like *Tales of Terror* was pre-empted.

08/21 *My Son the Vampire* (1952—aka *Mother Riley Meets the Vampire*) **Arthur Lucan**—A durable charwoman (played by a male actor in drag) battles a mad scientist. An interesting Bela Lugosi comedy that would become a staple over at Channel 5's *Creature Feature.*

08/28 *Dead Man's Eyes* (1944)

09/04 *The Werewolf* (1956) **Joyce Holden**—a future *Fright Night* feature.

09/11 *Hangover Square* (1945) **Laird Cregar**—a future *Fright Night* feature.

09/18 *Tales of Terror* was not shown, replaced by a special showing of *Citizen Kane.*

09/25 *The Man Who Turned to Stone* (1957) **Victor Jory**—*Hidden Fear* (1957) **John Payne**—*Stone* would become a future *Fright Night* feature. *Hidden* was a somewhat routine mystery thriller.

10/02 *Strangler of Blackmore Castle* (1963) **Karin Dor**—A series of eerie murders are committed in an English castle by a strangler with only nine fingers. *I Love a Mystery* (1945) **Nina Foch**—Another odd pairing, this time combining a traditional murderer-in-a-mansion German crime thriller in the Edgar Wallace style with an old-fashioned, good-natured U.S. mystery based on a popular radio program.

10/09 *The Son of Dr. Jekyll* (1951) **Louis Hayward**—The title character continues his father's work and rediscovers the formula which turned Dad into the monstrous Mr. Hyde. *Creature with the Atom Brain* (1955) **Richard Denning**—Cool B-movie duo from Columbia Pictures, with *Creature* a future *Fright Night* feature.

10/16 *Invasion of the Body Snatchers* (1956) **Kevin McCarthy**—Southern California is invaded by giant seed pods capable of duplicating the human form. *Fog Island* (1945) **Lionel Atwill**—A strange group of people meet at an old mansion on Fog Island and a man seeks revenge for his wife's murder. *Invasion* would become a scare-fest synonymous with Channel 5's *Creature Feature*, and *Fog* was a rarely seen PRC quickie, pretty gruesome for its time.

10/23 *The Werewolf* (1956)

10/30 *The Undying Monster* (1942) **John Howard**—*The Leopard Man* (1943) **Dennis O'Keefe**—both high quality B-thrillers from Fox and RKO respectively.

11/06 *The Mad Magician* (1954) Vincent Price — *The Body Snatcher* (1945) Boris Karloff — both future *Fright Night* features.

11/13 *The Man Who Turned to Stone — Cry of the Werewolf* (1944) Nina Foch — *Stone* was a future *Fright Night* feature, while *Cry of the Werewolf* would migrate over to Channel 5's *Creature Feature*.

11/20 *The Thing from Another World* (1951) Kenneth Tobey — a future *Fright Night* feature.

11/27 *The Human Duplicators* (1965) George Nader — An alien agent is sent to Earth to establish a colony of human-like robots that will infiltrate key governmental and industrial positions. Really low-budget silliness, better suited for a Saturday morning.

12/04 *The Devil Commands* (1941) Boris Karloff — A mad doctor forces a household to aid him with a brain machine so he can communicate with his dead wife. *Isle of the Dead* (1945) — *Devil* would migrate over to Channel 5's *Creature Feature*; *Isle* would be a future *Fright Night* feature.

12/11 Return of the Vampire (1944) Bela Lugosi/So Dark the Night (1946) Stephen Geray — *Return* would migrate over to Channel 5's *Creature Feature*, *So Dark* was a dull mystery drama wherein an annoying detective investigates a disappearance in rural France.

12/18 *Island of Doomed Men* (1940)

12/25 *Return of Dr. Mabuse* (1961) Lex Barker — Mysterious murders lead a police commissioner to a penitentiary and a criminal mastermind. From German director Harald Reinl, who was responsible for one of *Fright Night*'s best features, *Torture Chamber of Dr. Sadism*.

1972

01/01 *Mystery of Marie Roget* (1942)

01/08 *Calling Dr. Death* (1943)

01/15 *She Wolf of London* (1946) — *I Wake Up Screaming* (1941) Victor Mature — The latter is a mystery drama told in flashback about a promoter who is accused of the murder of a beautiful model.

01/22 *Murders in the Rue Morgue* (1932) — *So Soon to Die* (1957) Richard Basehart — The latter film was an obscure and odd drama lifted from the *Playhouse 90* television series (1956–1961).

01/29 *Tales of Terror* bumped for a telethon.

02/05 *The Mummy's Ghost* (1944)

02/12 *Bride of Frankenstein* (1935) Elsa Lanchester — *Pillow of Death* (1945) — *Bride* was a future *Fright Night* feature.

02/19 *Tales of Terror* replaced by special movie showing of *A Star Is Born*.

02/26 ***Mummy's Hand*** **(1940)—*Man Made Monster*** **(1941)**— both future *Fright Night* features.

03/04 ***Son of Frankenstein*** **(1939) Basil Rathbone —*The Wolf Man*** **(1941) Claude Rains**— both future *Fright Night* features.

03/11 ***Frankenstein*** **(1931) Boris Karloff —*The Human Monster*** **(1940) Bela Lugosi**— both future *Fright Night* features. From March 18 through September 24, *Tales of Terror* went on a long hiatus in favor of other entertainment programming not generally in the horror genre. When the show returned on September 30, it took the traditional midnight time slot. One may have been able to safely conclude that the audience for horror was equal to or better than any other programming the station had been able to come up with.

09/30 ***The Werewolf*** **(1956)**

10/07 ***The Mummy's Ghost*** **(1944)**

10/14 ***The Mummy's Tomb*** **(1942)**

10/21 ***The Devil Commands*** **(1941)**

10/28 ***Phantom of the Rue Morgue*** **(1954)**— a future *Fright Night* feature.

11/04 Looks like *Tales of Terror* was pre-empted.

11/11 ***Bride of Frankenstein*** **(1935)**

11/18 ***The Beast from 20,000 Fathoms*** **(1953) Paula Raymond**— this film would migrate over to Channel 5's *Creature Feature*.

11/25 ***The Sniper*** **(1952) Arthur Franz**— A sniper with a high-powered rifle takes aim at beautiful young women as police attempt to unlock his psychological profile in this cold, hard-hitting, ahead-of-its-time thriller.

12/02 ***Five*** **(1951) William Phipps**— Five survivors of a nuclear holocaust struggle with their hostile environment and the brutality of raw human emotion in a film that is both a thought-provoking drama and an absorbing sci-fi thriller. This film would migrate over to Channel 11's *Chiller*.

12/09 Looks like *Tales of Terror* was pre-empted.

12/16 ***Philo Vance Returns*** **(1947) William Wright**— A playboy's beautiful young fiancée is murdered and he enlists the help of detective Philo Vance to investigate shortly before his own death. Yawn ... just a routine murder mystery.

12/23 ***Night Monster*** **(1942) Bela Lugosi**— a future *Fright Night* feature.

12/30 ***The Undying Monster*** **(1942)**

1973

01/05 ***The Human Duplicators*** **(1965)**

01/13 ***Dr. Satan's Robot*** **(1966) Eduardo Ciannelli**— This was the Republic serial *Mysterious Doctor Satan* from 1940, edited down into a feature-length movie for television distribution.

01/20 ***Invasion of the Animal People*** **(1959) John Carradine**— a future *Fright Night* feature.

01/27 Looks like *Tales of Terror* was pre-empted for a telethon.

02/03 ***Serpent Island*** **(1954) Sonny Tufts**— A decidedly rock-bottom budget kept thrills to a bare minimum as a woman enlists the help of a down-on-his-luck seaman to help her retrieve a treasure of gold guarded by a voodoo cult somewhere on a remote island. It looked like an old home movie.

02/10 ***House of the Black Death*** **(1965) John Carradine**— a future *Fright Night* feature

02/17 ***To the Ends of the Earth*** **(1948) Dick Powell**— There must have been slim pickings for Channel 9 to have selected this lackluster film about drug smugglers in Shanghai as a *Tales of Terror* feature.

02/24 ***The Crawling Hand*** **(1963) Peter Breck**— An astronaut's hand, severed in a mysterious outer space explosion, falls to Earth and carries on a deadly rampage of murder. Nasty but fun horror movie with an attractively sleazy edge.

03/03 ***Untamed Women*** **(1952) Mikel Conrad**— a future *Fright Night* feature.

03/10 ***The Raven*** **(1935)**— a future *Fright Night* feature.

03/17 Looks like *Tales of Terror* was pre-empted for a telethon.

03/24 ***The Werewolf*** **(1956)**

03/31 ***Captain Mephisto and the Transformation Machine*** **(1966) Roy Barcroft**— Another '40s adventure serial, *Manhunt of Mystery Island,* cut into a feature-length film.

04/07 ***House of Dracula*** **(1945) Onslow Stevens**— a future *Fright Night* feature.

04/14 ***Spy Strikes Silently*** **(1966) Lang Jeffries**— a future *Fright Night* feature.

04/21 ***Phantom Lady*** **(1944) Ella Raines**— A man is accused of murdering his wife because his only alibi, a girl he met in the night, seems to have disappeared like a phantom. An engaging noir-ish mystery from Universal.

04/28 ***Who Killed Teddy Bear?*** **(1965) Sal Mineo**— Living alone in New York, a young discotheque hostess becomes the victim of a telephone psychotic. A real down and dirty "adults only" feature for its time.

05/05 ***Son of Frankenstein*** **(1939)**

05/12 ***Creature from the Black Lagoon*** **(1954) Richard Carlson**— An expedition to the Amazon discovers an aquatic creature with man-like features.

Universal's last great monster, and an exemplary piece of '50s sci-fi moviemaking.

05/19 Looks like *Tales of Terror* was pre-empted.

05/26 ***Phantom of the Rue Morgue*** (1954) — a future *Fright Night* feature.

06/02 ***The Killers*** (1946) **Burt Lancaster** — A boxer is pulled into a payroll robbery and then finds himself hounded by his former partners in crime. Interesting film noir, but a real stretch as a feature for *Tales of Terror*.

06/09 Looks like *Tales of Terror* was pre-empted.

06/16 Looks like *Tales of Terror* was pre-empted.

06/23 ***Strangler of Blackmore Castle*** (1963)

06/30 ***Sherlock Holmes and the Deadly Necklace*** (1962) **Christopher Lee** — The master detective Sherlock Holmes and his assistant Dr. Watson are called in to solve the theft of an Egyptian necklace in a rather atmospheric but flat thriller that was miserably dubbed. A German import directed by the legendary Terence Fisher.

07/07 ***Mystery of Marie Roget*** (1942)

07/14 ***The Black Cat*** (1941) **Basil Rathbone** — A woman's devotion to cats leads to her murder as greedy heirs gather in her brooding mansion waiting to collect their inheritances. A unique telecast for Channel 9: In an apparent attempt to avoid confusion with the 1934 Universal film *The Black Cat*, someone oddly decided to alter the name of this picture and have the word "Murders" superimposed underneath the title on this telecast. (Steinbrunner would be both a logical and illogical candidate, as he was reportedly a stickler for details and film purist but also was the man in charge.)

07/21 ***I've Lived Before*** (1956) **Jock Mahoney** — a future *Fright Night* feature.

07/28 ***The Invisible Man*** (1933) **Claude Rains** — a future *Fright Night* feature.

08/04 ***Dead Eyes of London*** (1964) **Joachim Fuchsberger** — A German version of the Edgar Wallace story previously filmed as *The Dark Eyes of London* (aka *Human Monster*) and a terrifically spooky and fun chiller.

08/11 ***Serpent Island*** (1954)

08/18 ***Who Killed Teddy Bear?*** (1965)

08/25 ***Ring of Terror*** (1963) **George Mather** — a future *Fright Night* feature.

09/01 ***Bedlam*** (1946)

09/08 ***Man Beast*** (1956) **Rock Madison** — a future *Fright Night* feature.

09/15 ***Cult of the Cobra*** (1955) **Faith Domergue** — a future *Fright Night* feature.

09/22 ***Untamed Women*** (1952) — a future *Fright Night* feature. The showcase was listed in TV guides as *Midnight Movie*.

09/29 *The Vampire Bat* (1933) **Fay Wray**—a future *Fright Night* feature. When Steinbrunner moved up the corporate ladder, Casey eventually began to take over movie duties at Channel 9. At the same time, station executives were looking at their Saturday night programming and brainstorming ways to revitalize it. *Tales of Terror* had been running for nearly two and a half years and it was time for a change, but nobody wanted to rock the boat too much.

4. It's Alive!

Saturday, October 6, 1973, was a rather ordinary day as far as horror on television was concerned. At 9:30 A.M., Channel 9's *Thriller Theatre* program presented *The Son of Dr. Jekyll*, Channel 5 showed *Frankenstein 1970* (1958) starring Boris Karloff on *Creature Feature Too* at noon, *Chiller Theatre* on Channel 11 served up *Night Tide* (1963) with Dennis Hopper at 8 P.M., Channel 9 ran an episode of *Thriller* (aka *Boris Karloff Presents*) at 11 P.M. and on *The 11:30 Movie*, Channel 5 offered viewers *Horror of Frankenstein* (1971) with Ralph Bates. In prime time, *The Partridge Family* was chirping on ABC, Lou Grant confessed to the newsroom he was having marital problems on CBS' *The Mary Tyler Moore Show*, and the *NBC Saturday Night Movie* was *Support Your Local Sheriff* (1969) with James Garner. All quite normal, all quite routine … until the clock struck midnight. At that moment, *Fright Night* debuted with the film *Decoy for Terror* (1970) and history was made.

Casey says *Fright Night*'s origins were based on the success of a show with the same name at the KHJ Los Angeles affiliate station, although some sources disagree about which station actually first launched the program. "We were looking for a new name and horror movie program to replace *Tales of Terror* and saw the success *Fright Night* was enjoying at KHJ, so we decided to try it here in New York," Casey says. "I think it may have been the station's general manager, Bob Williamson, who originally suggested it."

While the *Fright Night* program title may have originated over at KHJ, Casey says the Channel 9–produced bumper to introduce the program was completely original. It consisted of a series of color-tinted stills, mostly familiar publicity portraits of well-known monsters along with Kong, Dracula, the Wolf Man, the Bride of Frankenstein, and a few other creatures quickly fading in and out as chilling music builds to a crescendo. The final portrait of Glenn Strange as the Frankenstein Monster dissolves into a ceramic skull. Flowing from the eye sockets of the skull is a stream of dry ice wisps from which the words FRIGHT NIGHT appear in one socket. It was fast-moving, energetic and mood-setting. "We wanted to come up with something that gave the show a real personality," says Casey.

He adds, "I have to give the credit to our art director at the time, Jerry Miller, for coming up with that introduction. He did a brilliant job. He had promotional materials and stills from almost everything the station had produced since it went on the air in 1949. I had always said to him, 'Save that stuff! You never know when we'll need it,' and it came in handy for *Fright Night*. I also recall we purchased some additional stills from a local memorabilia store. Jerry Miller did everything — all the movie openings and closes from that time. Standby slides, bumper slides, all of it. We had worked together on the opening to *Million Dollar Movie* that a lot of people still remember, traveling all over New York to get those shots that comprise its well-known city sights montage with the score from *Gone with the Wind*." For those wondering about the history behind the skull used in the *Fright Night* bumper, Casey recalls that it was ceramic and purchased by Miller from a nearby junk store in the Times Square area at the time. He suspects that iconic piece of memorabilia was later tossed in the trash when Channel 9 relocated to New Jersey.

The *Fright Night* monster parade bumper was used until about 1985 when Channel 9 revamped most of its station graphics and began using more sophisticated video technology. For *Fright Night*, Miller's classic monster lineup was replaced with a side view of a nighttime movie theater marquee as a thunderstorm rumbles in the background. The letters spelling out F-R-I-G-H-T N-I-G-H-T make their appearance accompanied by ominous-sounding piano chords. The feel was slower and decidedly ominous and sinister. Most of Channel 9's movie bumpers took on a downtown movie theater motif in keeping with the rise of multiplexes springing up everywhere.

The bumper set the eerie tone, but the movies made *Fright Night* the unique experience it was. "We were a small, independent station and we were heavily in the movie business. That was our bread and butter," says Casey. "We licensed these films for a predetermined period of time and number of runs. The movies shown on Channel 9 were always purchased in packages and many of the packages were purchased with *Fright Night* in mind."

WOR-TV Art Director Jerry Miller

5. *Dissecting* Fright Night

The core of the *Fright Night* experience could be found in its film package purchases, an eclectic mix of chillers and bizarre movies that defy easy classification. According to Casey, the movies themselves were mostly 16mm, although 35mm was used in the early days for better quality. "The movies were edited to format by film editors who added leader to mark where the commercial breaks were," he says. "The leader was a clock that counted down from :08 and went to black at :02. There were metal foil 'stops' placed on the leader which caused the projector to stop during the commercial breaks. When things got messed up, you saw the clock on the air. The video tape commercials were run from the Tape Room next door to projection."

"Film package discussions with studios were usually handled in a very informal manner," says Casey. "All the big major and independent studios and distribution companies had shows or movies to pitch and had salesmen who were familiar with the people who purchased programming at the various stations. They'd check in and, for example, ask me if I was looking for any horror films and would pitch me whatever new stuff they were offering. Sometimes a salesman might get in touch with me and tell me he was going to be screening a bunch of movies his company might be considering for distribution. He'd invite me to watch them with him and if I was interested in any, they'd work out a deal with me. But they also sometimes put out a formal print package and they'd send out this promotional material to all the stations giving the details about the movies being offered. The *Fright Night* program certainly gave us a vehicle for getting our money's worth out of these movie packages."

Part of the typical contract was an exclusivity clause, ensuring Channel 9 was the only station in the area showing the films. Says Casey, "A color, contemporary theatrical film that was seen on *Fright Night* may have cost the station about $10,000. Many movie packages were a real mixed bag and may have consisted of maybe seven pictures, of which only two were really good films. An example might be a package from Avco-Embassy. It was a small company owned by Joseph E. Levine and I would buy a picture here and there from them. They had horror films like *A Bell from Hell* [1973] in some of the movie packages I purchased. But no matter what movie was shown, I can tell you, we never lost a dime on *Fright Night*. In fact, the program was a big help to us in making the most of these packages and some of the lesser films they contained.

"We had a tremendous amount of material purchased from Universal Pictures on a long-term deal way before I ever had the responsibility of film programming and acquiring product. The Universal deal had been in place for quite a while and I believe at that time, the Universal package was called simply 'Horror Greats.' Universal was a very professional studio to deal with. But in the time I was there, believe it or not, I don't think we bought anything more from Universal ... we just had so much on hand already. The average deal on those films was about seven years as I recall ... and that was a long time. But the Universal horror package was actually quite problematic for us. The biggest problem was one of logistics and physicality more than anything else. Their movies were all so damn short! At Channel 9 at the time, a film was basically slotted for about a two-hour film showcase. A two-hour slot in those days meant the movie was cut to about 95 minutes.

"Most of the Universal movies were far too short for that. The only two in the whole package that were long enough for a two-hour slot were *Son of Franken-stein* [1939] and *Phantom of the Opera* [1943]. Universal's B-films were always on the short side — generally between 59 and 65 minutes running time. *Dracula* [1931], *Frankenstein* [1931], and *Bride of Frankenstein* [1935] were all considered 'A' features, major Broadway pictures, not intended to be second billed on a double feature. But even so, they were only 72 or 75 minutes long. The Universal films were really a problem for Channel 9 to handle because of this, and also because they were all in black and white. Except for a handful like *Phantom of the Opera* and *The Climax* [1944]. Oh [laughs] ... and there was *Curucu, Beast of the Amazon* [1956]. That was a horror film all right! Just plain horrible!

"The great thing about *Fright Night* was it gave me a place to show those shorter features and not have the running time pressure we had in daytime and prime time. And, of course, they were perfect fodder for *Fright Night*. We also managed to fit a lot of them, including a few of the rarer Universal's like *Murder in the Blue Room* [1944] and *She-Wolf of London* [1946], into those one-hour open time slots we had before weekend New York Mets games. They were handy for that and gave the movie fans something before the air time was dominated by baseball."

As the years passed, color films became increasingly important to WOR. "I loved the old Universal movies, the RKO classics, and the Val Lewton pictures," Casey says, "but over time, Channel 9 didn't want to be known as just an 'old movie' station. Color televisions were becoming more and more common in households and the station became hyper-concerned about the films we were showing. So eventually a black and white film became a rarity on *Fright Night*. We needed to be more edgy."

"Edgy" is an understatement. *Fright Night* was a showcase for some of the most colorfully violent and bizarre horror and sci-fi films anyone could hope to see. Pictures like the gory, downright nasty *Night of the Sorcerers* (1973), the raunchy streetwalker exploitation thriller *Stone Cold Dead* (1979) and the perversely insane *The Baby* (1973) were just a few of the countless oddities that appeared on the show. Casey supervised the cutting of Channel 9's films, including those shown on *Fright Night*. "We tried to get away with as much as possible. We stretched the limits of what was permissible to show, and the late hour *Fright Night* was telecast gave us a bit more flexibility to do that.

"I always saw *Fright Night* as an escape. We showed films that gave people a chance to get away from reality. I did not feel any obligation to not run a picture or heavily cut a movie because of, for example, the Son of Sam killings or whatever else might be going on at the time. I tried to exercise good taste and sound judgment when scheduling films for *Fright Night* or any of our movie shows. I tried not show anything too disgusting or offensive. But really, when it came to *Fright Night*, you paid your money and you took your chance, so to speak. If you're going to stay up late to watch a horror movie, if it's got blood in it ... well ... excuse me! What do you expect to see ... a pie fight?

"There was a period right after I left Channel 9 and the people at the station were still calling me. I think it may have been my old boss at the station, George Snowden, who was faced with a problem when Channel 9 was offered the film *The Deer Hunter* [1978]. The suicide scene in the film was causing quite a commotion. They had called me to discuss their second thoughts about running it. They were afraid someone viewing the movie might try to imitate the Russian roulette scene. I was of the opinion that they've already bought the movie and scheduled it ... so what can you do? It's too important a scene to remove. If they cut it, they destroyed the integrity of the movie. If they didn't cut it and some poor guy went over the edge and killed himself after seeing it, they were screwed. One way or the other, they'd have been in trouble. But I never had that difficulty with current events and my film programming choices. *Fright Night* and some of the other shows were, no pun intended, truly the Inner Sanctum ... nothing affected them. And the people watching may have appreciated that."

So who exactly was watching *Fright Night*? Well, I sure was. Based on Internet blogs and horror movie message board feedback today, we can assume a large number of horror and sci-fi movie fans, insomniacs, night workers and assorted weirdoes were as well. The actual number was never established. "The problem was, back in that era, at that late hour, they weren't rating

Larry Casey with actor Andy Devine on the set of *The Joe Franklin Show.*

audiences," says Casey. "Especially after 1 A.M. It was sometimes referred to as 'hash and the dash.' *Fright Night* would have no rating and no share. But that wasn't indicative of how many were watching. The New York market was huge and in those days the ratings system was so flawed anyway. I think there was something like 500 FCC reporting diaries going out to cover the whole broadcast market to determine what people were watching. There could have been a million people viewing *Fright Night* and it wouldn't have shown up in the ratings because not one of them had one of those reporting diaries. Had one chosen oddball watched *Fright Night* and reported it, it would have been considered a monster hit instead of the sort of underground phenomenon that it ended up being."

If ratings for *Fright Night* weren't important, neither was competition from other stations. "We always were mindful of the competition, but never worried that someone might watch a horror movie on Channel 11 and, as a result, not watch ours. We weren't usually running head to head with other stations' horror movie programs that often anyway. Our station was considered *the* movie station in the New York market and we knew we usually had the best selection of films at any hour. And viewers knew it too. I would sometimes go into a bar and if the TV was on Channel 9, I'd listen to what the people were saying about what we were showing. I'd sometimes hear them say something about what a great station Channel 9 was for movies. I was like a one-man focus group and I was doing market research over a beer! I often got a lot of good feedback."

And advertising for *Fright Night*? Forget about it! "To be honest, *Fright Night* simply wasn't worth advertising from a business point of view. What ads we placed in *TV Guide* we usually reserved for bigger fish. The way it worked in *TV Guide* was as sort of a trade deal arrangement. We would run *TV Guide* commercials on Channel 9 and they would take our print ads. That's how it was with most television stations in the day. As you ran their commercials, you accrued points towards ads in their publications. It was kind of a screwy deal, but everyone did it because no station could sell every space they had in the course of a 24-hour day. It was almost like a ten-to-one deal. For something like every ten dollars of air time *TV Guide* received on Channel 9, we accrued a dollar's worth of print space. We usually reserved it for something really big like a first-run movie or major hockey or baseball game. We seldom advertised any of the movies in the time period we are talking about, and *Fright Night* was simply too low on the totem poll to merit the effort. I do recall one ad we took out for a prime time horror film at the time when we managed to get the uncut version of *King Kong*. We may have also advertised *Phantom of the Opera* when it was shown on *Million Dollar Movie*."

6. Sam Sherman
Invades Channel 9

The story of *Fright Night* would not be as interesting and intriguing as it is without the film contributions of Independent-International Pictures Corp., a bizarre mix of unusual horror movies by anyone's standards. The company was, and continues to be, presided over by Samuel M. Sherman. Born in 1940, Sam, a longtime horror movie fan, was a writer for many of the Warren publications (*Screen Thrills Illustrated, Famous Monsters of Filmland*) before serving in the publicity department of Hemisphere Pictures and starting his own small-scale film distribution efforts. With years of genre film marketing and distribution experience under his belt, he later formed the extremely successful production company Independent-International. Sherman was a notorious drive-in movie producer in the '60s and '70s, churning out an endless stream of campy horror, motorcycle, martial arts and other exploitation films, many with partner and director Al Adamson. Adamson had grown up in the film industry in Hollywood and was the son of silent film star Denver Dixon. When Sam began making his own films, Adamson's outrageous directorial style was the perfect compliment to his over-the-top subjects. The director's mysterious murder in 1995, just three years after his wife, actress Regina Carrol, passed away from cancer, focused a great deal of media attention on his life and career and solidified his status in the world of cult movies. Among his most infamous creations were the exploitation classics *Satan's Sadists* (1969), *Hell's Bloody Devils* (1970) as well as the horror extravaganzas *Dracula vs. Frankenstein* (1971) starring J. Carrol Naish and *Brain of Blood* (1971), which was shown on *Fright Night* under the title *The Creature's Revenge,* with Kent Taylor. It seemed absolutely inevitable that the paths of Sherman and Adamson would cross with *Fright Night*.

Sherman had enjoyed a long and close social relationship with Chris Steinbrunner and Larry Casey for years before they would meet to do business together. The three relished conversations about classic Universal pictures over lunch at a gothic motif restaurant in New York's Edison Hotel. Sherman's syndication efforts would bring them together once again, this time in a business deal that would add to *Fright Night*'s unique roster of horror films and create more than a few headaches for the producer.

"American International Pictures and Allied Artists handled the original television distribution of our films under a long-term deal," says Sherman. "Al and I were more theatrically oriented, so this arrangement worked well for us. We went along for a number of years quite comfortably in that relationship until AIP moved their television operations from New York to Los Angeles where people we didn't know were in charge. And then Allied Artists filed Chapter 11. In that process, we had to fight to get certain TV rights and original materials back ... which we did. But it was quite a bit of work!"

After the long, drawn-out process of reclaiming their catalog of product was behind him, Sherman realized they were now sitting once again on a large library of movies that could still be making money. Around this time, Larry Casey contacted Sherman. "Larry and Chris Steinbrunner and I were already enjoying a good friendship. We were mutual collectors and of course had a great love for the horror genre and for film in general. Larry came to me suggesting that Channel 9, actually the whole string of RKO stations, might be able to use some of my films. So I gathered up a lot of the pictures. I always kept a number of 16mm or 35mm prints in my office over at 165 West 46th Street and I invited them over and screened the movies for them. We'd look at part of this and part of that. I remember I threw on this German-American movie called *How Did a Nice Girl Like You ...* (1970) starring Barbi Benton, who was then best known as Hugh Heffner's girlfriend. It was a really awful picture and it made no sense at all. I put reel one on the projector, and there was this opening scene where Barbi stops on her way home at a big empty stadium and starts doing an act like she was a cheerleader. Her boyfriend comes along and picks her up on a motorcycle and she wiggles around to the front of it and faces him. It was, of course, implied sex. Chris was astounded! Well, actually *offended*, I guess. 'Why are you running this? We can't show anything like this at Channel 9!' he demanded. I apologized and said, 'I didn't really know what it was.' It kind of put a damper on the whole evening. Chris and Larry must have been thinking I was crazy because they knew that I knew they couldn't show anything like this on broadcast television. But at the same time, I'm thinking maybe I *can* do something with it. They're rejecting it and I am accepting it. I re-titled it *Naughty Cheerleaders* and it ended up doing great box office for Independent-International!

Sam continues, "I ran some other horror films for them that night, but it wasn't a really successful evening because I think they had hoped Channel 9 was going to find a treasure trove of movies they could use. But they did find a few. They made their choices and that became the package used by Channel 9 and actually the whole RKO chain."

During this period, Channel 9 wasn't the only New York station with an interest in Sam's film properties. Channel 11 gained a bit of publicity when they showed Sam's then brand-new and most infamous film, *Dracula vs. Frankenstein*, on their prime-time Saturday night *Chiller* program. "That deal came about as part of the deal with American International Television," says Sherman. "We were very friendly with Bill Cooper, who I believe was the program director over at Channel 11 at the time, and he was a very nice person to know. He suggested to my partner, Dan Kennis, that we should start a deal with American International Pictures because he was buying a lot of his movies from them. He was responsible for us getting together with American International, but it was strictly AIP who then sold the movies to Channel 11."

Left to right: John Bloom (The Monster), Sam Sherman, Zandor Vorkov (The Count) and Al Adamson on a break during the shooting of *Dracula vs. Frankenstein* (1971).

"We were on such an incredibly tight schedule in those days. We were still in the middle of distributing *Dracula vs. Frankenstein* to theaters. In those days, that was kind of unheard-of, although today the window of time between a theatrical run and television and home distribution is becoming much more narrow. So I had to rush to play the movie the week before Christmas and I believe it was to be shown on *Chiller* some time in February or March. I really pushed to get it played in theaters in New York because once it was played on television, it was almost impossible to get in theaters. Theater owners didn't want to play anything that people could see for free on TV." Other films in the package shown by Channel 11 included two horror films imported from Spain, the original theatrical co-feature to *Dracula vs. Frankenstein* called *Frankenstein's Bloody Terror* (1968) starring Paul Naschy and the obscure but atmospheric chiller *Graveyard of Horror* (1971) with Bill Curran.

Sam Sherman, despite the restrictions of the television and theatrical markets, was still looking to maximize returns on his film properties and always pushed the envelope. The producer kept his eye open for any theatrical opportunities on his other films that were about to be licensed to television. *Vampire Men of the Lost Planet* (1970), a *Fright Night* and Saturday morning favorite, was another such a movie. "It was a goofy, insane horror film," says Sherman. "It started off as a black and white Filipino movie and Al Adamson shot a framing story around it. It was pretty awful but very successful for us theatrically. I thought I could get more mileage out of this thing by getting it into theaters. But to do that, I had to change the title. So we released it in theaters as *Horror of the Blood Monsters* which was somewhere around the same time it was on television as *Vampire Men of the Lost Planet.*"

The television package seen on Channel 9 that contained *Vampire Men of the Lost Planet* turned out to be a potpourri of bizarre horror films from Sherman's archives. One of the films was *Night Fiend* (1973). "That picture came to us as what was called a 'tax shelter movie.' A lot of these foreign pictures like this came to us through arrangements with people from overseas we knew were licensing pictures to investment groups who got a credit write-off. Eventually films like *Night Fiend* and a number of others were either bought out by us or returned to their owners. This movie, which had a number of previous titles including *Violent Blood Bath*, didn't do well theatrically but I liked Fernando Rey and I thought it was a pretty good picture. *Night Fiend* was a great, alluring title for the late night hour *Fright Night* was broadcast."

Exorcism at Midnight (1966) was another in Sherman's film package that had a long and laborious history before it made it to the TV screen. Says Sherman, "There's an interesting story behind *Exorcism at Midnight*. That picture had come to me from my friend Richard Gordon. He had a black and white film that he was involved in producing called *Naked Evil* about a school for black students in England who became immersed in voodoo. The picture was actually quite good, but unfortunately black and white was 'out' so I wasn't able to do anything with it. So I turned it down at the time. A man named Bob Saxton had a film company I believe called Hampton International and he eventually took over Richard Gordon's films. For some reason, he tinted *Naked Evil* to make it sort of a color film, but without any real rationale, and it still had done nothing theatrically. Then Hampton International went bankrupt. Richard's brother Alex Gordon, who was somehow involved with Hampton at that point, then asked me to take over a number of these films from that company.

"Both Alex and Richard were very good friends of mine. And in our industry, relationships were very important — and Alex was stuck. We had money and we were doing well so we worked with our friends. We figured we'd find a way to make money off of these pictures from Bob Saxton. We played a number of these films theatrically, but we almost couldn't give them away. We were booking them for like $20 to $30 a date, just to play them off. As you can imagine, that's not a very lucrative business. The prints were run into the ground and were often badly scratched. What a mess. But I didn't care — I didn't like the films and, to be honest, I just didn't care about them. If I hated a picture, I just didn't want to be involved with it. So giving them away at $20 a pop ... well, it was either that or just keep paying storage on them."

Sherman adds, "Keep in mind, we were preparing the film package for all of the RKO stations, not just Channel 9. RKO was relying on Casey and Steinbrunner to buy a good package of horror films and we alleged in our contract that they were all color. *Naked Evil* was a good movie to include, but the only way we could add it to a color horror package was by shooting some real color footage. And tint some of the original black and white footage in a more meaningful way. So I handed the film over to Steve Jacobson, who was our editor and the man who handled post-production and the cuts that were made to our movies. I framed out a basic storyline, which takes place in a hospital where a doctor is looking at these black students and they have fallen under some kind of voodoo spells. I put actor Lawrence Tierney in it and arranged to have it shot at Roosevelt Island Hospital. I had no intention of being involved in this part of the production at all. Well, some time goes by and nothing got done. I asked Steve how he was progressing and he told me he was unsure of what I wanted. So I explained it again. It was only going to amount to twenty minutes of film — one day's shooting. And I set him out to do the shoot.

"I was with my partner, Dan Kennis, out in New Jersey and all of a sudden I get a psychic message in my brain that they are in trouble out there. I couldn't reach anyone on the phone and couldn't get anyone to call us. It's now noon. Even though the footage could be shot by a five-year-old child, I had this gut feeling something was going wrong. This feeling was so strong, I decided that I had to go out there myself and see what was going on. I drive out to Roosevelt Island and I get there by 1 P.M. Everyone, the actors and crew, was standing around and nothing was happening at all. Steve was going up and down the hallways, looking here, looking there, through his director's finder. Lawrence was very angry and spots me. He demanded to know why I hadn't been there, saying, 'I've been here since six in the morning and we haven't shot a single frame of anything. You knew what you wanted! You should have come out here and directed it yourself.'"

"Steve couldn't tell me what was wrong. I don't know why, but he froze for some unknown reason. Maybe battle fatigue or fear of something. He had already done a picture for us, so I knew he had the necessary experience. But for some reason he was just intimidated by this film. We were paying these

Actor Lawrence Tierney (left) with Sam Sherman on the Roosevelt Island Hospital "set" of *Exorcism at Midnight* (1966).

people and I had to get this done. He just kept saying he didn't know what I wanted. So I agreed to direct him and then he would direct everything else. From that point on, 'til almost 11 P.M., I told him what to do. Lawrence was under an SAG contract and he hit us up for overtime. I couldn't fight him on it. Later, we edited in the footage and did some optical work on the picture, and all in all the film didn't turn out bad. It was a crazy amount of work for just 20 minutes of additional footage, but it did make *Naked Evil* a color film that we were able to sell all over the country. Cashing in on *The Exorcist*, I changed the name to *Exorcism at Midnight*. It played on Channel 9, the USA Network, all over. Eventually, I sold my interest in the picture and got out from under it. But it received the most doctoring of anything in the RKO package."

Sherman's *Man with the Synthetic Brain* (1969) starring John Carradine and Tommy Kirk was the story of a half-human zombie, the brainchild of a mad doctor who is avenging the death of his son. The zombie is unleashed on Los Angeles and causes a reign of terror. This film also had a few secrets. According to Sam, "You'll notice that Regina Carrol says 'Arco' instead of the creature's real name Acro because Arco was the most popular gas station at the time and that must have been stuck in her head." He adds, "There's another scene where Acro or Arco is coming down a dark alley, and you can hear him grunting and gasping. He's coming down the alley ... and his grunting is giving himself away! That's me doing the gasping overdubs. It always seemed to me that monsters had asthma or bronchitis ... I don't know why, but whenever I did monster effects they always had problems breathing. Like when Lon Chaney, Jr., was in a scene in *Dracula vs. Frankenstein* ... again, that was me doing the heavy breathing."

Sherman also helped introduce *Fright Night* audiences to a name that would become synonymous with Euro-horror. "I made a contribution to *Fright Night* with a picture from the great actor Paul Naschy called *House of Doom* [1976]," says Sherman. "The picture was originally called *Blue Eyes of the Broken Doll*. It was quite well-made. I had been invited to a screening where several rival distributors were viewing it. That turned off a lot of distributors who did not want to be in such direct competition for films that way. I didn't care that much about all that, but I recognized this particular movie as a good picture and knew that I could make it successful. Other distributors may have had some interest in it, but I got a call from the producer and he asked me what I thought of it. I told him I would like to handle it and we made a deal. First thing I did was change the title to *House of Psychotic Women*, which I thought was a great name for it, and it did some very good business and we made some money off it. It was a chore to cut that one down for television because of all the sex and gore. We also had to do optical work to zoom in on scenes, which was another way of editing out adult material. Steve Jacobson did much of this post-production work, especially for the editing of the television versions. We re-titled the film for the TV package and *Fright Night* as *House of Doom,* but went back to *Psychotic Women* for the video release. I remember a great line from the movie in which someone asked Naschy what he thought of the three crazy sisters in the story. He responded, "Me? I like them all!"

"I discovered Naschy's existence when I was looking for a replacement picture for *Dracula vs. Frankenstein.* One of the Naschy films that came my way was *Assignment Terror,* which I believe was shown on *Fright Night.* The owners of the film wanted a ridiculous sum of money for it ... fifty thousand dollars for theatrical rights to it, even though it was due to be on TV in five or six months. I told them not only was I not going to pay that absurd price, but neither would anyone else. $50,000 for six months use of a bad picture? Nobody was going to take it. And ... the picture really stank! I offered them

Spain's legendary horror film star Paul Naschy made several appearances on *Fright Night.* He starred in *House of Doom* (above, with unidentified actress), *Horror Rises from the Tomb* and *Assignment Terror.*

$10,000 and not a penny more. Of course they refused and they ended up getting stuck with it and it just went right to television. We did, however, end up handling several pictures for Naschy and I did eventually meet him. I introduced him on stage at a *Fangoria* convention. I was the first to introduce him to U.S. movie audiences through the movie *Frankenstein's Bloody Terror*. I didn't have that much information on him at the time, but I always claimed he was the world's greatest horror star and, as it turned out, it all came true!"

Terror of Frankenstein (1977) was probably one of Sam's most sophisticated film properties to make it into the television package. "The film was made by a friend of mine, Calvin Floyd. He had originally made *In Search of Dracula* [1975] and was going to do the same type of film about Frankenstein. But we had decided documentaries weren't as popular or marketable, so he instead decided to make a new version of the Mary Shelley novel. It was originally titled *Victor Frankenstein* and it's been said to be the truest to the original book. When we screened it for the first time, I recall thinking it was a very good production and had a truly artistic quality about it. However, we only released it to television because, at the time, we just didn't feel there was strong enough interest in a period piece to give it a theatrical run. Later it was released on DVD, and the film has received very good notices over the years. But it was unfortunately never a very big picture for us."

Sam had another tax shelter picture on his hands with *Ghost Galleon* (1974), which later became *Ship of Zombies* (often listed in TV guides as *Ship of the Zombies*). "We released it theatrically as *Horror of the Zombies*. It was a typical tax shelter picture. The idea behind tax shelters was that instead of buying the picture outright, we would get the film for nothing from its European owners and we would have the responsibility of releasing the picture and reporting back any profits to the owners. The process involved non-recourse notes. These were notes that indicated the producers were owed several thousand dollars, but that they could only be paid from the proceeds of the film. If the film was distributed and it made money, a share was paid back to the owners. They were writing off these notes, which eventually became a practice that was outlawed. But for a while, there were a lot of pictures like *Ship of Zombies* floating around in that tax shelter mode. The arrangements prevented us from buying a lot of films, and it forced us to acquire movies from these investment groups. At the time, we ended up with some films that were difficult to market and generally did not make money. They were often very challenging to make a profit with. But there were exceptions. *House of Psychotic Women* was a tax shelter picture we actually did well with and made some money from. We also had a film in the '70s we called *The Boob Tube* [1975] which started off as a tax shelter film, but actually ended up being extremely successful for us. We had to pay a lot of money to the owners and they ended up making so much that they were unable to continue classifying the film as a tax shelter. The proceeds then became income from profit for them. It was a period I didn't like very much as I was dealing with people from the financial world rather than the film industry."

Demons of the Dead (1972) was one of Sherman's most interesting film contributions made to *Fright Night*. "I got hold of the film in yet another tax shelter arrangement, and it was a picture I liked very much. It was very well made by Sergio Martino, extremely stylish, and shot in England. I had released it theatrically as *They're Coming to Get You* and it did absolutely no business. We changed the name to *Demons of the Dead* and did some replacement work on the ending to make it seem like the events in the picture had actually happened, and then, of course, we cut most of the blood and sex. Years later the film's producer came to New York looking for some new horror film properties. I screened my film *Nurse Sheri* [1978] for him. He detested it. He called it cheap and boring. Ironically, *Nurse Sheri* ended up being a huge hit for my company and we couldn't give his supposedly better picture away. Yet he had no problem tearing my film apart."

Though the film bore release information credited to Sam Sherman's Independent-International Pictures when shown on Channel 9, *Creature with the Blue Hand* (1967), possibly one of the most entertaining horror films shown on *Fright Night*, was a German-made movie Sherman had imported. "Beverly Miller, a man heavily involved in the drive-in movie industry and who had a cameo role in *Beast of the Dead*, alerted me that Roger Corman needed a horror film to go with his forthcoming John Ashley feature *Beast of the Yellow Night* [1971], which he had imported from the Philippines," Sherman says. "I didn't care for the *Beast* picture; I didn't think it was very good. The movie's backers, called Four Associates I believe, were originally going to release it through Hemisphere Pictures and Kane Lynn, but that deal fell through and they negotiated another deal for it through Roger Corman. I think that the Corman camp knew it wasn't a great movie so they wanted it to be on a double bill. They were very enthusiastic about doing a deal with me for *Creature with the Blue Hand*, which I had just bought the U.S. theatrical rights to. But nothing happened and the deal just wasn't taking off. So eventually they told me Roger Corman would be in New York and I could meet with him at the Algonquin Hotel to discuss the project and finalize the deal personally.

"Corman had just married his wife Julie, a very pretty young girl. She had been a model and was quite attractive. I met with Corman and explained the deal about *Creature with the Blue Hand* to him. But Roger seemed to know nothing of this deal and I had to go through the entire negotiation

This publicity still from *Creature with the Blue Hand* (1967) depicts a scene that never takes place in the movie.

process all over again with him. It went well and afterward, he told me to meet him back at the hotel at 3 P.M. and he'd sign the contract. I quickly drew up the paperwork and got back to the hotel lobby, but ... no Roger. His wife Julie suddenly rushes over to me with tears in her eyes and is completely distraught. All at once, her arms were around me and she was hugging me. Crying, crying, crying! 'Oh Sam, where is Roger? He went out and hasn't come back!' Well, I'm thinking, 'Here I am trying to make a deal with Roger Corman, he's going to walk in and find me hugging his wife and she's crying!' I was in a panic! I was facing the door to the hotel and she was facing away from it. Just then, I saw Roger walk in the front door. I was thinking that in seconds this deal is going to be ruined and the movie will end up being called *Blood on Sherman's Floor*! I instantly spun her around 180 degrees so she would be facing the door and said, 'Julie ... there he is!' And I pushed her in his direction and she ran into his arms. Thank God! And Roger and I made the deal. And Julie went on to have several kids with Roger and she went on to be head of the NYU film school and a movie producer.

"Roger and I have always been friends since then. I signed over *Creature with the Blue Hand* to him for seven years theatrical and then gave the television rights to American International Pictures. When Channel 9 got it for *Fright Night*, it was from their dealings with AIP."

7. Enter the Devil

Sherman's film package story turned out to be far more dramatic than just picking some movies for Channel 9 to show on *Fright Night*. His adventures in syndication illustrated that the business was certainly not for the faint of heart. "There's an old expression which goes like 'No good deed should go unpunished.' If ever that expression was true, it's in the case of the ordeal behind Independent-International Pictures making 16mm prints for our television package to WOR. I don't remember the exact number of films ... it may have been 20 or 25. Most of them were horror and sci-fi films. Many were intended for *Fright Night* and other horror movie programs that WOR was producing. We had been using Movielab and some others processors because when you are working on getting these prints made, you can't rely on just one lab to get it all done. So we used a company called Precision as well. Then someone had recommended to me a full service lab called Triangle who could handle work like ours. Apparently they needed work desperately and we were glad to give them some. I remember I gave them at least two films, *Exorcism at Midnight* and *House of Doom* in their original forms. At that point I walked away from it. Steve Jacobson was in charge of our post-production unit and he handled it from there with his assistant Sam Kamporeale.

"It was very simple. We had to deliver the number of films stated in the contract. WOR wasn't going to pay us until they had full delivery of all the films in the contract. One day Steve came up to me and said we couldn't get anything back from Triangle. He told me all the other films were ready except for those two films. So I called a contact over there, a man named Joe, whom I had a good relationship with, and asked him what the problem was. I knew there was no problem with money because we had paid them. So I couldn't imagine what the hold-up could be. Well, my contact finally admitted the lab was going bankrupt. I said how sorry I was to hear it and suggested that he just pack our films up and we'd just bring them to another lab. His response was, 'I can't give them back to you because of the bankruptcy.' I was stunned. Why couldn't he? It was our material; they did no work and we owed them no money. And this was holding up payment for us on a major contract. To further complicate matters, the elements they were holding were not necessarily our property. The fine grain 35mm master of *Naked Evil* belonged to Richard Gordon. We couldn't lose that! He trusted us with the licensing of his film and expected to get it back.

"So I get on the phone with the attorney who is handling Triangle's bankruptcy. I immediately smell what this is ... this guy is a crook. He tells me that if I want my materials back, I will have to pay him a fee of $2000 per title. I said that's crazy ... what are we paying a fee for? It's our property, we want to pick it up and take it somewhere else. He says, 'Well, that's the way it is.' The guy was nothing more than a thief, a conman. He was trying to extort money from us. He said to me that if I didn't like it, when they filed full bankruptcy, I would be forced to make an application to the court and maybe ... maybe ... I'd get them back a few years later.

"We worked so hard to put this package together for Channel 9 and RKO, and of course nobody at the station knew any of this was going on. I didn't know what to do; I was just so upset and didn't know who to turn to. Al Adamson was on the other coast and he didn't have anything to really do with the day-to-day operations or television sales and I didn't want to bother him with it. I sat on the whole thing for a few days, pondering it. I called the attorney back, but he wouldn't budge. Then I made a decision. The only thing I could do was hijack our material. There was no other way to go. It was going to be tied up for years otherwise. So, as a fan of old westerns, I thought, well, sometimes people have to become vigilantes. I'm not advocating that choice, but sometimes a person is being harmed and he's up against a wall and there simply is no choice. I told Steve we needed some big strong guys and that we'd go over to the lab and we'd just say, 'Give us the stuff and we'll go.' And that's what we were gonna do! We weren't going to break into the building or anything, just go there and get what was rightfully ours.

"It turns out that the lab was closed almost all the time because of the bankruptcy. I got my Triangle contact's home phone number and asked Joe if there was ever a time that the lab was open. He said it was open for the attorneys on Tuesday at 1 P.M. I told him I was coming over there at that time with a bunch of big strong guys. I told him to put our negatives on a rack near the door and just point our way to them. We'll just take them out quietly. And I warned him not to let anybody get in our way. Pretty bold talk! But honestly, I didn't know if I could pull it off.

"Well, we looked and looked and couldn't find any big strong guys or great heroes or anyone to help us! Nobody would join us in this scheme. Steve Jacobson was extremely worried about the whole plan and the fact that we were going to go ahead with this potentially dangerous scheme. The only one who would come with me was my partner Dan, who was a gutsy guy, but older than I was. Steve and his assistant Sam then agreed to come with us but would stay along the perimeter of the building. We drove over there, knocked on the door, found it was unlocked and we walked in. We saw Joe and said, 'Where is our stuff!' Now remember he thought I was there with a big gang waiting outside. He pointed to where our stuff was, we grabbed it and as we attempted to open the back door to leave, a guy we thought was another Triangle employee or someone from the place tried to bar our way. Dan pushed the guy out of the way, we opened the door and Steve and Sam took the movies. They went off in one car and Dan and I went off in another.

"I didn't go back to my office, but I called in. My people said the police were calling, the Triangle attorney was calling, and that they were looking for me. Blah, blah, blah. I said, 'Hey, these people were holding my films in violation of federal law. I should call the FBI and let them know they were trying to extort money from us. We were only acting in our own best interests. We didn't hurt anybody and we didn't steal anything. We were just taking our own property back!' They told me that the attorney went crazy when he heard I did this. Apparently, the guy we pushed out of the way from the exit door turned out to be his father."

Sam pauses and laughs at the enormity of the situation. "I called my own attorney who handled the matter and he managed to get the police called off. I went back to my main office in East Brunswick, New Jersey, and Steve, by now, was back in our New York office with all the films. The Triangle attorney talked to my attorney and he said he would settle for nothing less than us bringing back those films to his office or pay the $2000 per title. I couldn't believe this was happening! Was I going to hire attorneys, go to court, wait six months or a year or more and then *maybe* I might get the films back? What the heck was I gonna do now?

"Well, I told Steve *exactly* what we were going to do! I told him to go to our film depot and find the absolute worst scratched-up print he could find for each of these titles. Then, he was to take the cans we took from the labs and take out the fine grain masters and put them in other cans and re-label them. Then he was to take those miserable prints that we were gonna junk anyway and put them on cores that we'd normally use for a negative or fine grain print. And then put them in the cans we got from the labs. He was to then pack them in the same box we had taken them away in. I told him to sit tight and wait for word from me. I called the Triangle attorney back and acted furious. I *was* furious, but I laid it on really thick. I yelled that they were corrupt, that they were extorting money from us and really tried to dramatize the whole situation. I said I was telling my attorney that we are returning these films but under the loudest possible protest. And that I refused to pay a cent to him because it was nothing short of blackmail! Then I had Steve drive to this crooked attorney with the box of crummy prints and hand them over. I knew the attorney wouldn't open the cans and I knew if he did he wouldn't be able to tell if it wasn't a fine grain master or not. He wouldn't know what to look for. We ended up taking the good material we had rescued over to Movielab, who handled the films properly, and the two pictures finally made it onto *Fright Night*."

"That was just the short version. People came to our door threatening to kill us! You know a lot of people apparently had buckled under to this corrupt attorney. By the time he got to me, he was pretty adept at putting a gun to people's heads to get that $2000. What a business to be in. I once wrote on the beginning of a trailer script something about 'The shocking scenes you are about to see are not suggested for the weak or immature. If you can't take it, we suggest you now patronize the concession stand or look away from this preview of *Satan's Sadists*!' Film distribution is not suggested for the weak or immature. What the hell kind of business is this? My God!

"There was another guy, an oldtime distributor named Hal Campbell, and his company was called Prime TV I believe. Even though he was an old man, he was a tough old bird. He was in the same spot as us and we had no idea he had been put through the same paces by that attorney. He said he had paid the $2000 for each of whatever amount of titles he had stuck over there at Triangle. He couldn't believe we had the nerve to do what we did and that we did it successfully. He said we should have called him and he would have gone with us! You know, I'm not going to say I was proud of it. But I was proud that I didn't knuckle under. We tried to do Triangle a favor. They needed work and I tried to give them some. But I was lucky I didn't get too stupid with this, like having weapons, or clubs, or big brutes when I stormed the place. It was one of those strange things that just did work out. And by the way, we never again saw the crummy prints we had switched. Those prints went into the black hole of Calcutta!"

Despite the enormous difficulties of getting prints made and the stress of entering the syndication business, the venture ended up a reasonably successful one. "It was very difficult to make a profit selling films for *Fright Night*, Channel 9 and other television outlets to use at the time," Sam says. "When you make a small movie, the expenses to put it on the market are tremendous. You have to make all that money back. And pay your overhead. Syndication is a help in recovering those costs, but it sure isn't an easy business. I believe we made a pretty good contract with RKO that they paid over time and, fortunately, it worked out well for all of us."

Sherman says that after he and his team handled most of the editing chores to make his movies suitable for television, the package that was used by all five of the RKO-owned stations was good for approximately five years and that the films had initially been stored largely in Sam's office during the years he ran them in syndication. "At some point we had a lot of them in our office stored on big racks that could hold the 16mm prints. Our editors would fix them up and send them off to the various stations. The 16mm films were easier and more manageable to deal with than 35mm. A certain amount of these movies were lost over time to attrition. They might have been fading, turning pink and experiencing problems like that. Eventually TV stations went to video tape and some of our original 16mm television prints were simply sold off to collectors."

For a period of time after he left WOR, Larry Casey handled Sherman's syndication efforts, but it was short-lived. Says Sherman, "We started to distribute our films on video tape through our Super Video Company. At that point, we eased out of the television syndication business." Today, Sherman continues to actively utilize the latest technologies and media hubs available to keep his films in the public eye and many of the Sherman-Adamson flicks are available for viewing on his YouTube channel (iipaladamsonmania) and popular streaming websites like Hulu.

8. A Ticket to the Tropics

During *Fright Night*'s first years, film product from another small motion picture company named Hemisphere Pictures Inc. would provide a significant portion of the color thrills Channel 9 increasingly sought. Casey does not recall dealing directly with Hemisphere, but publicity materials for the company's film package, a combination of self-made and imported chillers called the *Block of Shock*, indicate that the company was directly and actively seeking a television audience for their movies.

The company's long history is well known to producer Sam Sherman, though he says "People tend to associate me a little too closely with Hemisphere, although I did work for them and was actively involved in their campaigns at the peak of their success." According to Sam, "Hemisphere Pictures' origins can be traced back to the late '50s and early '60s. Hemisphere began to come about when Irwin Pizor, the son of William Pizor, an important producer and player in the early days of international movie distribution, teamed up with Kane Lynn, a former World War II Navy pilot. They were joined by Lynn's friend Eddie Romero, a producer and director with whom Lynn had already made two pictures out of the Philippines, *Terror Is a Man* [1959] and *The Scavengers* [1963]. The three were distributing mostly war-themed movies. Hemisphere Pictures eventually evolved out of that relationship. They had enjoyed a good deal of international success initially with the war films, but those movies were much less popular in the U.S.

"I became involved with Hemisphere around 1963 when the company was newly formed. I met Irwin at his beautiful office on Seventh Ave in New York City. "I had been looking for films to purchase and was just starting out with my own little distribution business. I obtained an old picture from him called *The Scarlet Letter* [1934], which I re-issued in the South. That started my career off in theatrical distribution. I began hanging out at Hemisphere quite a bit and developed a good relationship with the people in Irwin's office and became very friendly with Kane Lynn. He appreciated my enthusiasm and was quite surprised by the success I had with my reissue work on *The Scarlet Letter*. I suggested to Kane and Irwin that the war films they were

46

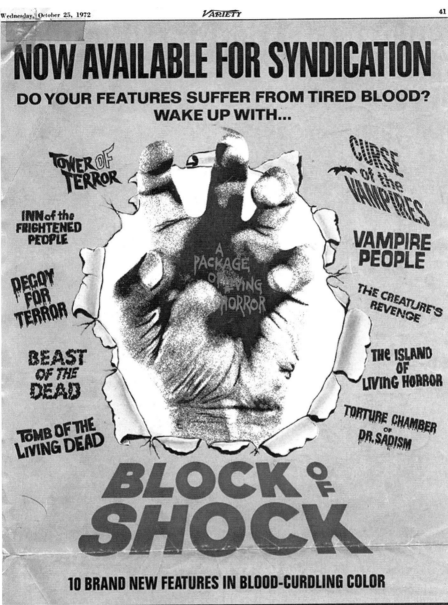

Hemisphere Pictures' *Block of Shock* TV campaign folder cover.

focused on, such as *Walls of Hell* [1964], weren't doing well in the U.S. because they were not what American movie audiences were looking for any more. Instead, I suggested that they consider making horror films for the American market. I feel a bit proud to have suggested or influenced that change in direction for them and that's what Hemisphere became known for."

Says Sherman, "We took Kane's film, *Terror Is a Man*, which had originally gone nowhere for them with that artsy title, and changed it to *Blood Creature*. Joel Ornstein, a sort of a renegade agent for Hemisphere Pictures' distribution, came up with the idea to package Hemisphere's *Walls of Hell* and *Blood Creature* together. He booked the double feature in Pennsylvania and it went through the roof! It was a blockbuster, making more money for Hemisphere at one theater than all their other movies in distribution at the time combined. That got their attention in a big way and began the cycle of horror films they became very well-known for.

"They were sitting on a Filipino vampire film from Eddie Romero that needed to be cut, dubbed and really punched up for an American audience. It was re-titled to *The Blood Drinkers* [1966]. It's really an outstanding film, perhaps even a classic. Based on the box office success of *Walls of Hell* and *Blood Creature*, they knew double features were the way to go. They paired up *The Blood Drinkers* with a U.S.–produced movie they'd gotten their hands on that had a really violent scene in it involving an axe to the head called *The Black Cat* and it worked out very well. *The Blood Drinkers* was added later to other double and triple feature showcases Hemisphere developed and eventually was re-titled to *Vampire People,* where it was run into the ground as a co-feature for my film for Hemisphere Pictures, *Brain of Blood* [1971], and then in scratchy 16mm prints for their television package."

Hemisphere went on to create an infamous trilogy of Philippine-made horror films based on the mysterious Blood Island first alluded to in *Terror Is a Man*. These three movies gave the company its reputation for drive-in gore films. The movies *Brides of Blood* (1968), *Mad Doctor of Blood Island* (1968) and *Beast of Blood* (1970)—sometimes referred to as the Blood Island series— all featured a handful of lower-ranking but familiar U.S. actors such as Kent Taylor, John Ashley, Angelique Pettijohn, Celeste Yarnall and Beverly Hills who shared screen time with the native actors of the Philippines. According to Sherman, "Kane was picking up overseas pictures for U.S. distribution at the same time that some of these pictures were being made in the Philippines, such as *Theatre of Death* [1967] with Christopher Lee. I began developing some of the trailers and campaigns in-house for Hemisphere, including *Theatre of Death*, which I re-titled to *Blood Fiend*. Irwin and Kane were being influenced by some of the gorier, sexier films that started coming out at that time. Things like *Two Thousand Maniacs!* [1964]. They wanted to hit the drive-in market hard with rougher material that had not been widely seen before. From those expectations came the Blood Island pictures.

"*Brides of Blood*, released to television as *Island of Living Horror*, really began Hemisphere's use of gimmicky marketing campaigns created in-house," says Sherman. "It was decided that *Brides* would be paired up with *Blood Fiend* and some ideas were being thrown around regarding what promotional gimmicks could be developed to play off the wedding and bridal theme of the feature picture. Though Pizor and Kane had different opinions about how to advertise it, and they often disagreed, I had a background in exploitive marketing and I was very enthused to implement whatever ideas they came up with. Kane got hold of some cheap plastic rings and wanted to give them out at drive-ins. The wedding rings seemed like a far-fetched idea to me because the film didn't have much to do with traditional brides. Pizor didn't like the idea at all, but I was open to discussing it and suggested in addition to the ring set, maybe we include some kind of marriage certificate.

"I also created the famous prologue for *Mad Doctor of Blood Island* which was seen intact on the *Fright Night* broadcasts under the name *Tomb of the Living Dead*. 'Blood' was really the focus now for Hemisphere, and Kane and Irwin wanted some kind of audience participation gimmick related to blood for the picture. So they ordered some kind of liquid substance that came in gel packs that they intended audiences to drink and I came up with that prologue where the audience would take the green blood oath before swallowing it. Well, I thought I better test it out the stuff we'd be asking them to swallow and make sure it was okay. It tasted like some kind of fruit-flavored punch and I actually got quite sick from it. Hopefully everyone at a drive-in who swallowed it was filled up with popcorn and theater junk food and never got affected by it the way I did. But I heard people really did stand up and recite the oath and drank the stuff as instructed in my prologue. The movie intro was shot in the Philippines using Caucasian types who would look like the young people that would be seeing the film in the U.S., once again in an effort to Americanize the picture.

"*Mad Doctor of Blood Island*, which became known on TV as *Tomb of the Living Dead*, was probably one of the best known movies in the Blood Island trilogy. There was no real connection between this film and *Brides of Blood*, but they did bring back John Ashley. Again, it was a project developed by Eddie Romero, who was focused on characterization, and director Gerry de Leone, who was more into the stories. The movie, while a bit overly complex as far as plot was concerned, was very multi-layered with a substantial increase in the levels of graphic horror and sex. I'd say this film was my favorite of the trio of Blood Island pictures. I think it's a very well-acted film and I think it was a better production than *Brides*. The music score was simply amazing, just beautifully done by Tito Arevalo. I was delighted when Kane Lynn was able to bring the master recordings back to the U.S. as I had asked him to, and having those tracks allowed us to use the music cues over and over again. *Mad Doctor of Blood Island* got paired up with a great Christopher Lee movie we imported from a German company called *Blood Demon*, which was seen on Channel 9 as *Torture Chamber of Dr. Sadism,* and I think it was a really great double feature.

"As the pictures began to get older, Hemisphere got the idea to start packaging the films together. Three, sometimes four movies were distributed together to extend their life at the box office. They believed in developing new ad campaigns to make them seem fresh and I was heavily involved in that. The first one was called *The Blood-O-Rama Shock Show*. I developed some trailers for it that were very loud with screaming and shouts and carrying on and all kinds of dramatic scenes from the films. I remember John Ashley saw it and was laughing out loud. He thought it was quite hysterical. It was followed by *The Chiller Carnival of Blood*, and that trailer had a narration that went something like 'Step right up to the greatest show on earth ... or six feet under!' It was at that point that Kane decided all these films had to start with the word *Blood*. So a film like *Mad Doctor of Blood Island* became *Blood Doctor*. I think Hemisphere was pushing their luck a little with that decision. But they wanted to brand themselves stronger and to be known as 'Hemisphere ... The House of Horror.'"

Hemisphere returned to Blood Island one last time for *Beast of Blood*. "I thought of this picture a bit more as an adventure film," says Sherman. "We brought back John Ashley again, as he was a good actor and he enjoyed going to the Philippines to make these pictures. The movie was again crafted by Eddie Romero. Hemisphere was still interested in staying in the *Blood* business, but this ended up being the last one made with the original production crew. Over time, it seems that this movie ended up being the fan favorite of the three Blood Island pictures. *Beast of Blood* was again teamed with a second feature, another Filipino vampire movie called *Curse of the Vampires*. We also had a piece of wonderful art obtained from a Filipino artist who did a great rendering of the decapitated beast holding its own head, which became very famous. The double feature did very, very well at the box office. When the movie was released to television, it was re-titled to *Beast of the Dead*.

"At the time of the theatrical release of this picture, Irwin and Kane had quite a serious falling-out over financial matters. They got to the point where there was a fight for control of the company. And right around that time I had started a company with Al Adamson and Dan Kennis, Independent-International, but managed to keep my hand in Hemisphere. Admittedly, that was a strange situation to have one's own production company and yet also be working for a competitor. As the tensions at Hemisphere progressed, Kane traveled to Manila and bought out Eddie Romero's interests and removed Irwin from the company. It was an unfortunate situation, but some time after the fallout, they both ended up respecting each other I think and appreciating their teamwork together and what they had accomplished."

As far as the television releases of their films were concerned, Hemisphere apparently wanted no part of the censorship process. Sherman concurs that Hemisphere left the editing of their films to the hands of station splicers, which would account for variations in what was shown in, for example, the rape sequences contained in *In the Devil's Garden* (1972, aka *Tower of Terror*) on Channel 9 or Long Island's far more conservative Channel 67. It would also account for the fact that some nudity slipped through when Channel 9 broadcast *Island of Living Horror* in early *Fright Night* telecasts.

I managed to catch a few of Hemisphere's movies at the drive-in and was seeing them increasingly on *Fright Night*. At the same time I was contacting Channel 9 about *Fright Night* and supporting their horror movie programming, I was also busy writing to Hemisphere Pictures, then located at 445 Park Avenue in New York City, singing their praises with equal enthusiasm. They were busy marketing their last major theatrical foray into horror with some three-year-old films called *The Devil's Nightmare* (1972) and *In the Devil's Garden*, selling them to drive-ins looking for *Exorcist*-themed product as if they were newly made. But they took the time on January 17, 1975, to send me a long letter of appreciation. Like the less than perfect movie product they were peddling, the typed letter was filled with cross-outs, white-outs and handwritten corrections, but it expressed a humility that was not lost on me at even a young age. Signed by a Hemisphere representative named Maurice Rabinoff, the letter alerted me that even though I was not old enough to see *In the Devil's Garden* in theaters, I would be able to see the film when WOR-TV would broadcast it on February 22 under the name *Tower of Terror*. Maurice added that I was probably one of the only fans Hemisphere Pictures had and how delighted he was that I noticed their devilish double feature.

He humbly admitted, "It's true we too would like to see our films playing in New York or in neighboring suburban areas, but it is not just up to us to decide. A theater is like your local supermarket or book store ... they will buy any product they feel will make money for them and in turn for us. Theaters cannot play a film or play it for more than one week if money is not coming in ... they have to pay their employees and other costs necessary to maintain

Hemisphere Pictures' Devil combo from 1971, one of the company's last ventures into horror.

themselves. Therefore, we, like many other small companies, can only play [our films] in this region on a multiple basis like the Devil's combination if the major competing films aren't biting the bulk of the business." My friends at Hemisphere Pictures assured me they would let me know if *The Devil's Nightmare* would appear on television and included with their letter a few stills, posters, pressbooks and ad mats for some of their films. But for Hemisphere, the sands of their horror movie hourglass had just about run out and the company spent most of its final days of theatrical distribution releasing imported German soft-core sexploitation features like *Swingin' Stewardesses* (1971) and *The Young Seducers* (1974).

9. Holiday Affairs

Despite Casey and Steinbrunner's passion for the genre, some of the films shown on *Fright Night*, on rare occasion, missed the mark. *Really* missed the mark. One can only assume they were broadcast when absolutely nothing else was available, as it was impossible to classify them as horror, sci-fi or fantasy. Considering the depth of their in-house film library as reported by Casey, this might seem to be an unlikely situation for the station to find itself in. Films like the admittedly thought-provoking drama *B ... Must Die* (1975) starring Darren McGavin and the Boris Karloff drama *Island Monster* (1954) (a despicably dull film despite its title) come to mind. "Sometimes a title fell quite a bit short of its description in the press material we received," says Casey. "But to be honest and with all due respect to *Fright Night*'s many fans, the show was sometimes referred to at the station as *Crap Playhouse*. If we had a really obscure, bad film collecting dust, *Fright Night* was a great place to make some money off of it. Not that we didn't try to get some great movies on the program, but the quality of the films shown on *Fright Night* didn't really matter. Just like running time didn't really matter. *Fright Night* and the Saturday morning horror movie shows were a great place to schedule movies that were difficult to slot in other time periods."

When it came to frequency of repeat telecasts for these films, even the dreck got more than one shot in the spotlight. "We were usually able to use a film for several years with unlimited runs. My personal philosophy was to try to avoid showing a film more than twice a year. Twice a year was my yardstick, but I often violated my own rule on a number of pictures, because I knew the film would deliver the same rating no matter how many times I showed it. *King Kong* was certainly one of those pictures and many of the *Fright Night* features were as well. Also, some movies may have turned up more frequently on the program because otherwise the film would just be sitting around gathering dust for a long time after you've paid for it. It's possible some of the really odd, really bad films shown on *Fright Night* weren't shown very often, but not likely that they were only shown once. Every film got multiple runs — though maybe some received a good deal less rotation than others. Some of the movies were obtained very cheaply so it didn't quite matter as much if they weren't telecast that often. It's also very possible that someone at the station may have seen a movie and it was so dreadful they bristled at its content and said, 'Don't ever run that again or you're fired!' I don't recall that ever happening in my time at the station."

But most of the film choices were wonderful, fun and entertaining experiences whether the films themselves were critically considered good, bad or mediocre. Whatever film package Casey was working with, he always tried to dig deep. "Universal's *Horror Greats* package was a turn-key source for titles for us, however old they may have been. I liked to root through our packages and try to find something unique and different, especially for *Fright Night*," he says.

A few of them were divinely inspired, especially around holidays. Halloween was an obvious holiday to celebrate for any American who enjoyed horror films. In the New York tri-state area in the '70s, horror movie mania would spread far beyond the confines of Channel 9 to other stations that would join in the seasonal fun. The afternoon and evenings surrounding Halloween were packed with great movies. A sampling of Halloween film telecasts during the years at the beginning of the *Fright Night* reign shows the depth of spirit among all the stations in the area.

1973

WOR-TV Channel 9: *The Seventh Victim* (1943) Kim Hunter; *Eye of the Cat* (1969) Michael Sarrazin; *The Raven* (1935) Boris Karloff
WCBS-TV Channel 2: *Who Slew Auntie Roo* (1972) Shelley Winters; *Theater of Death* (1967) Christopher Lee
WNEW-TV Channel 5: *Horror Hotel* (1960) Betta St. John

1974

WOR-TV Channel 9: *Fear No Evil* (1969) Louis Jourdan
WCBS-TV Channel 2: *The Canterville Ghost* (1944) Charles Laughton; *The Navy vs. the Night Monsters* (1966) Mamie Van Doren
WNEW-TV Channel 5: *Lust for a Vampire* (1971) Ralph Bates

1975

WOR-TV Channel 9: *Son of Frankenstein* (1939) Boris Karloff; *Psycho* (1960) Anthony Perkins

WCBS-TV Channel 2: *House of Wax* (1953) Vincent Price; *The Canterville Ghost* (1944) Charles Laughton

WABC-TV Channel 7: *Scream, Blacula, Scream* (1973) William Marshall; *The Ghost in the Invisible Bikini* (1966) Tommy Kirk

1976

WOR-TV Channel 9: *Tower of London* (1939) Basil Rathbone; *Phantom of the Opera* (1943) Claude Rains; *Brotherhood of Satan* (1971) Strother Martin

WCBS-TV Channel 2: *House of Wax* (1953) Vincent Price

WPIX-TV Channel 11: *Hold That Ghost* (1941) Abbott & Costello

1977

WOR-TV Channel 9: *Flesh and Fantasy* (1943) Edward G. Robinson; *The Revenge of Frankenstein* (1958) Peter Cushing

WCBS-TV Channel 2: *House of Wax* (1953) Vincent Price

1978

WOR-TV Channel 9: *Touch of Satan* (1971) Lee Amber; *Mr. Sardonicus* (1961) Ronald Lewis

WNET-TV (Public Television) Channel 13: *Nosferatu* (1922) Max Schreck

When the usually peaceful and joyous Christmas season rolled around, programming choices may have seemed like far more of a challenge for the producers of a show like *Fright Night*. But not for Casey. *The Invisible Man* (1933) was the first film to become something of a *Fright Night* Christmas tradition, airing on the show's 1976 and 1977 telecasts falling on or just before the holiday. "I picked that film because of the snowy motif ... the opening scenes just had a great wintry feel. It was light; it was a classic. It seemed ideal for the *Fright Night* programs that fell around Christmas," says Casey.

Later, the Christmas spirit would take a decidedly Grinch-like turn with the regular telecast of *Silent Night Bloody Night* (1974), a violent, frightening tale of a murderer's rampage in a rural community around the holidays. The film also had the distinction of being one of the most often telecast movies on *Fright Night.* "Don't get me wrong," says Casey, "I loved *White Christmas* [1954] and traditional holiday movies. But how many times can you watch those things? I refuse to watch *It's a Wonderful Life* [1946] one more time; I couldn't take it! We always pushed the envelope on *Fright Night* and *Silent Night Bloody Night* was a great fit. WOR never got any complaints for showing it that I heard about ... and if they did, who cares? And, just for the record, I believe I also showed a more traditional Christmas movie on some of our other film shows called *Silent Night Lonely Night* [1969] ... so you could take your pick!"

Casey adds, "One other Christmas picture I would have liked to have shown that came along later was *Black Christmas* [1974]." This blood-curdling film actually did become a macabre Christmas telecast tradition when it was picked up by the USA cable network in the mid–1980s and became a regular broadcast around the holidays on their *Saturday Nightmares* program.

Equally offbeat and clever was the scheduling of director Larry Buchanan's movie monstrosity *In the Year 2889* (1967), shown on or about New Year's Eve. "*2889* was scheduled because it was about the future and was a cheap monster movie we had bought from American International and

The inmates escape in *Silent Night Bloody Night* (1974), one of the most often-broadcast movies in *Fright Night*'s history and a Yuletide favorite.

good for New Year's," says Casey. Buchanan's relationship with *Fright Night* was a natural, with the program spotlighting three of the moviemaker's most infamous and bizarre horror productions under the Azalea Pictures banner. Rob Craig, whose book *The Films of Larry Buchanan* (2007, McFarland) is essential reading for any connoisseur of the infamous director's bad cult movies, reflects on Buchanan's inclusion in *Fright Night*'s vast repertoire. Says Craig, "Being a fan and addict of the films of Larry Buchanan ever since one sunny Sunday afternoon, circa 1967, when I experienced the New York television premiere of Buchanan's seminal, minimalist *Zontar, the Thing from Venus* [1966], I was more than thrilled when my favorite New York television station, the beloved Channel 9, aired several of Buchanan's mesmerizing made-for-television wonders on their long-running, sorely missed genre film omnibus, *Fright Night*. Although I had seen all the Azaleas (with the exception of the legendary *Hell Raiders* [1968] on ABC affiliate Channel 7 previously), it was always a joy to watch them again, deep in the heart of the night, when these astounding quasi-experimental films, in my opinion, were made to be seen."

The selection of *In the Year 2889* as a New Year's kick-off on *Fright Night* was a brilliant programming decision in Craig's view. "Buchanan's morose and melancholy remake of Roger Corman's 1956 breakthrough picture *Day the World Ended* was a great choice for the show. I was so enamored of Corman's film, that for many years I disliked Buchanan's remake, and it wasn't until this broadcast that I saw clearly that Buchanan had modified and, in some cases, improved the basic scenario, and how *2889* was, in many ways, an entirely different film from Corman's grim low-rent apocalypse. Thanks to this and subsequent screenings, *2889* has become one of my favorite Azaleas."

This film had also achieved a warm spot in my heart and I became curious what those who performed in Buchanan's movies thought of their experiences. I was inspired in the late '90s to contact the star of *In the Year 2889*, singer-actor Paul Petersen. By return letter, Petersen related how he came to be involved in this *Fright Night* anti-classic. Petersen had initially turned down the project, as any self-respecting star-on-the-rise would, but the film's tenacious director had supporters, both small and surprisingly big, including Paul's studio teacher and the legendary Bob Hope, who persuaded the young actor to take the job. "The simple fact is, I had a ball," said Petersen in his letter. "To me, the hilarious part was that so many of the other actors took their roles seriously ... 'What's my motivation?' and crap like that. Larry had a pat response to the motivation question: 'Your salary!'

"And Larry and I got along very well indeed. I think he appreciated the fact that I was prepared and accommodating. This was not brain surgery after all." Petersen also mentioned his small role in another *Fright Night* movie telecast in 1975. "Years before ... I did a movie over at Universal ... a small part ... in a movie called *The Monolith Monsters* [1957]. Buchanan knew the movie and we chewed over the absurdity of giant rocks capable of moving about and killing. Ah, sci-fi!"

Buchanan's other *Fright Night* contributions, *The Eye Creatures* (1965) and *Curse of the Swamp Creature* (1966), are noted by Craig with equal passion. "The 1979 *Fright Night* screening of *The Eye Creatures* was a revelation to me, because although I had seen the film before, this was the first time I became consciously aware of the entirely new subplot which Buchanan added to the scenario of the film's prototype, *Invasion of the Saucer Men* [1957]. This subplot, wherein two goofy military men spy on everything which goes on around their base, including teenagers making out, via a bank of video surveillance cameras, is an Orwellian stroke of genius. Although these scenes are played largely for laughs, the sheer paranoia implicit in the notion that the government watches every single move of its citizens unawares, made *The Eye Creatures*, to me, overall the 'darkest' Azalea, an admittedly dark canon to begin with.

"Although I had for many years owned a battered 16mm print of the film, I never missed an opportunity to watch *Curse of the Swamp Creature* when it was infrequently telecast, and *Fright Night*'s February 1978 telecast was a delight, as their print beat mine by a mile, although the depressing, grim atmosphere of the film still came shining through, as did John Agar's stoic performance — which he would later consider the nadir of his career." According to Craig, when Agar was asked about working with Buchanan by a fanzine interviewer in the early 1980s, his recollections weren't warm and fuzzy. "Agar lamented, 'The guy is strictly an amateur. I mean, he wouldn't even take the time to film an establishing shot! He always told me, 'We can fix it in editing!' Some time later, Agar softened his opinion towards his work with Buchanan, probably after realizing that the three Azalea films he made for American International Television [*Zontar* and *Hell Raiders* were the others] were considered the most popular amongst his devoted fan base."

The almost bootleg appearance of Buchanan movies, especially evident in *Fright Night*'s late night telecasts of scratchy, faded prints, may have fueled speculation about the legitimacy of the films. Says Craig, "During [the mid– to late 1970s], there was still the general perception amongst fans of the Azalea films that they may have been unauthorized, even outlaw remakes of the older American International theatrical features. There was nothing officially in print clarifying that Sam Arkoff and James Nicholson had in fact commissioned Buchanan, circa 1964, to make a series of cheap color genre features for their fledgling television syndication arm. Therefore, the fact that these no-budget, scruffy counterfeits appeared to be near-amateur knock-offs of beloved AIP classics like *The She-Creature* [1956] and *It Conquered the World* [1956] made them all the more addictive and hypnotizing to fans of the genre, myself included. Watching the Azalea films unspooling late at night on a flickering television screen was often more like suffering a hallucination than enjoying an identifiable movie experience, and it is doubtful that anyone encountering an Azalea film for the first time via a late-night broadcast like *Fright Night* has ever forgotten the experience!

"My own personal opinion," says Craig, "is that, in addition to the creepy *déjà vu* feeling one always had when watching Buchanan's cheap color remake of an already-familiar black and white monster movie on *Fright Night*, as well as his astute use of strict budget constraints, the use of some of the most evocative, melancholy music cues from Ronald Stein, Les Baxter and others greatly heightened the 'spooky' sense that imbued all of the Azalea films, and gave them much of their unshakable other-worldly patina. As it turns out, those rascals at AIP didn't bother to clear the re-use of these cues with their creators, assuming them to be owned by AIP as they were used previously in their productions. According to Ronald Stein's widow Harlene, Stein was unaware for years that AIP had 'borrowed' some of his best scores [from 1957's *The Undead* as well as *It Conquered the World* and *The She-Creature*] and when he discovered this wholesale theft years later he was not amused, but apparently saw no convenient way to attempt, at this late date, to regain through legal action some compensation for the misuse of his intellectual property. While we can certainly side with Mr. Stein, who most assuredly should have been compensated for the use of his work, we can also be thankful that Buchanan and company saw fit to use them, because frankly, if the Azaleas had been scored with cheap, generic stock library music of the type that was making the rounds at the time, thanks to libraries such as DeWolfe and Valentino, the films would have been entirely different creatures, and not nearly as haunting as they became with the help of Ronald Stein's magnificent music."

10. Voices in the Night

Part of the almost small-town charm of WOR and *Fright Night* came from the voiceover announcers who would alert viewers what was coming up next on Channel 9. Among the most memorable were Phil Tonken (1919–2000) and Ted Mallie (1924–1999), both of whom had a long association with WOR and careers in the old-time radio era. Mallie was an announcer with a flair for the dramatic. According to Casey, "The announcer copy was provided by the promotions department and generally didn't provide stage directions. Some announcers read it straight, while some did provide a little ham acting or a spooky whisper like Ted Mallie." Art Helmer was another familiar voice. Joining this boy's club later was Jesse Elin Browne.

Browne, an accomplished voice artist, was the first female staff announcer at Channel 9 (and proudly clarifies *all* of New York) in 1977. Browne's vocal work would later be heard in projects for such major organizations as McDonald's, Sears, Hallmark and even the U.S. Air Force, among many others. In August 1977, I may have developed an infatuation with the announcer's charming voice which prompted me to write directly to her and express my appreciation for her work. She responded with a warm and detailed letter of gratitude. I had amusingly wondered if working at the station was anything like life on the then hugely popular *The Mary Tyler Moore Show*, as if such a thing were actually possible. In her honest and articulate response, she said "[I]t's a field of specialists who simply do their job — their function — to contribute to the overall picture, which is to produce one thing: WOR-TV Channel 9. It can be fun sometimes. But most of the time, it's a job just like anyone else's."

Today, Ms. Browne remembers working the late shift and handling the announcing duties for *Fright Night* in the 8' × 8' booth with fondness. "What I can tell you about being on duty during *Fright Night* Saturdays is that it was always a blast. Sure, there were times when I had seen some of the movies previously, especially the movies which were produced when I was younger. But in other cases, there were movies I had never seen in that genre." Browne says she worked the night shift at Channel 9 most of the time and few if any in upper management were around during those hours.

She adds, "Most of the employees working in the middle of the night at the old Times Square station watched those movies. We talked to the screen, we critiqued what we watched, and sometimes we discussed the cheesy effects. Yet we were glued to the screen, just the same." Browne says there was more work involved than just announcing the name of the movie being shown or that "*Fright Night* will return in a moment" during a commercial break. She says, "Our job required that we watch the show to be certain that the films aired properly. We kept the official FCC log book, which was kept manually back then, and made certain that the start and end times were all noted correctly. And we attested that all the commercials ran correctly so that the sponsors were assured that the time they purchased was used properly."

I wondered if, at the time, Ms. Browne was aware of the impact *Fright Night* movies might have been having on viewers or the actual numbers listening to her voice on those Saturday nights. "I was not aware of the size of our audience," she says. "I worked the night shift most of the time. The jobs were very compartmentalized." It seems like the impact of *Fright Night* may have been accidental, with cost and efficiency being WOR's primary concern. "The only observations I had were that they showed whatever movie they could lease least expensively. In some cases they were movies they owned because they had ownership of RKO properties. But with most other movies, they had the right to air them a certain amount of times in a given period of time for one flat fee."

The *Fright Night* experience seems to have given Browne a true appreciation for the genre. "I can say now that I have seen and appreciate all the films of, for example, Christopher Lee and while I may not have had an appreciation for them at the time, I've learned over the years that he was always a well respected actor ... a master at his craft ... Watching all the Japanese-produced films with the (rubber suit) animation seemed so silly and campy during the time but, again, with the passage of time and an improvement in the technique, films like *The Nightmare Before Christmas* [1993] and *James and the Giant Peach* [1996] evolved and directors like Tim Burton have become wildly popular even today. It's easy to see the influence movies like *Godzilla, King of the Monsters!* [1956], *Mothra* [1961] and even *King Kong* had on the kids who watched them with aspirations of directing their own movies one day. In a way, I think the 1970s were still early days in both the science fiction and horror genres. It actually makes me proud that I was part of the independent television station movement that showed the films during those years, in a major American city."

Although Browne does not recall any specific films shown on *Fright Night*, both Sam Sherman and Larry Casey do. Casey is quick to identify his favorite of the Universal movies he scheduled: *House of Dracula* (1945). "The studio knew it was the end of the era even before the picture was made, but it had a great atmosphere about it. All the monsters were together and the film is creepy and entertaining despite some of its drawbacks," he says. Ironically, *House of Dracula* was only shown on *Fright Night* once, and apparently as an afterthought. It was a last-minute substitute in 1976 when the originally scheduled film, *The Last Man on Earth* (1964), was bumped for unknown reasons. Equally ironic is Casey's favorite horror film of all time, the Vincent Price classic *House on Haunted Hill* (1959), which was locked up at competing station WNEW for many years and never made a *Fright Night* appearance. Casey notes, however, that the film actually had its New York television premiere on Channel 9.

"I am quite sure I saw many of the *Fright Night* shows. I was always up late. And WOR was a home for horror!" says Sam Sherman. For him, a major stand-out was one of his own releases, *Night of the Laughing Dead* (1977), a British comedy-horror film he had licensed for the U.S. under a tax shelter arrangement. Originally called *House in Nightmare Park*, the film told the amusing turn-of-the century story of a bad actor summoned to an isolated

Frankie Howerd and Ray Milland take a stab at comedy-horror in *Night of the Laughing Dead* (1977).

mansion where dark secrets are revealed and murder is committed in order to find a stash of diamonds.

Sherman's clever re-titling of comedienne Frankie Howerd's extremely funny old dark house thriller, directed with a flair for gothic comedy by Peter Sykes, is reflective of the producer's appreciation for the genre and the film. "It was incredibly unsuccessful for us and it died at the box office when I released it domestically as *Crazy House*," says Sherman. "Funny thing about movies ... sometimes no matter what you do to market a film, it will just defy you. Like *Night of the Laughing Dead*. No matter what I did to make that picture work, it failed. Maybe it was too British or too laid back. Bob Glazer, a big executive at RKO television, and I seemed to be the only people who liked the film at the time. I decided to goose it up for television distribution. I tightened up some of the scenes, pumped up the soundtrack so the dialogue was clearer and added some music cues and special sound effects." Comparison of the original, longer UK cut and Sherman's edit proves Sam's take to clearly be the lighter and more enjoyable version. Recollecting an amusing scene in the film where actor Howerd reacts to the sudden appearance of a deadly snake ("I hope it's a crusher, not a biter!") instantly generates a hearty laugh from Sherman. But he concedes, "Another one of those 'Sam Sherman likes a picture to his own detriment' situations. But it did make for a good *Fright Night* feature."

One film Casey was eager to show on *Fright Night* (and no doubt several of its other movie programs) was Tobe Hooper's *The Texas Chain Saw Massacre*, a 1974 film that was actually far more disturbing than it was gory. "I could have gotten that film ... and really cheap too! Two or three cuts and we could have played that film in prime time for nuns with no problem," Casey says. Station management refused however, insisting the title alone would cause too much controversy.

Ironically, WOR rarely received complaints about its film programming. "Late night shows like *Fright Night* never generated much controversy. We never received too many complaints about the content on shows like that. Maybe once in a while we'd hear from a purist who was angry at us for cutting a film because of length restrictions, but content at that hour was never much of an issue. However, I do remember one mother calling the station after she had discovered her child watching some horror movie on one of our Saturday morning movie shows. She was all pissed off and felt she should be able to lock her child in a room and not have to worry about what he's watching on TV on a Saturday morning. I tried to explain that most stations offered kiddie programming and cartoons and that we were offering adults and more mature viewers an alternative experience."

11. It Doesn't Always Happen at Night

Channel 9's Saturday morning movie programming offered viewers many of the same movie titles that late night viewers of the station were also enjoying. *Science Fiction Theater* was seen on WOR in various time slots ranging from 10 A.M. to 11:30 A.M. on Saturday mornings beginning in late 1971 and running until 1973. *Thriller Theatre* ran Saturday mornings generally at 9:30 A.M. from 1973 through 1975 and featured another great Jerry Miller bumper, a collage of famous monsters appearing within the large T-H-R-I-L-L-E-R letters passing across the screen and accompanied by a haunting organ dirge. *Thriller Theatre* also was shown weekdays in the late afternoon for a time. The mix of films included on these programs featured a few more adventure dramas and sci-fi offerings in keeping with the day, hour and the broader definition of their program titles, but horror fans, looking for more than the cartoons found everywhere else, would get more than their fair share from *Fright Night*'s daytime cousins.

SCIENCE FICTION THEATER

1971

12/18 *S.O.S. Coast Guard* (1942) **Bela Lugosi**—Feature-length version of the 1937 adventure serial from Republic.
12/25 Looks like *Science Fiction Theater* was pre-empted.

1972

01/01 *The Strange Case of Dr. RX* (1942) **Lionel Atwill**—A killer called Dr. RX has a prescription that includes the murders of men who have been recently acquitted of crimes in this enjoyable Universal mystery quickie.

01/08 *Captain Mephisto and the Transformation Machine* (1966)

01/15 *Have Rocket Will Travel* (1959) **The Three Stooges**— The comedy team nyucked it up on Earth and in space.

01/22 *Dinosaurus!* (1960) **Ward Ramsey**— A caveman and dinosaurs are unearthed on an island construction site. An extremely juvenile but harmless piece of Saturday morning fluff.

01/29 *Day the Sky Exploded* (1958) **Paul Hubschmid**— Meteors headed for Earth threaten to destroy the planet.

02/05 *The Incredible Petrified World* (1957) **John Carradine**— A mysterious world is discovered by scientists descending in a diving bell to the ocean floor. A low-grade but not entirely uninteresting Jerry Warren clunker.

02/12 *The Invisible Ray* (1936)

02/19 *Cyclotrode X* (1966) **Linda Stirling**— Edited feature version of the 1946 Republic serial *The Crimson Ghost.*

02/26 *Unknown Island* (1948) **Virginia Grey**— Adventurers travel to an uncharted Pacific island and discover prehistoric monsters still roaming the land in a fun, lowbrow thriller.

03/04 Looks like *Science Fiction Movie* was pre-empted.

03/11 *The Day the Earth Caught Fire* (1961)

03/18 *Mutiny in Outer Space* (1965) **Richard Garland**— Astronauts battle a deadly fungus.

03/25 *Dr. Satan's Robot* (1966)

04/01 *Creature with the Atom Brain* (1955)

04/08 Looks like *Science Fiction Movie* was pre-empted.

04/15 *The Invisible Man* (1933)

04/22 *The Human Duplicators* (1965)

04/29 *The Mummy* (1932)

05/06 *Frankenstein Meets the Wolf Man* (1943)

05/13 *Dinosaurus!* (1960)

05/20 *House of Dracula* (1945)

05/27 *The Son of Dr. Jekyll* (1951) **Louis Hayward**

06/03 *20 Million Miles to Earth* (1957) **William Hopper**— A space expedition returns to Earth with a creature from Venus that mutates to gargantuan size. Stupendous special effects and a highly memorable creature are the highlights of this film from effects wizard Ray Harryhausen.

06/10 *Mutiny in Outer Space* (1965)

06/17 *The Werewolf* (1956)

06/24 *Earth vs. the Flying Saucers* (1956)

07/01 *Teenage Zombies* (1959) **Don Sullivan**— A mad female scientist uses a strange gas to turn young people into mindless slaves. More incredibly cheap fun from producer Jerry Warren.

07/08 ***Devil Bat's Daughter*** (1946) **Rosemary La Planche**— A ruthless psychiatrist convinces a patient that she is driven to kill in a weak, tepid sequel to the Bela Lugosi semi-classic, *The Devil Bat.*

07/15 ***Captive Wild Woman*** (1943)— a future *Fright Night* feature.

07/22 ***The Mad Doctor of Market Street*** (1942)— a future *Fright Night* feature.

07/29 ***The Mummy's Hand*** (1940)

08/05 ***The Return of the Vampire*** (1944)

08/12 ***Slaves of the Invisible Monster*** (1966) **Richard Webb**— Feature version of the Republic serial *The Invisible Monster* (1950).

08/19 ***Cry of the Werewolf*** (1944)

08/26 ***Cyclotrode X*** (1966)

09/02 ***Nyoka and the Lost Secrets of Hippocrates*** (1966) **Kay Aldridge**— Re-edit of the 1942 Republic serial *Perils of Nyoka.*

09/09 ***Spy Smasher Returns*** (1966) **Kane Richmond**— Republic's 1942 *Spy Smasher* serial gets the feature version treatment.

09/16 ***Missile Base at Taniak*** (1966) **Bill Henry**—*Canadian Mounties vs. Atomic Invaders*, a 1953 Republic serial, edited to feature length.

09/23 ***Captain Mephisto and the Transformation Machine*** (1966)

09/30 ***Have Rocket Will Travel*** (1959)

10/07 ***The Monster of Piedras Blancas*** (1959) **Les Tremayne.** A lighthouse keeper is convinced that a legendary monster lives in the caves beneath and will someday come out to kill. A great low-budget, independently made monster movie with an unexpectedly scary creature and nice a gory decapitation scene!

10/14 ***The Return of the Vampire*** (1944)

10/21 ***S.O.S. Coastguard*** (1937)

10/28 ***The Black Cat*** (1934)

11/04 ***The Claw Monsters*** (1966) **Phyllis Coates.** Feature version of the 1955 serial *Panther Girl of the Congo*, memorable for its slow-moving crawfish monsters poking around in the brush and scaring natives.

11/11 ***House of Dracula*** (1945)

11/18 ***The Flying Serpent*** (1946) **George Zucco.** A crazed archaeologist discovers an ancient winged serpent creature still living and uses it to kill his enemies.

11/25 ***Black Friday*** (1940)

12/02 ***The Man Who Turned to Stone*** (1957)

12/09 ***The Undying Monster*** (1942)

12/16 *Two Lost Worlds* (1950) James Arness. Sailors become shipwrecked on an island filled with prehistoric beasts. This movie wanted to be something big, but with no budget it ended up as wooden as the vessels it prominently features. Still, it was ideal for a Saturday morning.

12/23 *The Monster of Piedras Blancas* (1959)

12/30 *Fabulous Baron Munchausen* (1962) Karel Hoger. Director Karel Zeman's visually remarkable, dream-like Czech film incorporates unusual linear animation with live action. (His film *The Fabulous World of Jules Verne* is even more surreal and enjoyable.)

1973

01/15 *Creature of the Walking Dead* (1965) Rock Madison. Another Jerry Warren mix of footage from a Mexican film about a fountain of youth formula and U.S. scenes that made for a weird, incoherent viewing experience.

01/22 *Monster from the Ocean Floor* (1954) — a *Fright Night* feature

01/27 *Man Beast* (1956)

02/03 *Robot Monster* (1953) — a *Fright Night* feature

02/10 *Phantom from Space* (1953)

02/17 *The Snow Creature* (1954) Paul Langton. A giant Yeti is captured in the Himalayas and brought back to Los Angeles where it escapes. The monster's paws look like big mittens.

02/24 *Project Moon Base* (1953)

03/03 *Target Earth* (1954) Richard Denning. Giant robots from another planet invade the Earth.

03/10 *The Invisible Man* (1933)

03/17 *Curse of the Stone Hand* (1964) — a *Fright Night* feature

03/24 *Day the Sky Exploded* (1958)

03/31 *The Incredible Petrified World* (1957)

04/07 *The Human Duplicators* (1965)

04/14 *The Gamma People* (1956) Paul Douglas. Scientists in an Iron Curtain country perform mind-control experiments on children in a talky drama with elements of both comedy and sci-fi.

04/21 *The Man Who Turned to Stone* (1957)

04/28 *The Son of Dr. Jekyll* (1951)

05/05 *Two Lost Worlds* (1950)

05/12 *Creature with the Atom Brain* (1955)

05/19 *The Spider Woman Strikes Back* (1946) — a *Fright Night* feature.

05/26 *Jungle Woman* (1944)

06/02 *Invasion of the Animal People* (1959)

06/09 *Day the Sky Exploded* (1958)

06/16 *Teenage Zombies* (1959)

06/23 *The Incredible Petrified World* (1957)

06/30 *Phantom from Space* (1953) **Noreen Nash.** Old-fashioned tale of a space traveler, landing in California and met with hostility from humans. No surprise there.

07/07 *Target Earth* (1954)

07/14 *Monster from the Ocean Floor* (1954)

07/21 *The Snow Creature* (1954)

07/28 *The Slime People* (1963)

08/04 *The Man Who Turned to Stone* (1957)

08/11 *Dinosaurus!* (1960)

08/18 *The Ghost of Frankenstein* (1942)

08/25 *20 Million Miles to Earth* (1957)

09/01 *Cyclotrode X* (1966)

09/08 *Retik the Moon Menace* (1966) **George Wallace.** Feature-length version of the 1952 Republic serial *Radar Men from the Moon*.

09/15 *Sombra, the Spider Woman* (1966) **Carol Forman.** The 1947 Republic serial *The Black Widow* is given the feature film treatment.

THRILLER THEATRE

1973

09/29 *Creature with the Atom Brain* (1955)

10/06 *The Son of Dr. Jekyll* (1951)

10/13 *Phantom from Space* (1953)

10/20 *Face of a Fugitive* (1959) **Fred MacMurray**—Falsely accused of murder, a man escapes the law and starts a new life near the Mexican border.

10/27 *4D Man* (1959) **Robert Lansing**—A scientist uncovers the secret of moving through matter with dire consequences.

11/03 *The Son of Kong* (1933) **Robert Armstrong**—This quickie sequel to *King Kong* was churned out in a hurry but is still an enjoyable romp.

11/10 *Target Earth* (1954)

11/17 *Frankenstein Meets the Wolf Man* (1942)—a *Fright Night* feature.

11/24 *Robot Monster* (1953)—a *Fright Night* feature.

12/01 **Invasion of the Animal People** (1959)
12/08 **Ring of Terror** (1962) — a *Fright Night* feature.
12/15 **The Werewolf** (1956)
12/22 **The Crawling Hand** (1963)
12/29 **Creature with the Atom Brain** (1955)

1974

01/05 **The Body Snatcher** (1945) — a *Fright Night* feature.
01/12 **Untamed Women** (1952) — a *Fright Night* feature.
01/19 **Gamma People** (1956)
01/26 **Man Beast** (1956)
02/02 **Destination Space** (1959) **John Agar** — A TV pilot film that never became a series.
02/09 **Dillinger** (1945) **Lawrence Tierney, Edmund Lowe** — A petty thief begins a life of crime that leads to a daring series of robberies.
01/16 **The Monolith Monsters** (1957) — a *Fright Night* feature.
02/23 **Curse of the Undead** (1959) — a *Fright Night* feature.
03/02 **The Thing That Couldn't Die** (1958) — a *Fright Night* feature.
03/09 **The Invisible Ray** (1936) — a *Fright Night* feature.
03/16 **Godzilla's Revenge** (1969) **Kenji Sahara, Tomonori Yazaki** — A schoolboy tormented by bullies dreams of befriending Godzilla and his son. The goofy, pixie-like kid was painful to watch.
03/23 **Have Rocket Will Travel** (1959)
03/30 **Fabulous World of Jules Verne** (1961) **Ernest Navara.** In the early 1800s, a professor and his assistant, working on the forerunner of today's atomic energy, are abducted by a band of pirates whose leader hopes to conquer the world with their discovery. Director Karel Zeman's remarkable tale combines mesmerizing linear animation with live action. There's nothing like it and it remains a captivatingly unusual and original movie even today.
04/06 **The Black Castle** (1952) — a *Fright Night* feature.
04/13 **Dracula** (1931) — a *Fright Night* feature.
04/20 **The Brighton Strangler** (1945) — a future *Fright Night* feature.
04/27 **The Invisible Man's Revenge** (1944) — a *Fright Night* feature.
05/04 The program becomes *Blockbuster Movie* until 09–21 showing action films.
09/21 *Thriller Theatre* returns at 10 A.M. with **Jack and the Witch** (1969) — Cartoon animated feature.
09/28 **Little Norse Prince** (1968) — Cartoon animated feature.

10/05 *Bluebeard* (1944) **John Carradine.** A Parisian artist murders his models.

10/12 *Mermaids of Tiburon* (1962) — a *Fright Night* feature.

10/19 *Riders to the Stars* (1954) **William Lundigan** — Astronauts attempt to discover the secrets of meteors.

10/26 *Ghidorah, the Three Headed Monster* (1964) **Yuriko Hoshi** — Giant monsters unite to battle an invading three-headed creature that threatens to destroy Tokyo.

11/03 *Target Earth* (1954)

11/09 *The Crawling Eye* (1958) — a *Fright Night* feature.

11/16 *The Strange Door* (1951) — a *Fright Night* feature

11/30 *Curucu, Beast of the Amazon* (1956)

12/07 *Fog Island* (1945)

12/14 *Invisible Agent* (1942) **Peter Lorre** — An American agent uses invisibility to thwart the plans of Nazis in a Universal oldie originally designed to support the war effort.

12/21 *Mr. Moto in Danger Island* (1939) **Peter Lorre** — The master sleuth investigates diamond smuggling in Puerto Rico.

1975

01/04 *Godzilla's Revenge* (1969)

01/11 *Nabonga* (1944) **Buster Crabbe** — Deep in the jungle, an adventurer discovers a beautiful woman guarded by a huge gorilla. Quickie thriller from PRC, often used by Channel 9 to fill in open hour time slots.

01/18 *The Gamma People* (1956)

01/25 *The Son of Dr. Jekyll* (1951)

02/01 *Man Beast* (1956)

02/08 *The Disembodied* (1957) — a *Fright Night* feature

02/15 *Gorath* (1962) — a *Fright Night* feature

02/22 *It Came from Outer Space* (1953) **Richard Carlson** — A spaceship carrying an alien life form crashes near a desert town. An early 3-D sci-fi from Universal.

03/01 *Bride of Frankenstein* (1935)

03/08 *Creature from the Black Lagoon* (1954)

03/15 *Daughter of Dr. Jekyll* (1957) **John Agar** — A young woman fears she has a split personality when she discovers she is the daughter of the infamous doctor. Fun, enthusiastic chiller but with a poorly executed period setting and obvious use of miniatures.

03/22 *The Invisible Man Returns* (1940)

03/29 *20 Million Miles to Earth* (1957)

04/05 *Revenge of the Creature* (1955) **John Agar**— The Creature from the Black Lagoon is captured and transported to a Florida oceanarium for study.

04/12 *The Mole People* (1956)— a *Fright Night* feature.

04/19 *House of Frankenstein* (1944)— a *Fright Night* feature.

04/26 *Monster on the Campus* (1958)— a *Fright Night* feature.

05/03 *Tarantula* (1955)— a *Fright Night* feature.

05/10 *Curucu, Beast of the Amazon* (1956)

05/17 *White Zombie* (1932)— a *Fright Night* feature.

05/24 *The Creature Walks Among Us* (1956)— a *Fright Night* feature.

05/31 *Battle of the Worlds* (1961)— a *Fright Night* feature.

06/07 *Target Earth* (1954)

06/14 *The Wasp Woman* (1959)— a *Fright Night* feature.

06/21 *The Slime People* (1963)— a *Fright Night* feature.

06/28 *Creature with the Atom Brain* (1955)

07/05 *The Crawling Hand* (1963)

07/12 *Project Moon Base* (1953) **Donna Martell**

07/19 *Invasion of the Animal People* (1959)

07/26 *Wild Youth* (1965) **Robert Hutton**

08/02 *I Walked with a Zombie* (1943)— a *Fright Night* feature.

08/09 *Cell 2455 Death Row* (1955) **William Campbell**— A man awaits execution on Death Row.

08/16 *Isle of the Dead* (1945)

08/23 *Man in the Dark* (1953) **Edmond O'Brien, Audrey Totter**— Doctors attempt experimental surgery to remove the criminal element in a man's brain. A remake of 1936's *The Man Who Lived Twice*, *Man in the Dark* was originally in 3-D.

08/30 *The Body Snatcher* (1945)

09/06 *House of Dracula* (1945)

After the *House of Dracula* telecast, *Thriller Theatre* became *Action Theater* but continued to show a similar mix of science fiction, horror and, of course, action films. Larry Casey masterminded another Saturday morning program that would pair like-titled horror movies for a clever show called *Spaced-Out Films*. "That was a fun program to schedule for," he says. "We'd pair up movies like *The Son of Dr. Jekyll* and *Daughter of Dr. Jekyll* and create these crazy double features. They didn't always have the same theme in common, usually just similar title elements."

12. More, More, More

What remains remarkable about *Fright Night* is that in the demanding, ever-changing New York television entertainment market, the show managed to endure for well over a decade, and with its formula relatively unchanged. Every once in a while, the show was pre-empted for a telethon, put on a brief hiatus for non-genre programming like the sports series *The Champions* or comedy-variety show *Steve Allen's Laughback*, or moved to a later time slot to make way for momentarily hotter music shows like *Disco '77*.

Apparently fatigued by my endless letter campaign to restore the show each time it disappeared, Chris Steinbrunner, in the capacity of Manager of Program and Film Services, wrote me on September 29, 1975, to explain: "Unfortunately, all our Saturday late night supernatural film programming has been eliminated by executive decision in favor of sporting events like the wrestling show and *The Best of Joe Franklin* which unfortunately we cannot air during the week and have relegated to the weekend." He added, "In the meanwhile, I am trying to schedule horror films on Friday nights on *Showcase 9*. Even though the show will not be called *Fright Night*, and because it starts very late — half past midnight, it will be available for no one but the most diehard viewers." Fortunately, Steinbrunner and management came to their senses and *Fright Night* was restored in 1976.

"*Disco '77* probably bumped *Fright Night* later for monetary reasons," explained Larry Casey. "The advertisers probably requested a 1:00 A.M. start time." Furious that I'd have to wait an additional 30 minutes for my favorite program, I reluctantly watched *Disco '77* to see what it was all about. The program was also being simulcast on New York's WBLS-FM. A thumping dance beat came out of my television and an announcer said: "From Miami Beach and Fort Lauderdale, Florida ... the disco capital of the world! *Disco '77*!" Then porn star-turned pop star Andrea True of *More, More, More* fame took the stage and sang her dance hit "New York, You Got Me Dancing."

But despite these setbacks, *Fright Night* persevered.

If Larry Casey had been able to call all the shots, *Fright Night* might have conceivably been something different or perhaps never come about. At least

WOR-TV / 1440 BROADWAY / NEW YORK, NY 10018 / (212) 764-7000

September 19, 1975

Mr. James Arena

Dear Mr. Arena:

Everyone around here was impressed by your art work. You are certainly devoted to "FRIGHT NIGHT" and we will do our best to please you in the future.

Keep watching WOR-TV.

Cordially,

Chris Steinbrunner
Manager,
Program and Film Services

CS/hw

RKO
TELEVISION

One of several letters sent by Chris Steinbrunner and others at WOR-TV thanking this author for his support of *Fright Night* during the first years of the program.

not as we knew it. "As a kid," he says, "I idolized legendary horror movie host John Zacherle. My generation was all about *Shock Theater*. It was my dream to bring him back to New York. Even Zacherle himself was agreeable to the idea, provided we could give him the exact same show he had in Philadelphia. He wanted the identical ability he once had to participate in the films being shown, the jokes, the whole thing. But union rules and the cost to produce such a show would have made it impossible for our station. The project got priced out of do-ability for us." Might Zacherle have been the host for *Fright Night*? After a pause to ponder the idea, Casey says, "Well, probably not. It's unlikely we'd have wasted him in such a late time slot."

Casey's tenure at WOR lasted until about 1979 or 1980, when he moved on to positions at Showtime and other major television and cable companies. It is his recollection that his position at Channel 9 was not immediately filled and that his boss George Snowden, with the aid of Casey's trusty secretary Rose Marie Sullivan, handled the movies thereafter. If that's the case, Snowden, and any other film programmers who came along, never tampered much with the *Fright Night* formula and the show continued without interruption or formula change until its demise in 1987.

13. Postmortem

In the wake of *Fright Night*'s departure, horror movie fans were not exactly left high and dry and the impact of the loss of the program was not immediately palpable. A few short-lived shows like USA Network's *Saturday Nightmares*, Joe Bob Briggs' *Monstervision* and *100% Weird* on TNT, and even a syndicated program of public domain horror flicks called *Haunted Hollywood*, filled the void to some extent, enjoying bigger audiences thanks to the arrival of cable super-stations. Grandpa Munster himself, Al Lewis, helped bridge the past with the contemporary when he hosted TBS' *Super Scary Saturday*, an afternoon horror program that played briefly on the station. Once in a blue full moon, Channel 9 might even still telecast an old horror or sci-fi flick such as *Them!* (1954), though it was a rarity.

With the explosive expansion of cable's channel assortment, there were a lot more viewing choices, not the least of which was the Sci-Fi Channel, which showed promise as a new source of classic and cult horror movie programming for quite a while. And, before *Madmen* dominated the network's programming, AMC's annual month-long Halloween movie schedule and attention to cult and drive-in movies in the '90s and early 2000s were fine momentary distractions in the absence of *Fright Night*. When WPIX began reviving their prime-time Saturday telecast of *Chiller* around Halloween in 2008, I'm sure many New York fans' hearts began to beat with excitement and hope. Alas, those same hearts had a stake driven through them when it was announced by management that the station's economics would not allow for anything more than a once-a-year special. As younger audiences and changing tastes drive modern programming decisions, all these resources inevitably dry up. It would become the responsibility of the fan to fill *Fright Night*'s Frankenstein-sized boots through the support of DVD releases and online websites, message boards and blogs.

Few of the elements that existed in the broadcasting glory days of *Fright Night* exist in the present day. Says Larry Casey, "Today, the whole dynamics of the business is much different. You'll rarely see an older movie turn up except on specialized outlets like TMC or sometimes AMC. Most of the movies you see on television are what are called 'barter movies.' They are films with pre-sold commercial time. They are always highly visible, well-known, popular movies made during the last few years. The stations showing these films generally have to run these pictures in a prime time period first and then again within seven days at another time or some other similar arrangement. The movies are generally free to the stations and they profit by getting some of the ad time to sell their own commercials."

Even if one never goes to the trouble of viewing all the films ever shown on *Fright Night*, it's still impossible to escape the conclusion that the program was a unique and extraordinary experience. Whether the program was tele-casting the security of a golden oldie in black and white or shocking the senses through the world of more contemporary color films, *Fright Night* was a nuclear reactor supplying a seemingly limitless energy current of horror. Only looking back, seeing its staggering array of movies and the uniqueness the show possessed for such a long period of time, can one begin to appreciate what a gift this program was to viewers in the tri-state broadcast area. Casey makes an interesting observation about this program and this era in Channel 9's history: "I have to personalize this because I think it's really true." "I think if it weren't for Chris Steinbrunner, and if he hadn't been there before me to get the ball rolling with *Mystery Museum, Tales of Terror*, and programming like that, *Fright Night*, and all the other programs horror fans enjoyed on WOR-TV, might not have come to be. To be honest, I loved the genre very much, but I don't know if I would have come on board and said, 'That's what this station needs ... more horror movies!' It bears repeating that this was the station Kong built and in many ways Chris built, and I simply inherited the raw clay and continued to mold it."

Fright Night's producers, although clearly demonstrating an appreciation for the horror film genre at the time, may not have realized what a dependable and thrilling resource they had developed for fans of the genre with this pro-gram. It's clear that Channel 9 was a business and that money had to be made. They may have often been forced to think of *Fright Night* as, primarily and simply, an easy revenue generator and a place to economically run movies that fell short of prime-time caliber. But Steinbrunner and Casey's love of the genre was, more often than not, evident in so many of their film choices for the program that it seems clear there was a genuine affection percolating at WOR for *Fright Night* and the Saturday night horror movie experience. Over three decades later, Casey seems a bit surprised, humbled and very pleased to hear that the *Fright Night* experience provided more than just revenue to Channel 9 and serviced an incredible education in the glorious art of the horror film to countless horror fans. "It's very gratifying to know *Fright Night* was so appreciated and that it is still remembered today," he almost blushingly admits.

Sam Sherman reflects on the show's legacy. "*Fright Night* was just one great example of a multitude of shows in this country that specialized in science fiction and horror films at the time. Back then, the stations weren't all showing the same syndicated programs like they do today. Each station was unique and they were distinctive entities that showed unique programming. I guess it started in the '50s with Universal's *Shock* package distributed through Screen Gems and the great horror hosts like Seymour and Zacherley and the tradition that was carried on in later years by Elvira. Shows like *Fright Night* were great ... they gave people a place to find these movies on a Saturday night and it's really a shame they are gone."

Even with the ability today to possess and view, at will, nearly the entire line-up of *Fright Night* movies, it's still not quite the same as waiting up late for those original telecasts. After completing my own experiment to relive the *Fright Night* experience, though completely successful and satisfying on many levels, I kept hearing those faint but familiar words, "You can't go back." Sam concurs: "Personally, I don't feel that watching a DVD or downloading a movie replaces watching a film the way we did on TV in the era of *Fright Night*. You can own every film that was ever played on that show, but it doesn't have exactly the same feeling. If an old movie is shown on television today by some chance, even though it's not like those days in the past, it's almost like it feels better to watch it on TV than to just pop in the DVD. I can't explain it, but the best reason I can come up with is that a broadcast feels live at that moment. With a DVD, you don't have to watch it now. You can watch it another time. But all of a sudden, the same films shows up on the air and you'll watch it right then and there. And that's because it becomes a special event. Even though you own the DVD.

"When these movies showed on up *Fright Night*, it was like the movie was being brought to you for possibly one and only one time, broadcast live. It was unrolling and being projected and you *had* to watch it when *they* were showing it. You wanted to be there for the event. You might even set your clock by it. You knew on Saturday night at midnight or 1 A.M., *Fright Night* was going to show something special. It was almost like you were going to see a live play, not some movie where all the actors died forty years ago. Many times we didn't know what was going to be shown until maybe the week before or sometimes even the day of the telecast. The TV guides didn't always tell you ... they'd sometimes just say 'movie' and give you no information. It was exciting anticipating what the movie might be. Back in those days, the first thing I'd do was go through the TV guide from beginning to end each

Producer Sam Sherman creating fuel for *Fright Night*.

week to see what horror movies were going to be shown. I'd mark them with a big X so I knew I had to watch it. And with some of the unusual movies that were shown late on a Saturday night, as was often the case on *Fright Night*, I had no idea what to expect.

"I wouldn't care what anyone else may have wanted to watch," laughs Sam. "Oooh, *The Devil Bat* is on and that's what I wanted to see! That's what I *had* to see!"

Sam says there was a sense of the subliminal in watching programs like *Fright Night*. "You knew were part of an audience even though you may have been watching the show in your darkened den completely alone." "You knew in the back of your head that there may have been thousands or millions watching the show in their homes just like you were. And let's say that during the movie Channel 9 didn't edit out some nudity and the next day you asked your friends, 'Did you see that scene last night on *Fright Night*?' It became a shared experience. And anything could happen with those 16mm prints too.

They could rip or jam as you were watching a movie or something could have happened earlier and a whole different movie had to get substituted. There was a real sense that anything was possible and the element of the unexpected was always present and really added to the experience. With a DVD, well ... it is what it is. There's nothing unpredictable. But with broadcasts like *Fright Night*, there was that entertaining element of unpredictability. It was being broadcast live and you just never knew how it would go down. If you go back further to the days of Zacherley, he was *really* live and you never knew what he was going to do. Once, he took a meat cleaver and slammed it into a head of cabbage like it was somebody's skull. Who the heck expected that?

"*Fright Night* might show some weird picture you never heard of and never saw before. It was like you had a sense of discovery watching it. Oh boy ... it was just all so good. Today everything is kind of homogenized and if something is shown on TV, you just don't get any of that sense of audience or excitement we once had."

For me, and many like me, the impact of *Fright Night* has not lessened over time, but the generation that I am part of, the one that can truly appreciate this era, is rapidly aging. It's not difficult to imagine a point in the not too distant future where *Fright Night*, and all the programs like it, may be lost to fading memories and a society no longer interested in such antiquities.

For the longest time in my world, from my earliest childhood memories until young adulthood, entertainment stayed rather stagnant. There were magazines, comic books, records, some toys and games, movies in theaters and movies on TV and the good old reliable book. Maybe the occasional live concert or Broadway show once in a while. That was pretty much it. And it stayed that way. But throughout that whole period, *Fright Night* was there ... a loyal, dependable companion. Almost always feeling fresh and exciting and quite reliably showing me sights I had never seen before ... and would probably never have been able to see any other way. And like a faithful friend, the show brought out the best in me. I watched it with rabid anticipation and was completely absorbed in the moment when it was on. I was transported to other worlds, both good and evil, amusing and horrifying. It taught me endlessly about right and wrong and helped me face my worst fears early on. It showed me that sometimes life doesn't have a happy ending. But in the end, and more often than not, good will triumph over evil. It allowed me a chance to escape from some of those uncomfortable pressures and realities of real-life and growing up. It made me less afraid of the real life horrors that were so abundant when the sun came up.

Fright Night stimulated my imagination and it brought out tremendous creativity in me, as a writer, amateur moviemaker and artist. I was blessed to have parents who allowed me to explore my interests and never passed judgment on what I was into. I recall my father walking into the den one night while *Fright Night* was on and seeing some creature clawing at the TV screen, shaking his head in amusement and going back to bed. My parents may not have understood my fascination with horror, but they never discouraged my enjoyment of it. Ironically, Larry Casey related a story to me that his wife at the time, a schoolteacher, thought my numerous letters about the show and devotion to horror movies might be the sign of a disturbed mind. But somehow I managed to keep the freak in me in check. And I'll wager that most of the youth who enjoyed this and similar programs across the country did as well. *Fright Night* never left me in a stupor, foggy or naïve. It never interfered with social relationships, family, friends, school or faith. In fact, it made me sharper, more aware and, I'd like to think, more intelligent and observant than I might otherwise have been. And in comparison to the stimuli available to today's youth, it all seems rather tame and harmless now.

Today it's still a world of scary monsters and fear. But it's different from the unearthly realm that *Fright Night* created. Now I regularly see misshapen humanoids stumbling on the subway. I witness zombies texting on cell phones (or whatever the latest futuristic device is) as they wander aimlessly into the boulevard traffic, and cringe as tsunamis, toxic chemicals and political madmen, violence and inhumanity regularly transform my world into a horror planet. I'm less concerned today about a spaceship crashing and unleashing a creature to destroy mankind than the stock market tanking and destroying my 401K. And damn it, I still feel like I'm on that geek radar. But thanks to *Fright Night*, I can summon up the skills to handle it and to face it all with courage. Just like I did every time the television announcer let me know that *Fright Night* was coming up next on Channel 9.

And we all have, for a while anyway, our still very vivid memories, that take us right back to those gloriously primitive Saturday nights sitting in front of a TV and a giant WOR-TV logo on the screen dissolving into a parade of monsters that we will forever remember and love.

Part Two: The Films of *Fright Night*

Time Travelers

I decided some time ago that the *Fright Night* experience, which actually encompassed any viewer sitting in front of a TV for any horror movie program shown in the United States during the '70s and '80s, shouldn't have to end entirely simply because those days are long gone. Technology has advanced to a point where it is now possible to obtain almost all these films and conveniently view them in order, easily and with nearly the same presentation and ambience created by Channel 9. And so my project to recreate the *Fright Night* experience began.

It helped to have that "collector's mentality," an inner drive that began when I started getting a mania for back issues of *Famous Monster of Filmland*. I guess the project officially started when *Fright Night* was still being telecast and I began making VHS recordings of the show and collecting video tapes in the late '80s, later converting those to DVD. I then decided to obtain a DVD copy of nearly every film shown on the program — and with the exception of *The Nylon Noose* and *The Chilling* I did. (It's only a matter of time before I track down those.) Having friends like movie collector–author Rob Craig helping hunt down the more obscure titles from *Fright Night's* repertoire didn't hurt either. The DVDs are available today on numerous low-priced online retail sites, as well as on specialized collector sites from around the world and bidding services like iOffer and eBay.

In Part Two, I list every film shown on *Fright Night* during its stellar 14 year run so you'll know what you need to find. After the synopsis and review, I indicate if the film is available in a commercial U.S. format by putting a C after the review. The availability status of these movies changes frequently, so always keep checking your suppliers. The quality of these movies, like the price, will of course vary from source to source. Don't necessarily be scared off by a less than pristine copy of any movie. Remember that all the dirt and crackling and the lackluster color were all elements that added to the charm of *Fright Night* and never bothered most of us as kids. Criterion-level quality is the luxury of purists (and stronger economic times), but the *Fright Night* experience doesn't require it. I'd say the price I paid for each of these films in DVD or DVD-R format averaged $5 to $10 apiece and even the worst of them was worth every penny.

Viewing these movies on the soon-to-be-antiquated format of DVD involves storing the discs, pulling them out and loading into a player. And to view the original bumpers requires switching to yet another disc, DVD player and maybe even a VCR. I can tell you first hand that this annoying process will kill one's enthusiasm within seconds. It's also a method that's so old school that the instructions might as well be written out in hieroglyphics on a cave wall. Another and better option for the collector with no intentions of piracy (heed those copyright infringement warnings) would be to undertake the admittedly tedious task of transferring the films and bumpers where possible to MP4 formats for one's own personal use and storing them on two 1TB external hard drives, which are then connected to a tiny media player that allows them to be viewed on a big flat screen TV or simply on a laptop. The films could also be stored on devices like a Sony Playstation. Today, this can take quite a bit of time as the digital transfer from disc to MP4 or similar formats on your average home PC or Mac, depending on your capability, is still not exactly lightning fast. There are, no doubt, probably many faster, easier ways to accomplish all this for system-savvy geeks and those willing to do some online research. But even for the not-so adept, you can bet this whole process will get even quicker and simpler over the next few years, with technological advancements and entertainment enhancements such as streaming services that are already making many of these films available on demand in the blink of an eye. Ease of viewing is essential on a project like this; your collection of *Fright Night* films should be reasonably accessible with, ideally, no more than a click from an on-screen menu.

The *Fright Night* original bumpers that played right before the movie started are viewable today on YouTube and various retro-television forums and websites thanks to fans who preserved them on videotape from the original telecasts. The actual film or videotape bumpers produced by Channel 9 were destroyed long ago, back when WOR moved from New York City to its Secaucus location, according to a station representative.

Although the hunt for all the *Fright Night* movies can be exciting, once you've got your resources in place, the fun can really begin again.

So let's assume you're a true *Fright Night* experience devotee (you must be if you've made it this far) and are going to attempt to re-live the line-up once again as I did. Or you weren't lucky enough to have been around to enjoy the original *Fright Night* experience and want to know what it's all about now. Or maybe your memories of the show you watched as a kid somewhere in this nation strongly resemble the ones I am describing here in *Fright Night* on Channel 9. And let's say you're going to try and authenticate the experience by viewing the movies seen on this amazing program by watching them after midnight for the next several hundred Saturday nights. You've got to have a list of every movie shown on *Fright Night*. You may want to know what the flicks are going to be about, especially the more obscure titles. And with some of the dogs run on *Fright Night*, it may definitely be helpful to know how likely you are to fall asleep ... or if you should pass altogether. I've tried to take some of the guesswork out of it by throwing in some brief commentary for each film, a combination of my journalized reactions to the films as a young viewer and my opinions upon seeing the flicks today. These critiques are not meant to be NYU Film School analyses, but rather a homogenization of the everyday viewer's reaction to them in the context of viewing them on *Fright Night*. The movie plots are summarized using many of the actual local TV guide descriptions published back in the day and the featured media reviews were provided by major and local New York area newspapers, such as *Newsday*.

Keep in mind, *Fright Night* was generally shown between 12 midnight and 1:30 A.M. throughout most of its history, making the show available to only the most determined viewers or hopeless insomniacs. The late hour made viewing some of these films a genuine challenge, while enhancing the experience for others. I'm going to be brutally honest ... a lot of the movies *suck*. Larry Casey's amusing anecdote about the show being referred to as *Crap Playhouse* was often painfully spot-on. But it's not hypocrisy to both love and hate many of these clunkers. It's all just part of the human nature that genre fans possess when it comes to the *Fright Night* experience. The yin and the yang were never more present than in *Fright Night*'s overwhelmingly vast repertoire. For every classic, there's a bore or two. There are some real gems too ... genuinely great movies. A handful could be categorized as unique-to-*Fright Night* classics because of some special quality that the film possessed. And there are many, many more that are universally regarded as masterpieces of the horror genre.

Regardless of their ranking in horror movie history, each one contributed to *Fright Night*'s amazing story and, whether wretched or wonderful, the opportunity to see all these films should be cherished. So get ready ... when you have finished viewing all these amazing movies, you will be an entirely *different* person. You may feel shaken and even abused, but you'll be stronger, wiser and better able to face the challenges of our modern world.

"Well ... we've warned you!"

The Fright Night *Experience*

1973

As a large meteorite crashes into Fremont County, Colorado, and *Pioneer 10* sends back the first up-close images of Jupiter, *Fright Night* makes its splashy debut.

10/6 *Decoy for Terror* (1970—aka *Playgirl Killer, Portrait of Fear*) William Kirvin, Jean Christopher, Linda Christopher. A beautiful girl is set up as a police decoy in an attempt to capture a maniac artist whose models have disappeared. The debut feature for *Fright Night* came from the Hemisphere Pictures' *Block of Shock* TV package (which included a handful of licensed films from other production outfits in addition to Hemisphere's own drive-in features) and plodded along with an odd, sleazy, pre-porn 42nd Street feel and a plot reminiscent of *Track of the Vampire* (1966). Trouble was, both the murders and the sex were too tame to keep one's eyelids from drooping. Watching singer Neil Sedaka sing at a pool party

and play a "macho" cameo role added to the surreal weirdness. One of the victims (you can't miss her) had the biggest rack and the most atrocious acting skills I had ever seen. The film's climactic ten minutes were only modestly thrilling, mostly because you knew the 90 minutes was coming

The playgirl killer (William Kirvin) makes his move in *Decoy for Terror* (1970) the *Fright Night* debut feature.

to an end. But, despite its many flaws, this cheap movie was still an amusing and off beat beginning for the program. I couldn't get that French opening theme song, "Montage," out of my head: "...Oooh, mad people dancing...." C (Hemisphere, color)

10/13 Looks like *Fright Night* was pre-empted (already!) for a telethon.

10/20 *Island of Living Horror* (1968—aka *Brides of Blood*) John Ashley, Kent Taylor, Beverly Hills. **A scientist, his wife and a Peace Corps worker travel to a remote island to investigate reports of strange mutations of plant and animal life.** Wow ... it started off with a semi-rape scene, was punctuated by bloody, gruesome dismemberments, a hideous (and horny) half human-half blob creature and a jungle full of carnivorous plants. It ended with a mob of torch-bearing natives chasing a radioactive monster to its lair and letting off steam with a big, sexy mating luau. Again from Hemisphere's *Block of Shock* package, this incredibly fun, colorful drive-in classic from the Philippines never let up. Blood Island made for a great *Fright Night* destination and it was a completely over-the-top movie packed with chills. The cast members had to re-dub most of their dialogue in this picture, and actress–sex kitten Hills' (you couldn't pick a better drag name) breathy delivery of lines like "Maybe I can help keep the crew happy" was priceless. Channel 9 made only minimal cuts and some long distance nudity remained intact. What a fun night! C (Hemisphere, color)

10/20 *Psycho* (1960) Anthony Perkins, Janet Leigh, Vera Miles. **A young woman steals $10,000 and, while on the run, encounters a young man too long under the domination of his mother.** Just reading the name of Alfred Hitchcock's masterpiece listed in the TV guide generated tension and this telecast marked the first widely regarded genre film classic to appear on *Fright Night*. The haunting performances, grim visuals and multiple shock sequences suitably illustrated the diversity of film experiences one could begin to expect from the program. Something about viewing this chiller in the dead of night was truly unsettling. Man, I got the creeps when the sheriff asked who was buried out at Greenlawn Cemetery — which was mercifully followed by a commercial break. Perkins' thoughts about the fly on his hand, a skull face superimposed over his, and the emergence of the car from the swamp at the film's conclusion made sleep very difficult. Did I mention the shower sequence? *Newsday* gave it four stars and said it was Hitchcock's "best job of starting out with one kind of plot and sneaking into another.... [N]ot for the squeamish." C (Paramount, b/w)

11/03 Looks like *Fright Night* was pre-empted.

11/10 *Tomb of the Living Dead* (1970—aka *Mad Doctor of Blood Island*)

John Ashley, Angelique Pettijohn, Ronald Remy. A beautiful tropical island is terrorized by a strange green-skinned creature. The third installment from Hemisphere's *Block of Shock* package and yet another jaunt to Blood Island that was more infamous than its predecessor, *Island of Living Horror*, but a less cohesive Filipino production. You almost wanted to swat the mosquitoes feeding on the necks of actors as this drive-in quality trip to the steamy tropics weaved its chlorophyll tale of terror. Aside from the camera zooming in and out (a bit tough on the eyes at this late hour), the most memorable aspect of this telecast was the inclusion of the campy promotional intro (developed by Sam Sherman) that featured a group of young people swallowing a mysterious green blood potion, which the announcer warns "has been known to passionately affect some people after drinking it!" Watching it today, one might try downing a glass of Absinthe as a fine substitute! Good fun. C (Hemisphere, color)

11/17 *Torture Chamber of Dr. Sadism* (1967 — aka *Blood Demon, Castle of the Walking Dead*) Christopher Lee, Karin Dor, Lex Barker. A group of people journey to the remote castle of Count Regula who, years before, was sentenced to death for the murder of 12 virgins. Did Channel 9 realize this film was the original co-feature to *Tomb of the Living Dead* on the drive-in circuit when it telecast the movie the following week? Brilliant! Spooky as all hell, it dripped with a rich and evocative Euro-atmosphere ("Euro" will become a common adjective to describe *Fright Night* movies and this flick defines the term!). It was shown several times during the program's history; it's doubtful anyone would ever have tired of watching this *Wizard of Oz*–like journey into horror. The colorful band of travelers took a hair-raising trip in a horse-drawn coach through a forest of hanging corpses, shuddered at the echoing footsteps of a sinister one-legged messenger on a cobbled village street, and faced a castle full of torture traps — just a few of the creepy delights this film offered. It was a scary world that only the Germans could create, with a cast and crew that were well-established in the country's Edgar Wallace crime thrillers. A skillful blend of horror and adventure from director Harald Reinl and the Hemisphere *Block of Shock* package. A *Fright Night* classic. C (Hemisphere, color)

11/24 *Octaman* (1972) Pier Angeli, Kerwin Mathews, Jeff Morrow. A naturalist exploring rural Mexico is certain that man is destroying himself through underwater nuclear testing and pollution. What Channel 9's description failed to mention was that pollution also created a four-tentacled (eight would have been too much pressure on this film's budget) man-o-pus with adorable offspring. Cheap and grainy, this movie holds a fond place in my *Fright Night*–lovin' heart, especially with its narrator-whispered

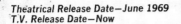

Theatrical Release Date—June 1969
T.V. Release Date—Now

TORTURE CHAMBER OF DR. SADISM

Starring

CHRISTOPHER LEE   LEX BARKER   KARIN DOR

RUNNING TIME: 90 MINUTES - IN COLOR

synopsis
(NOT FOR PUBLICATION)

Count Regula sends a sinister one-legged messenger to inform Baroness Lilian and Roger, her attorney, that they must travel to Sander Valley where Lilian is to receive a great inheritance. Once there, they enlist the aid of Fabian, a scurrilous monk, to guide them to the legendary "Blood Castle" where, years ago, the Count was accused of murdering twelve young maidens.

Traveling to the castle, black-hooded riders attack Lilian and her maid. Though Roger tries to protect them, eerie events cause the girls to disappear. Fabian, revealed as a highway bandit, is terrified by such events and helps Roger find the girls in a steel chamber beneath the castle. But they become prisoners as well, guarded by the diabolical Anatole. The evil servant announces that Count Regula, executed 40 years ago, has been reincarnated. With an iron mask for a face, the Count appears, proclaiming that all he requires to obtain complete immortality is the blood of a 13th virgin—which will be Lilian's

They try to escape. They are recaptured. Lilian is thrown into a pit of snakes and spiders, driving her insane. Barely escaping execution, Roger retrieves Lilian's diamond cross. Displaying it, he rids the castle of the evil spell, the Count and Anatole disappear, and Lilian returns to sanity and the open arms of Roger.

Hemisphere Pictures, Inc.

LOEW'S THEATRE BLDG. 1540 BROADWAY, SUITE 300 NEW YORK, N.Y. 10036 (212) CIRCLE 5-6874

Publicity art and TV promotional description from Hemisphere Pictures' *Torture Chamber of Dr. Sadism* (1967).

intro and eerie nighttime scenes. Though often maligned, *Octaman* was just a good old-fashioned monster movie with more than a passing resemblance to *Creature from the Black Lagoon* (both movies had the same writer). It had a distinctly '70s low budget style that was very entertaining. (Filmers Guild/Heritage, color)

12/01 ***Bride of Frankenstein*** **(1935) Boris Karloff, Elsa Lanchester, Colin Clive. Frankenstein's Monster learns the meaning of friendship and threatens vengeance unless his creator makes a mate for him.** Universal Pictures would play a big role in *Fright Night*'s history, and what an introduction to the studio's classics! With the Monster's mate featured prominently in the show's opening movie creature montage, this first-time telecast just seemed right! Creepy, weird, wryly humorous and oozing with Golden Age atmosphere, it was a legendary monster movie that needs no analysis ... it was a Universal classic. Something about Una O'Connor nervously muttering "Let them all be murdered in their beds!" stuck with and scared me as a young child when I first saw the movie on Channel 5, long before this telecast. *Newsday* wrote of it: "As good as, if not better than, the original. The mating of the monsters is a gem." Said the *New York Times*, "Ripe, knockout horror sequel, for a change." C (Universal, b/w)

12/08 ***Phantom of the Rue Morgue*** **(1954) Karl Malden, Patricia Medina, Steve Forrest. A mysterious killer, whose strength seems to exceed that of a normal man, prowls the streets of Paris in the early 1900s.** Certainly a loud movie (I remember having to turn down the volume during the opening minutes so the high-pitched screams of female victims would not awaken my sleeping parents), it was also a fun, old-fashioned horror mystery yarn loosely based on Poe's "The Murders in the Rue Morgue." The vibrant use of color, lavish sets and photography (intended for 3-D) were eye-catching and helped compensate for a slow first half. It was highly reminiscent of *House of Wax* (1953), made by the same studio. Merv Griffin was featured in a small role, long before he became a gazillionaire. (Warner, color)

12/15 ***Vampire People*** **(1971—aka** ***The Blood Drinkers***) **Ronald Remy, Amelia Fuentes, Eva Montes. A priest and police attempt to combat a group of vampires that has invaded their village.** Re-released on the drive-in circuit numerous times, this compelling Filipino vampire flick became well-known for its sepia-toned sequences and distinctive atmosphere. It's a very interesting and eerie movie, but viewing at a late hour could be a challenge through some its slower parts. I even recall dosing a bit while viewing it at a drive-in theater on a double bill with *Brain of Blood* with my dad (who was most definitely asleep). Long Island station

WSNL-TV would show the film on their Saturday afternoon *Shock Theater* show, where the movie and Basra the bat could be appreciated more fully. Another dubbed import from Hemisphere's *Block of Shock* package. C (Hemisphere, color)

12/22 *Operation Fear* **(1968 — aka** *Kill Baby Kill,* **Curse of the Living** *Dead***) Erica Blanc, Giacomo Rossi-Stuart, Piero Lulli. A young doctor finds himself wandering in a state of almost semi-consciousness, undergoing strange and incredible experiences.** Channel 9's odd description gave unsuspecting viewers little idea what to expect from this evocative Euro-thriller, and its almost espionage-style title did even less to help. Great costuming, spooky moods, rich color and striking photography punctuated this eerie ghost story that has attained a bit of a cult following. What it lacked in sensationalism and speed, it certainly made up for in atmosphere. Plenty of goosebumps surfaced when a dead little girl's hand or ghostly face appeared at the window. *Newsday*, reviewing the film under its *Curse of the Living Dead* title, said, "[T]he film is by Mario Bava, whose special pasta is psycho-gore, and whose works are never totally uninteresting." They also called the guy who re-titled the movie a "nit-wit," when actually the *Curse* title was probably the best-fitting of the three. C (FUL, color)

12/29 *Diabolical Dr. Z* **(1966) Howard Vernon, Estella Blain, Mabel Karr. A mad scientist uses a beautiful, sinister woman to lure his victims.** A well-photographed and visually stylish Jess Franco production with a kind of cool '60s vibe, but it was just a little too eccentric ... in that confusing kind of "foreign" way that can make for strained viewing at half past the witching hour. The strange robotic contraption used in the operating room was memorable. Weird stuff not often shown on TV; despite some pacing issues, it was worth catching. C (Speva, b/w)

1974

The Watergate scandal and subsequent resignation of President Nixon, along with the kidnapping of Patty Hearst, signals a real downer of a year. But it's a great time to escape reality with *Fright Night* and its line-up of classics, drive-in flicks and obscurities.

01/05 *Stranger on the Third Floor* **(1940) Peter Lorre, John McGuire, Margaret Tallichet. A reporter cannot believe that a man convicted of a strangling could possibly be innocent until he finds himself accused**

of a similar murder. The first of the RKO Pictures back catalog to make it to *Fright Night*, this tight, compelling film noir quickie had lots of dark New York streets to set a decidedly creepy mood. Lorre's sinister madman role lent just the right amount of uneasiness to keep things interesting and he created a genuinely disturbing vibe. The *New York Times* said, "[F]air idea turns pretentious, far-fetched." But *Newsday* said it was "Lorre at his maniacal best." C (RKO, b/w)

01/12 Looks like *Fright Night* was pre-empted.

01/19 *Monster on the Campus.* **(1958) Arthur Franz, Joanna Moore, Judson Pratt. The blood of a perfectly preserved prehistoric fish turns a scientist-experimenter into a horrible beast-like creature.** Some of the scenes with the Neanderthal monster running amok in the night were fun, but the clean-cut look of this Universal-International sci-fi B-picture made it a rather unremarkable event whenever it was shown. The giant rubber fish that causes all the trouble was kind of cute and I always felt bad for the dog locked in the cage being prompted to look ferocious. It was a mild and reasonably amusing time-waster. C (Universal-International, b/w)

01/26 *Vampire People* see 12/15/73.

02/02 Looks like *Fright Night* was pre-empted for a telethon.

02/09 *Tower of Terror* **(1972 aka** *In the Devil's Garden, Assault, The Creepers***) Suzy Kendall, Frank Finlay, Lesley-Anne Down. A pretty art teacher thinks she has seen the maniac responsible for killing several young girls in the woods behind an exclusive girl's school.** The British definitely had a knack for placing the spotlight on sexual deviants during this era of filmmaking. Not a whole heck of a lot happened in this picture, so perhaps my fondness for anything from Hemisphere Pictures' *Block of Shock* package made me really love it. The actual assaults appeared as little more than frantic groping with the camera zooming in on frantically twitching eyeballs; therefore, not much censorship was required. Viewers were presented with an array of suspects that failed to prompt much concern about who was behind it all. However, it all came together as an entertaining ensemble piece in kind of a naughty, casually sleazy way. It featured a host of familiar British genre actors of the time, but the real star of the picture was an electric power line tower that hovered menacingly over the woodsy shenanigans. "And don't forget to wash your brushes!" C (Rank/Hemisphere, color)

02/16 *The Hypnotic Eye* **(1960) Jacques Bergerac, Allison Hayes, Merry Anders. A mad stage hypnotist uses his powers to commit a series of ghastly murders.** Having never heard of this picture at the time, I felt like I was watching a real obscurity and something rare and unique. The first victim's flaming hair was burned in my brain for weeks and the gruesome taste of this mad hypnotist tale stayed in my mouth like a bad tuna fish sandwich. This movie cast a spell on me and its sensationalistic, gaudy, in-your-face horror made it a very memorable *Fright Night* experience. However, *Newsday* gave it one star and said, "Laugh along with the mad mesmerizer." C (Allied Artists, b/w)

02/23 *Beast of the Dead* (1970 — aka *Beast of Blood*) John Ashley, Celeste Yarnall, Eddie Garcia. A reporter travels to a Pacific outpost to check stories about green demons. Dr. Lorca, fresh from *Tomb of the Living Dead*, comes back in a somewhat less bloody and sexy sequel claiming, "I am madder than ever." This return visit to Blood Island started off with a great axe-wielding monster attack, but it was woefully slow hacking through the jungle thereafter until, at last, a head transplant and assault on Dr. Lorca's camp of horrors perked the picture up. It's another offering from Hemisphere's *Block of Shock* package, and one of the company's biggest grossing movies from the drive-in days, but it didn't have quite the relentless gusto of the company's previous efforts. Still, any visit to Blood Island is a trip to the tropics worth taking. C (Hemisphere, color)

This *Beast of Blood* (1970) was all washed up by the time he premiered on *Fright Night* under the name *Beast of the Dead* in 1974.

03/02 *Souls for Sale* (1962—aka *Confessions of an Opium Eater*) Vincent Price, Linda Ho, Richard Loo. **A 19th-century adventurer attempts to smash a slavery ring controlled by a strange woman.** Price made his *Fright Night* debut with this obscure, strange mystery-adventure picture, but his presence, which turns out to be in the form of a rare heroic role, does little to fit this square oddity into the show's round genre pool. Yes, there was plenty of tame Asian torture, drugs, underground catacombs, female slavery, and a sexy, devilish Chinese woman hell-bent on achieving power but, despite its sleazy feel, it failed to stop waves of drowsiness from overtaking me. Fortunately, there was always next week's installment to look forward to. (Photoplay, b/w)

03/09 *Spy Strikes Silently* (1965 — aka *Spies Strike Silently*) Lang Jeffries, Erica Blanc, Andrea Bosic. **An American Secret Service man must travel to exotic ports to unmask the power behind a fantastic new nuclear espionage ring.** Well, looks like "next week" wasn't much better. An international co-production, made at a time when early Bond mania was in vogue, it was certainly a lively movie filled with spies, intrigue, murder, mind control, and a madman set on world domination. But as a suitable telecast for *Fright Night* it was a stretch. Credit had to be given to Channel 9 for uncovering yet another scratchy obscurity, but it was a snoozer for anyone hoping for chills. (Terra/Estela, color)

03/16 *Inn of the Frightened People* (1972—aka *Revenge, Terror from Under the House, After Jenny Died*) Joan Collins, James Booth, Kenneth Griffith. **When a law-abiding citizen's young daughter is murdered, he decides to take vengeance into his own hands and abducts the suspect who has been released from custody for lack of evidence.** Channel 9 sure knew how to supply a spot-on synopsis! Great, believable performances from a well-seasoned British cast made the disturbing subject matter of this picture the kind of gritty "real life" horror that *Fright Night* was able to successfully showcase well on more than one occasion. The ending was great, shoving its blunt and bloody message about vigilantism right in your face. Sexy Joan was in fine form. Once again it was from Hemisphere's *Block of Shock* package. C (Rank/Hemisphere, color)

03/23 *Circus of Fear* (1966 aka *Psycho Circus*) Christopher Lee, Klaus Kinski, Leo Genn. **A million-dollar robbery leads to a rendezvous and murder at a circus.** This film made its way over to Channel 9 from WPIX's *Chiller* program. Despite a great cast and title that suggested a good horror romp, this movie was more in the style of the German bumper crop of Edgar Wallace '60s thrillers circulating at the time. Channel 9's print was quite grainy, which sometimes suggested an obscure and unusual film oddity might be in the offing, but it was instead just a rather bland whodunit with a few modest horror elements (like Lee in a black mask throwing knives). A pretty tough movie to make it through at this late hour for even a die-hard fan. C (Circus Films, color)

03/30 ***Curse of the Vampires*** **(1970—aka** ***Blood of the Vampires*** **) Amalia Fuentes, Eddie Garcia, Mary Walters. A young girl and her brother return to their family's tropical mansion to discover that their mother has become a vampire.** From the makers of *Vampire People*, and a step up in quality and sophistication, but it still retained the cheap Filipino jungle charm of its predecessor. It was a bit talky and slow in spots, but eerie lighting and big fangs helped create a spooky late night mood. I recall being surprised when a newly transformed vampire looked at his new choppers ... *in a mirror*! And that crazy mother of a vampire in the basement was a noisy pain in the ass. The Hemisphere Pictures' *Block of Shock* served up another oddity well worth catching. C (Hemisphere, color)

04/06 ***The Accursed*** **(1958—aka** ***The Traitor*** **) Christopher Lee, Donald Wolfit, Jane Griffiths. A British underground unit learns that their wartime leader has been murdered by one of their own members.** Listed in several TV guides as *The Accused*, it was a rarely televised UK whodunit even back then. The film had a very stagy feel and extremely civilized performances, and though not terribly exciting, it did offer a fine opportunity to see a great horror cast (that included a young Anton Diffring). Despite the nice English manor location and the threat of murder, it was a bit tough to make it to its rather unexciting conclusion at 1:30 in the morning. But the disciplined fan could hack it. Props went again to Channel 9 for the obscurity factor. (Fantur, b/w)

04/13 ***House of Frankenstein*** **(1944) Boris Karloff, John Carradine, Lon Chaney, Jr. A ruthless mad doctor surrounds himself with a hunchback, a gypsy girl, the Wolf Man and Frankenstein's Monster.** This Universal monster mash-up moved along at a brisk clip, even if some of the magic of previous entries in the franchise had begun to fade. The movie was slick-looking, but it was also a somewhat undistinguished horror show with Carradine's Dracula business running far too short. *Newsday* gave it two stars and said, "They were running out the string ... but it still has moments." True. C (Universal, b/w)

04/20 ***Night Monster*** **(1942) Bela Lugosi, Lionel Atwill, Ralph Morgan. A series of terrifying murders occur in the gloomy home of a crippled millionaire dabbling in the occult.** At the time, the *New York Times* called it "a real schlepper." I beg to differ. This movie's sinister goings-on scared the crap out of me when I had first seen it on Channel 5 a few years earlier. The shadow on the wall of the killer racing towards his next victim, the blood-splotch trails leading to hidden passageways and lines like "Sounds like you heard what's been seen walkin' 'round Pollard's Slough ... and how even the frogs quit croaking when it shows up" scared the bejesus out of me. *Newsday* thought it was only good for laughs, saying, "So bad it's funny." To quote beautiful cast member Irene Hervey (playing psychologist Dr. Harper), "Didn't seem funny to me." Truly a *Fright Night* classic and one of Universal's best and scariest B-pictures from producer-director Ford Beebe. C (Universal, b/w)

04/27 *Cat People* (1942) Simone Simon, Tom Conway, Kent Smith. A young woman fears that intimacy will trigger her reversion to the deadly cat creature of her ancestry. An undisputed classic of suggested horror from producer Val Lewton that was compelling from start to finish. And, in between, the menacing indoor swimming pool scene and a potential victim's walk down a seemingly empty street got the nail-biting started and suspense building to hazardous levels. My Aunt Adele recommended this movie to me when I was first discovering the world of monster movies. She claimed she didn't sleep for a week after seeing it when it first played in theaters. *Fright Night* gave me my first viewing of the film 32 years later and she was right ... it *was* scary! C (RKO, b/w)

05/04 *Bride of Frankenstein* see 12/01/73

05/11 *Island of Living Horror* scheduled. It was replaced by *Lost Flight* (1969) Lloyd Bridges, Anne Francis, Ralph Meeker. The captain of a downed airliner must help passengers survive on an uncharted island as a power struggle develops. Last-minute film switches rarely occurred on *Fright Night*, but this must have been *really* last minute as the movie choice was an odd and disappointing one at best. The first made-for-TV movie shown on *Fright Night*, it was a *Lord of the Flies*–themed adventure drama that was more suitable for a Movie-of-the-Week, which it once was. A talky, run-of-the mill drama; passable as ordinary prime-time filler but not a good choice for *Fright Night*. (Universal, color)

05/18 *Disciple of Death* (1972) Mike Raven, Ronald Lacey, Stephen Bradley. The leader of a devil worship cult takes up residence in a country manor and seeks new victims from a nearby village. Dark, gory and creepy Satanic rituals kept this British period piece interesting and it was probably the best use ever made of Christopher Lee wannabe Mike Raven's hammy talents and red eyes. Raven appeared to be channeling Tod Slaughter for this performance and it was a whole lot of over-the-top fun. There was a creepy title sequence and music score too. One of those early entries in *Fright Night*'s history that gave the show a real "drive-in theater" feel. C (Avco Embassy, color)

05/25 *King Kong* (1933) **Fay Wray, Robert Armstrong, Bruce Cabot. An explorer captures a giant ape and brings it to New York City, where the creature wreaks havoc.** While WOR made a Thanksgiving tradition out of its three-pack telecasts of *King Kong, The Son of Kong* and *Mighty Joe Young, Kong* surprisingly also made a one-shot appearance on *Fright Night.* Kong's promotional visage (a popular wall poster at the time) was part of the show's original opening montage and the film's inclusion on *Fright Night* couldn't have been more welcome. One of the biggest and best from Channel 9's RKO Radio Pictures stash. C (RKO, b/w)

06/01 Looks like *Fright Night* **was pre-empted for a telethon.**

06/08 *Island of Living Horror* **see 10/20/73**

06/15 *Octaman* **see 11/24/73**

06/22 *Decoy for Terror* **see 10/06/73**

06/29 *Torture Chamber of Dr. Sadism* **see 11/17/73**

07/06 *Beast of the Dead* **see 02/23/74**

07/13 *The Slime People* (1963) **Robert Hutton, Les Tremayne, Susan Hart. Disturbed by nuclear tests, huge, scaly creatures from the slimy regions under the Earth invade Los Angeles.** I was already a huge fan of *Night of the Living Dead* (1968) by this time, so this movie hit a chord with me thanks to its many plot similarities. (*The Killer Shrews* [1959] shown on WPIX's *Chiller Theater,* also seems to have been a blueprint for the *Night* film.) The creatures were genuinely slimy and kind of creepy as they crept across the screen looking for trouble. It was very low-budget moviemaking that thoroughly entertained in that "guilty pleasure" kind of way. The discovery of shish-kabobbed dead bodies in a car and the desperate main characters' frantic escape from the monsters in a television studio kept me quite alert that night. It's funny how movies like this stay in your memory longer than some of the so-called classics. C (Hutton-Robertson, b/w)

07/27 Looks like *Fright Night* **was pre-empted.**

08/03 *The Ringer* (1952) **Herbert Lom, Mai Zetterling, Greta Gynt. A wealthy but arrogant solicitor begins receiving threatening notes.** This dry British part-comedy, part-drama was in much the same vein and style as *The Accursed,* but had even fewer of the elements befitting a typical *Fright Night* presentation. Only the presence of Donald Wolfit and some cast members from *My Son the Vampire* (1952) and *The Human Monster* (1939) provided the viewer with points of interest. No doubt it was a telecast rarity, but it was hard to classify it as anything more than a bore. (British Lion, b/w)

08/10 *Love from a Stranger* (1947) **John Hodiak, Sylvia Sidney, Ann Richards. After winning the lottery, a woman fears that her new hus-**

band may have killed his previous wives and is plotting her death. Sidney seemed to have been channeling Bette Davis for her performance in this one. While the Basil Rathbone–Ann Harding version from 1937 directed by Rowland V. Lee (*Son of Frankenstein*) turned up on public television from time to time, this remake of the Agatha Christie story was rarely seen, once again proving that Channel 9 was a movie-lover's lost and found. It was an interesting late night mystery story and a decent entry for *Fright Night*, especially with its thunderstorm climax. But the '37 version with its better-suited cast and more contemporary setting might have been the better choice. Nice tension during the howling rainstorm. (Western Television, b/w)

08/17 *The Window* (1949) Bobby Driscoll, Arthur Kennedy, Ruth Roman. A young boy witnesses a murder but cannot convince anyone he is telling the truth about what he's seen. A well-acted, brisk, believable story and sturdy suspense provided some good (if kind of wholesome) chills. Children never struck me as the best subjects for a horror film, but as a young boy watching this movie it was easy to get caught up in Driscoll's drama. Though the killers weren't overly menacing, their everyday appearance and manner made them even scarier. C (RKO, b/w)

08/24 *The Wolf Man* (1941) Lon Chaney, Jr., Claude Rains, Evelyn Ankers. A man, bitten by a wolf, becomes a monster when the moon is full. Released theatrically around the time of the Pearl Harbor attack, Universal's surprise hit showed it wasn't too late for the studio to come up with a real classic. Chaney's showcase is so well-made and dripping with the best of the studios' atmospheric style, one could not resist getting caught up in its fast-paced, timeless story. The fog, the dead trees, the music, the gypsies packing up camp in a panic ... all added to a palpable sense of menace. Leaping from the *Fright Night* opening montage, make-up man Jack Pierce's immortal werewolf took his rightful place among the show's line-up of unforgettable creatures. The *New York Times* took a dimmer view in their TV review: "If you must, stand back" and "Can't touch the original *WereWolf of London*." A local TV critic was more enthusiastic, saying, "Good acting and direction heighten suspense." The 83rd Annual Academy Awards, held on February 27, 2011, not only awarded best makeup to Dave Elsey and Rick Baker for their memorable reinvention of the monster in the 2010 version of *The Wolfman*, but also gave the artists a chance to acknowledge the Universal horror legacy in front of 80 million-plus viewers. C (Universal, b/w)

08/31 *The Invisible Man Returns* (1940) Vincent Price, Nan Grey, Cedric Hardwicke. A man, falsely accused of murder, receives an injection

that renders him invisible so that he may catch the real killer. The invisible man was more of a hero in this picture. Universal's sequel to the 1933 original by James Whale had that high quality and unhurried classic charm of a studio still taking a lot of pride in its work. Vincent Price kicked off his horror career in fine form with *Tower of London* (1939) and this one. It was a thoroughly enjoyable piece of '40s escapism. C (Universal, b/w)

09/07 *Vampire People* see 12/15/73

09/17 *Tomb of the Living Dead* see 11/10/73

09/21 *Curse of the Vampires* see 03/30/74

09/28 *Inn of the Frightened People* see 03/16/73

10/05 *Honeymoon of Horror* **(1965) Robert Parsons, Abby Heller, Alexander Panas. A woman suspects that her new husband, an eccentric sculptor, and his strange friends may be plotting her murder.** Painfully cheesy production values, annoying acting and washed-out color were immediate tip-offs that this low-budget thriller might be either magnificent or brutally hard to get through ... and it was both! Lots of campy dialogue, '60s fashions, and threats of violence made it a bad-movie aficionado's dream, but even the most devoted masochist would have been tempted to turn off the tube and go to bed long before it was over. Wretched moviemaking, but, once again, it seemed like perfect material for *Fright Night*. C (Flamingo, color)

10/12 *Equinox* **(1969) Edward Connell, Barbara Hewitt, Frank Bonner. Four teenagers looking for a missing archaeologist in the California hills discover instead a 1,000-year-old book on devil worship.** I will forever associate this wonderful low-budget, decidedly entertaining bad movie marvel with *Fright Night*— where I saw it for the first time and anxiously, impatiently waited for it to be shown again. It was just a great story, with cool stop motion and photographic effects and a sense of ominous doom that sucked me right in. The film had a great sense of adventure and storytelling despite its severe budget limitations. It actually managed to serve up a decidedly eerie, even scary atmosphere at points. Having read about the film in the pages of *Famous Monsters of Filmland* magazine, it was extremely exciting to see it on TV. If there were any doubts that *Fright Night* would be my premier source for horror movies, they were now laid to rest. An absorbing, fascinating and thoroughly enjoyable horror movie experience! The satanic park ranger's twisted face gave me the creeps. A *Fright Night* classic. C (Harris/Tonylyn, color)

10/19 *Blood and Lace* **(1971) Gloria Grahame, Vic Tayback, Milton Selzer. A teenager seeks to find the maniac responsible for the brutal hammer killing of her prostitute mother.** Psychological drama and hard-hitting (literally) violence collided big-time in this warped, bloody and highly memorable film. Gloria's tight-lipped portrayal of the wicked housemother at an unsavory foster home was great and the nasty edge this movie possessed helped it earn a small cult following over the years. The flick had that cheap '70s drive-in quality that made it an ideal candidate for *Fright Night*. Even back then it left an unpleasant aftertaste following its grandiose but reasonably unpredictable ending. A local TV critic rightly called it a "grisly shocker." (Contemporary Filmakers, color)

10/26 *Deathmaster* **(1972) Robert Quarry, Bill Ewing, Brenda Dickson. A vampire chieftain poses as a guru to enslave the members of a California hippie commune.** I can recall the opening scenes of a coffin washing ashore like they were yesterday. This drive-in favorite was relatively new at the time, so seeing it turn up on the program so close to its theatrical run was a major thrill. It was a cool, creepy, bloody vampire flick and a great introduction to the hypnotic charms of Robert (*Count Yorga Vampire*) Quarry. I loved those vampire choppers where every tooth was a fang! *Newsday* gave it one star but said, "Add a star if you've got a weird sense of humor." You weren't going to fall asleep on this one. C (American International, color)

11/02 *The Creature's Revenge* **(1971 aka *Brain of Blood*) Kent Taylor, Regina Carrol, Zandor Vorkov. The brain of a dying Middle Eastern ruler is transplanted into the body of a monster that goes on a bloody rampage.** Having already overdosed on this film upon its original drive-in theater run (along with its co-feature *Vampire People*), I knew exactly what to expect from Al Adamson and Sam Sherman's extraordinarily cheap yet delightfully entertaining monster movie. There was no room for uncertainty and no cause to hesitate with a flick that promised a blood-dripping brain transplant that turned a maniac into a monster. "A cure as bad as the disease!" said one local newspaper. And if memory serves, Channel 9 left all that fake brain grafting virtually uncut! Regina Carrol looked and sounded like a chain-smoking cougar with a spray-on tan, perfect for her unsavory role in this cult favorite. She was reunited with Zandor Vorkov and John Bloom (the count and monster respectively from Adamson's previous masterpiece *Dracula vs. Frankenstein*). The terrorism overtones apparent in this movie escaped me back then ... it was just pure fun! Nice incorporation of Blood Island theme music cues from Tito Arevalo. Another astonishing selection from the Hemisphere *Block of Shock* package. "What do you think I am, an amateur?" C (Hemisphere, color)

11/09 Looks like *Fright Night* was pre-empted.

11/16 *Blood Rose* **(1970) Howard Vernon, Anny Duperey, Elizabeth Teissier. A surgeon murders beautiful girls in order to restore the face of a woman horribly scarred by fire.** The movie oozes with atmosphere and the kind of eerie style that can only be evoked in a spooky French chateau setting; the familiar storyline made for great horror movie material. In the late '70s the flick played on a local drive-in triple bill that I had missed, and Channel 9 once again came to the rescue with a late night opportunity to watch it. Lots of good, gruesome fun. (Oppenheimer, color)

11/30 *Phantom of the Rue Morgue* see 12/08/73

12/07 *Shock Corridor* (1963) **Peter Breck, Constance Towers, Gene Evans. A journalist seeking fame for his undercover work gets himself committed to an insane asylum in order to solve a murder.** While a highly acclaimed film in some circles, this ambitious movie from director Samuel Fuller still came off like a Broadway show with heavy acting and exaggerated situations. Twisted erotica, like a ward full of crazed nymphomaniacs, helped perk things up, but the psychological drama was a bit too dry and heavy for a kid looking for the menace promised in the title. This was the type of movie that requires more than one viewing (preferably at a not-too-late

Original theatrical ad mat for *The Deathmaster* (1972).

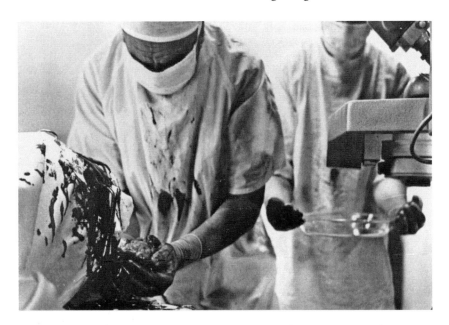

Messy surgical techniques by actors Kent Taylor, left, and Grant Williams kept the brain pulsating in *Brain of Blood* (1971). The movie was seen on *Fright Night* as *Creature's Revenge*.

hour) to appreciate fully, but it rarely showed up again on Channel 9. C (Allied Artists, color)

12/21 *Hand of Power* (1968 aka *The Zombie Walks*) Joachim Fuchsberger, Siw Mattson, Wolfgang Kieling. **A killer known as "The Laughing Corpse" murders with a poisoned ring.** One of a nearly uncountable number of director Alfred Vohrer's Edgar Wallace crime thrillers from Germany. Though not as entertaining as his yet-to-be shown *Fright Night* masterpiece *Creature with the Blue Hand*, this picture was a late night pleasure. Humorous dubbing, a cloaked madman in a cheap skull mask, creepy hidden passageways and bumbling detectives punctuated a movie that, like others in this genre, did not take itself too seriously. It was also thoroughly confusing and corny, but I had a ball with it. (Rialto, color)

12/28 Looks like *Fright Night* was pre-empted.

1975

While *Viking 1* begins its long journey from Earth to Mars and *Jaws* redefines the horror film (and seemingly making everyone but me avoid the beach), *Fright*

Night takes a fond look backward with a lineup that favored the Universal classics of the past. Unfortunately, the year is marred by two long breaks.

01/04 *The Hypnotic Eye* see 02/16/74

01/11 *Baraka X-77* (1966 aka Baraka X-13) **Gerard Barray, Sylva Koscina, Renato Baldini. A band of international criminals plots the abduction of a scientist whose secret formula will give them the power to create solid rocket fuel.** Channel 9 probably picked up this dubbed, Bond-like crime thriller, a French-Italian-Spanish collaboration, from the same package that contained *Spy Strikes Silently*. Though possessing a decent amount of intrigue, bizarre characters and a fairly brisk pace, it was still an actioner laced with only modest peripheral sci-fi elements. And, like *Souls for Sale*, it flirted with a little S&M. It was better suited for a movie show like TNT's *100% Weird*. (Cloche/Capitole Deutsche Exports, color)

01/18 *College Girl Murders* (1968) **Joachim Fuchsberger, Uschi Glass, Grit Boettcher. A mysterious man with an unknown form of poisonous gas causes Inspector Higgins of Scotland Yard to make his way to a boarding school for girls from well-to-do families.** The hooded killer was quite striking with his vibrant red get-up and white whip in this mystery thriller by way of Germany. It had some especially spooky, atmospheric visual touches, kooky sets and gimmicks that the Deutschland moviemakers were well known for. Great color too. But, again, the kind of '60s Bond-ish tone the picture had, often unavoidable in flicks of this era, just didn't quite hit the mark. After the first 20 minutes, I gave up trying to follow the plot, but I still had a good time. More insanity from director Alfred Vohrer. C (Rialto, color)

01/25 Looks like *Fright Night* was pre-empted for a telethon.

02/01 *Man Made Monster* (1941) **Lon Chaney Jr., Lionel Atwill, Anne Nagel. A circus performer survives electrocution when his bus crashes into a power line. An evil scientist experiments with transforming him into a human electrical dynamo.** Universal B-pictures like this one never failed to be entertaining, brisk and fun. With just a 60-minute running time, it was completely painless — especially in a post-midnight *Fright Night* time slot. Chaney lays the innocent-guy-turned-monster ham on thick as Dynamo Dan, but that's the '40s for you. C (Universal, b/w)

02/08 Looks like *Fright Night* was pre-empted.

02/15 *The Mad Doctor of Market Street* (1942) **Lionel Atwill, Claire Dodd, Una Merkel. A doctor who believes he can revive the dead is shipwrecked on a tropical island with other castaways on whom to experiment.** *Fright Night* took viewers into the jungle many times during its long history; the tropics of Universal's back lot certainly weren't the most threatening or atmospheric of sets. Still, it was a lot of fun and Lionel Atwill gave another flawless menacing performance. His crazy, obsessive scientist character operates at full tilt in a typically hokey B-picture that featured a frantic *Titanic*-like ship sinking. This movie turned up frequently on Saturday and Sunday afternoons when Channel 9 needed to fill in an hour-long time slot before the Mets took the field, but it was just as entertaining late at night. C (Universal, b/w)

02/22 *Horror Island* (1941) Dick Foran, Leo Carrillo, Peggy Moran. A band of people find themselves on an island off the California coast on which pirates' treasure is rumored to have been buried. The *New York Times*

The Phantom from *Horror Island* (1941) strikes a menacing pose in a publicity still.

described *Horror Island* as "Not Coney," "lousy" and "crummy" for their TV reviews on separate occasions. I wondered how much they got paid to come up with those insights with which I could have not have disagreed more. A charming, innocent, spirited, and really fun adventure thriller that packed a haunted castle, phantom, secret passageways, treasure and a great assortment of colorful characters into the fastest hour one could ever ask for. Much of the original opening footage (taking place on Universal's wet and foggy dock sets) was cut by Channel 9, but it didn't take anything away from the experience. Universal reused well-worn sets from their previous horror films and I was able to see the primary doorway from the original 1931 *Dracula* put to good use as the characters arrive on Morgan's Island. And there was the main entrance area of Ingston Manor from *Night Monster* used as part of the castle interior. It all added up to a great horror show, albeit very lightweight fare. In fact, I was so taken with this Universal quickie that I wrote to Channel 9 literally begging them to show it again as soon as possible. Fortunately, like *The Mad Doctor of Market Street*, it was re-broadcast a number of times before baseball games and again on *Fright Night*. A hugely entertaining slice of '40s nostalgia and a *Fright Night* classic! C (Universal, b/w)

03/01 *The Mummy's Tomb* (1942) Lon Chaney, Jr., Elyse Knox, John Hubbard. The high priest of an ancient Egyptian cult travels to America to seek revenge on those who desecrated the tomb of a mummy. Another Universal 60-minute feature that moved so fast with its predictable plot and monster movie elements, it was over before you knew it. You knew exactly what you were getting ... not a classic but a whole lot of fun just the same. The *New York Times* seemed to think it was anything but, saying, "Go ahead, serves you right." C (Universal, b/w)

03/08 *Calling Dr. Death* (1943) Lon Chaney, Jr., J. Carrol Naish, Patricia Morison. A doctor experiences a memory lapse and discovers his wife was murdered during the blackout. A title from Universal's Inner Sanctum series. With its meager, bland goings-on, it's pretty much just a time killer. I was never much of a fan of these films and often found Chaney's whispery narration and the dull plots a little irritating. When one of these films showed up in the TV guide listings, it was always a bit of a buzz kill. C (Universal, b/w)

From 03/15 through 04/19, *Fright Night* was now temporarily and inexplicably called *Mystery Movie* (not to be confused with Channel 9's earlier horror movie program *The Mystery Museum*).

***The Frozen Ghost* (1945) Lon Chaney, Jr., Evelyn Ankers. A hypnotist whose subject dies blames himself and goes to work in a wax museum where he uncovers a series of terrible murders.** Another hour-long quickie. *Newsday* said of this Universal Inner Sanctum series entry, "Nothing much in the way of thrills, but a neat B-movie cast." I agreed. At least you wouldn't be up too late. C (Universal, b/w)

03/22 Looks like *Fright Night* was pre-empted for a telethon.

03/29 *She-Wolf of London* (1946) June Lockhart, Don Porter, Sara Haden. When hideous murders occur on the grounds of her ancestral estate, a girl, dreaming horrifying dreams, fears that she is the victim of an ancient werewolf curse. *Newsday* gave it one star and added, "The mental warpage is infectious." This was another film widely used by Channel 9 to fill in 60-minute time slots on weekend afternoons. This Universal quickie was a bit duller than most of their '40s material. Lockhart's depressing demeanor throughout the film was unquestionably a bit of a downer. This movie had gotten more than its share of boos and hisses over the years for its lack of a genuine monster, but as a fan of Universal and cheap quickies like this, I had to say I still managed to love it. Let's face it, like other things in life, you just can't always explain why. A local TV guide critic harshly dismissed it by saying, "Nair needed!" and "Nothing worse than a woman's bite." I actually passed on going to the beach with my family to watch this again when it was shown one Sunday afternoon, so it couldn't have been that bad. C (Universal, b/w)

04/05 *The Raven* (1935) Boris Karloff, Bela Lugosi, Lester Matthews. A mad surgeon reconstructs torture devices in his isolated home to use against his enemies. Watching this controversial picture some 40 years after Universal released it to theater screens, a young kid (me) sitting in front of the TV could tell the studio was pushing the envelope. Its cruelty and violence seemed remarkably out of place for a '30s movie but that's probably what made it so entertaining. C (Universal, b/w)

04/12 *Captive Wild Woman* (1943) John Carradine, Evelyn Ankers, Acquanetta. A scientist engaged in glandular research believes he can transform a female gorilla into a woman. The Ape Woman, Paula Dupree, was at her best in this, the first of the three-film series. (The sequels would be seen on *Fright Night* as well.) It had a couple of good, creepy, mood-inducing shots, such as the classic Wolf Man–like transformation sequence, but the recycled circus footage was a bore. The film's sequels would make recycling almost an art form. C (Universal, b/w)

04/19 *Fright Night* took its first hiatus and was replaced by *The Joe Franklin Show* until 6/28.

06/28 *The Thing That Couldn't Die* (1958) William Reynolds, Andra Martin, Jeffrey Stone. The remains of a beheaded criminal who died centuries before are found buried on a desert ranch. Having seen this film before on other Channel 9 movie shows and found it reasonably entertaining, this showcase on *Fright Night* was nothing new for me. But such re-broadcasts allowed me an opportunity to look at the movies a little bit closer. I failed, however, to come up with any new insights on this one. The scene with the severed head being held up in the window and the big resurrection climax were pretty decent and creepy money shots. (Universal-International, b/w)

07/12 *Night Monster* see 04/20/74

07/19 *Track of the Vampire* (1966 aka *Blood Bath*) **William Campbell, Luana Anders, Sandra Knight. In modern-day Venice, a succession of beautiful girls mysteriously disappears.** This movie had a long, involved history of being nipped and tucked from another movie with a decidedly different storyline, but the end result shown here was pretty good. The nighttime shots of shadowy, empty Venice streets and the lengthy sequence where a trench-coat-clad vampire chases a young girl for what seems like miles right into the sea (and even then it *still* wasn't over) are as fresh in my brain today as the hot summer night I first saw it on *Fright Night*. It was a dark, hard-hitting horror flick and actually unsettling in spots. C (American International, b/w)

07/26 *Son of Dracula* (1943) **Lon Chaney, Jr., Robert Paige, Louise Allbritton. The mysterious Count Alucard marries a pretty girl and makes her into his vampire partner.** The eerie opening title sequence where gloved hands brushed cobwebs aside to reveal the picture's name, an idea no doubt borrowed from the silent film *The Cat and the Canary* (1927), kicked off a movie that's much better than one's memory may initially recall. Dracula is often called an inappropriate role for Chaney but I didn't find him that distracting as the count and, taken as a whole, the film was completely entertaining and even energetic. I loved the vapor transformation gimmick and Alucard's ferocious anger at the film's climax. It seemed like Chaney was truly giving his all to this role, and for once he was spared hours in the makeup chair. C (Universal, b/w)

08/02 *The Wolf Man*

08/09 *The Mad Ghoul* (1943) **George Zucco, Evelyn Ankers, David Bruce. Using mysterious gas, a professor turns one of his students into a zombie.** Another great little Universal quickie with a good story and nice '40s flavor. Though the monster looked like he just needed moisturizer, it wasn't half-bad. Zucco, equally dry and understated, was really every bit as good as Lionel Atwill at portraying a madman and he delivered the goods in this picture. C (Universal, b/w)

08/23 *World of the Vampires* (1964) **Mauricia Garces, Silvia Fornier, Erna Martha Bauman. A man and woman become prisoners of a vampire who uses haunting music to control an army of undead creatures.** The first of the wonderfully zany, wacky K. Gordon Murray Mexican monster movies to be shown on *Fright Night* was a typically bizarre, hypnotic film with a captivating big-fanged Dracula character playing an organ made of skulls (quite badly I might add) to raise his undead followers from their cardboard coffins. The diabolical vampire's almost orgasmic abandon at the keyboard was something to see! The followers had faces that resembled pillows with fangs painted on them. I had never seen anything quite like it and never forgot it. This movie got me forever hooked on south-of-the-border horror. (AIP Television, b/w)

08/30 *The Creature's Revenge*

09/06 *Untamed Women* (1952) Doris Merrick, Mikel Conrad, Richard Monahan. An Air Force captain tells the story of how he escaped from an uncharted island which was inhabited by lovely girls and prehistoric monsters. Even a kid in the unsophisticated '70s had to notice how unbelievably corny and campy this movie was. While the disappointing dinosaur stock footage couldn't have been too much of a surprise, how the actors managed to keep straight faces making this picture was! The late night experience of watching this hysterical movie was something every horror movie fan should have had to endure as a rite of passage. A hack job, to say the least, but so amateurish it had a kind of magic quality about it. (Jewell, b/w)

09/13 *The Monolith Monsters* (1957) Grant Williams, Lola Albright, Les Tremayne. A meteor crashes on the outskirts of a small desert town, unleashing stone monstrosities with the power to grow and reproduce. This telecast stands out as one of my most vivid *Fright Night* recollections, for a combination of reasons. From the off-screen announcer advising that "Grant Williams and Lola Albright star in *The Monolith Monster* [sic], next on Channel 9" during the closing credits of *Championship Wrestling* to the stone monoliths (there was more than one, to correct the announcer) rising from and crashing to the ground, to the film's memorable music score, it was a Universal-International B-picture that vividly stayed with me. The film's original opening monologue was cut from this telecast. It was an inventive, original, well-paced sci-fi thriller and a great way to spend a Saturday night. C (Universal-International, b/w)

09/20 *Fright Night* took another hiatus and was replaced again by *The Joe Franklin Show* until 01/03/76.

1976

While the "Son of Sam" serial killer is terrorizing the streets of New York, nervous residents find little relief from the uneasiness by watching *Fright*

Night. But it's a fun year for the show, with Mexican monsters, more RKO classics and Mr. Moto added into the brew. Unfortunately, *Fright Night* also takes another major hiatus.

01/03 *Night of the Blood Monster* **(1972) Christopher Lee, Maria Schell, Leo Genn. During the struggles of King Henry V against the rebellious William of Orange, a charge of witchcraft condemns a hapless young woman to the stake. A soldier fights dark forces to save her.** Honestly, it felt like this film would never end. I had hoped for something along the lines of the brutal *Mark of the Devil*, but instead was subjected to a tedious history lesson with only modest peripheral horror elements. Probably the most misleading title ever! I found it impossibly dull, but *Newsday* opined, "Interesting.... If you're into such things it's worth a look." Nice music score though. C (American International, color)

01/10 *Creature with the Blue Hand* **(1967 aka *Bloody Dead*) Klaus Kinski, Diana Korner, Harald Leipnitz. A madman escapes from an institution**

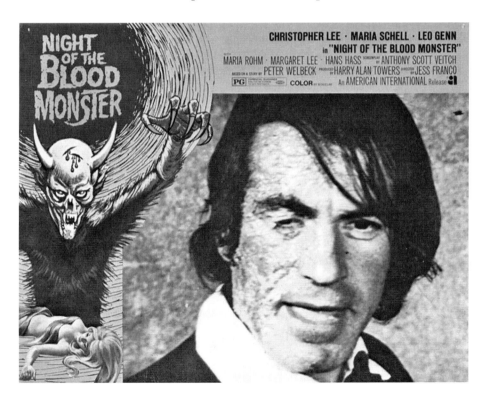

An original theatrical lobby card for *Night of the Blood Monster* (1972) accentuating horror elements that were pitifully scarce in the actual movie.

to be accused of further murders, actually the work of a mysterious figure with a metallic blue hand. Upon this movie's first *Fright Night* telecast, the *New York Times* simply said, "Like it says." I always thought those *Times* TV critics sounded like uppity snobs. Maybe after publishing that lackluster review, they actually watched the movie, because the *Times'* comments when the picture was shown again were quite different. The revised commentary exclaimed, "Fast, funny and gory. Good late hour chills. Last time round, it hooked us." Having only seen a TV spot and a brief portion of the film from a distance on a drive-in theater screen during its original theatrical run with *Beast of the Yellow Night*, I was elated to see this movie being shown on *Fright Night*. Something about the phantom and his pre–Freddy Kreuger hand, the eerie mansion and its secret passageways, bizarre butler, mad asylum doctor, strange dialogue and the tongue-in-cheek humor mixed with menace just completely exhilarated me. Wonderful closing line from the butler: "I've always had a great deal of admiration and respect for the aristocracy, but lately I'd say things were getting out of hand." Channel 9's print had the Independent-International copyright on it, but Sam Sherman tells me it was released to TV by AIP Television. A *Fright Night* classic from director Alfred Vohrer! C (Rialto/AIP Television, color)

01/17 *In the Year 2889* (1965) Paul Petersen, Charla Daurte, Quinn O'Hara. Seven people remain alive after the Earth has been annihilated in a nuclear holocaust, in a valley surrounded by mutants. This astonishingly low-budget production was a must-see for me after I read about it in the "Worst Horror Films of All-Time" issue of a kid's favorite newspaper of the day, *The Monster Times*. But, like so many films on their list, it was a movie I never thought I'd get a chance to view until *Fright Night* came along and made it possible. Larry Buchanan's masterpiece of bad moviemaking was ... *fantastic*! I loved the rubber-masked monster wearing a cheap business suit, the backyard look of its locations, and the dialogue lifted from the script of Roger Corman's 1956 *Day the World Ended*. Part of the fascination about watching a Buchanan movie was to see just how bad the movie could get as the frames went by. This movie got a two-star (fair) rating from one local newspaper, so you *know* they never saw it. But I loved it and prayed that other Buchanan movies would eventually turn up. They did. C (AIP Television, color)

01/24 *The Last Man on Earth* scheduled. Replaced by *House of Dracula* (1945) Lon Chaney, Jr., John Carradine, Onslow Stevens. A benevolent scientist seeks to help the infamous Count Dracula and is himself infected with the dread vampire taint. It would have been hard to choose between Vincent Price's zombie jamboree and this nifty Universal mad monster party. It was merely a rehashing of *House of Frankenstein*, but I found its darker mood and spookier atmosphere much more entertaining. It was my first viewing of the movie since reading the filmbook published in issue #84 of *Famous Monsters of Filmland* (the one with the great Christopher Lee close-up cover). *Newsday* gave it two stars and called it "buff stuff." The film later resurfaced as a Halloween movie special on Channel 5 several years later. C (Universal, b/w)

01/31 Looks like *Fright Night* was pre-empted for a telethon.

02/07 *The Man Who Turned to Stone* **(1957) Victor Jory, Charlotte Austin, William Hudson. A group of scientists prolong their lives by absorbing the bio-electrical energy of girls.** Like *Creature with the Atom Brain* and other Columbia Pictures horror efforts of the 1950s, this movie was real simple, offered no frills, but supplied all the murder and monsters one could hope for. And anything taking place in a girl's detention home was always going to be a hoot. If I was able to remember it some 35+ years later, it must have had something going for it! C (Columbia, b/w)

02/14 *Murders in the Rue Morgue* **(1932) Bela Lugosi, Sidney Fox, Leon Ames. A mad doctor seeks to mate ape and woman, and trains the beast to kidnap a woman for the experiment.** This movie had the creaky atmosphere and style of an old silent picture. The distracting close-ups of a real chimp cross-cut with a guy in a completely different-looking monkey suit, and Lugosi's curly hair in contrast to his slick-back in *Dracula*, were off-putting, but the actor's hammy mad scientist portrayal really sold the picture. Not exactly a true classic, but a nice selection for *Fright Night* from the early days of horror cinema. C (Universal, b/w)

02/21 *The Raven*

02/28 *Weird Woman* **(1944) Lon Chaney, Jr., Evelyn Ankers, Anne Gwynne. An exotic woman's use of voodoo upsets her college professor husband.** I recall being initially unenthused to watch this movie, the second in Universal's Inner Sanctum series. Unfortunately, these movies so often missed the mark with their pseudo-horror trappings. But *Weird Woman* wasn't half-bad. It was also cool to see Evelyn Ankers portraying a villain instead of a helpless victim. C (Universal, b/w)

03/06 *The Frozen Ghost*

03/13 *Captive Wild Woman*

03/20 *The Mummy's Curse* **(1944) Lon Chaney, Jr., Virginia Christine, Peter Coe. The mummies of an Egyptian priest and priestess are brought to life by a secret potion.** The final entry in the Universal

Mummy series brought a Cajun flavor to the storyline and was a pretty decent chiller. Southern superstitions blended surprisingly well with Egyptian mummy folklore and created a mood that was eerier than usual. Not as absorbing and fun as *The Mummy's Hand*, but I was definitely into it. The local newspaper, however, advised viewers to "Dig Karloff's Mummy instead." C (Universal, b/w)

03/27 *The Mummy's Tomb*

04/03 *Curse of the Vampires*

04/10 *I've Lived Before* (1956) Jock Mahoney, Ann Harding, Leigh Snowden. A pilot believes he may be the reincarnation of a World War I flyer. Though the film had more psychological drama than scares, it was somewhat interesting and took its subject matter surprisingly seriously. A bit too tepid and flat for the late hour, though. And Mahoney was not the most spirited of actors. (Universal-International, b/w)

04/17 *Hypnotic Eye*

04/24 *The Living Coffin* (1965) Gaston Santos, Mary Duval, Pedro de Aguillon. A woman fears being buried prematurely in the tomb of her family estate. I loved this flick! Unquestionably one of the most enjoyable movies I ever watched on *Fright Night*, this unlikely hybrid bridged the western and horror film genres magnificently. I was hooked the minute the cheap K. Gordon Murray hand-painted title card came up featuring skeletal remains lying in the desert. I had to endure some boring fight scenes and awful dubbing and dialogue, but the spooky characters and moody atmosphere, swamps, sinister under-lit faces and great use of color made for a surprisingly satisfying night of south-of-the-border shudders. I just wish the hero's companion hadn't always been talking about a nice soft mattress and going to bed when watching this at one in the morning. *Newsday* said, "Buried alive down Mexico way. Send flowers." I considered it a *Fright Night* classic. C (AIP Television, color)

05/01 *The Black Raven* scheduled. Replaced by *White Zombie* (1932) Bela Lugosi, Madge Bellamy, Joseph Cawthorn. In Haiti, a necromancer uses his power to cloud minds in order to change a girl into a zombie. One of those last-minute switches where the substitute was better than the original programming choice. *White Zombie* is an absorbing and haunting classic, especially in fascinating scenes like that in which Lugosi condescendingly converses with a man (Robert Frazer, who looks like Lugosi in 1933's *The Vampire Bat*) who is slowly being crippled by a zombifying drug. The film had a fairy tale–like quality about it and was great entertainment. In 2010, New York fans were delighted when this now public-domain movie made a very rare prime-time appearance on Channel 11's

Halloween revival of *Chiller*, paired with *Bride of the Monster*. "For you ... they are the angels of death!" C (Halperin, b/w)

05/08 *Unknown World* (1951) Bruce Kellogg, Marilyn Nash, Otto Waldis. Scientists seeking to escape the inevitable destruction of the environment create a tank-like vehicle that can burrow down into the Earth's core. The *New York Daily News* thought it was a "boring journey to the center of the earth" and gave it one star. It may not have been the most nerve-shattering experience ever put on film, but the scientists' crazy beetle-craft and the strange, somewhat realistic environments they encounter kept me quite interested. A low-budget but passable sci-fi adventure that Channel 9 paired with *Unknown Island* on their Saturday morning *Spaced Out Films* program not long after. C (Lippert, b/w)

05/15 *Dracula's Daughter* (1936) Otto Kruger, Gloria Holden, Edward Van Sloan. The daughter of the infamous vampire count opens an artist's studio in Soho. The *New York Times* said, "Beautiful moving work by Miss Holden on delicate ground," and they hit the stake right on the head! While fans continued to wonder why Universal failed to revive the count and Bela Lugosi for this sequel to the 1931 original, his daughter proved a classy and worthy torch-bearer. Sophisticated chills blended with dark moodiness, and weren't uninterrupted by too much comic relief. Even Holden's retake of the "I never drink ... wine" line made so famous by Lugosi was subtly effective. C (Universal, b/w)

05/22 *The Mummy's Hand* (1940) Dick Foran, Wallace Ford, Peggy Moran. A group of archaeologists search for the tomb of an ancient Egyptian princess. What could a young horror movie fan find to criticize in this well-paced, exciting monster movie that was responsible for creating more popular mummy lore than the Karloff original? A great set of characters, some genuinely spooky moments (like the howling jackals), and a powerful, creepy-looking mummy fleshed out by actor Tom Tyler added up to a perfect, old-fashioned *Fright Night* feature and a terrific Saturday night. C (Universal, b/w)

05/29 *The Mad Ghoul*

06/05 *The Black Castle* (1953) Richard Greene, Boris Karloff, Stephen McNally. When friends fail to return from a hunting party, an adventurer travels to a sinister castle to find them. The local newspaper gave this medieval horror melodrama three stars, an unusually positive rating for a genre film. A movie that bridged the old Universal with the new Universal-International, this film had a bit of both worlds: some of the old charm of the '40s and the polished, sophisticated look of the studio's emerging new style that became the norm in the '50s. The end result was a modestly entertaining mix of gothic horror, romance and adventure, but it just wasn't terribly earth-shaking. C (Universal-International, b/w)

06/12 *The Vampire Bat* scheduled. Looks like *Fright Night* was preempted by a soccer game.

06/19 *Frankenstein Meets the Wolf Man* (1943) Lon Chaney, Jr., Bela Lugosi, Patric Knowles. Larry Talbot, aka the Wolf Man seeks Dr. Frankenstein but instead finds the Monster. A local newspaper described it as "wonderfully creepy and atmospheric." I was in complete agreement and actually got chills during the opening sequence in the graveyard, shuddering as the music score so perfectly peaked when Chaney's hand clutched the arm of a fear-frozen graverobber. While some analysts wasted time criticizing Lugosi's interpretation of Frankenstein's creation, I found the studio's first dip into multiple monsters to be a horror movie fan's dream. Great fun! C (Universal, b/w)

06/26 *Nylon Noose* (1963) Richard Goodman, Olga Summerfield, Curt Beck. A group of investors gather in a sinister mansion where a murderer stalks them. Another ultra-rare German import from the catalog of U.S. TV distributor Medallion Films, this was an atmospheric old dark house thriller featuring a hooded killer and mad scientist. A *Fright Night* journal I was keeping at the time indicated that I loved the film, but my recollections about its content are extremely vague today, except for its grim black and white photography. At the time of this writing, the film has all but vanished and remains impossible to find in any format except in 16mm television prints that turn up on online dealer sites from time to time. For now, it is for me a *Fright Night* "lost" film. *Newsday* gave it one star and warned "Steer clear." That means see it (if you can find it)! (Medallion, b/w)

07/03 *Earth Vs. the Flying Saucers* (1956) Hugh Marlowe, Joan Taylor, Donald Curtis. When flying saucers shoot down secret military rockets, scientists must develop a new weapon before the saucer men can conquer the earth. The local newspaper gave it just two stars, but this fantastic UFO extravaganza was mesmerizing. It was my first up-close TV brush with Ray Harryhausen's incredible stop-motion animation work; the huge, menacing saucers were amazing to watch. The battle in Washington, D.C., was a sight to behold and the movie was an unforgettable kid's dream. The sound of those saucers stayed with me forever. C (Columbia, b/w)

07/10 *The Brainiac* (1963) Abel Salazar, Carmen Montejo, David Silva. A man vows revenge when he is executed for sorcery. He returns hundreds of years later in the form of a brain-eating monster. Probably the most infamous of the many south-of-the-border monster mashes that now have huge followings. A stunning Mexican horror classic from importer K. Gordon Murray that was simply unbelievable. After trying to absorb as a kid what half the crimes the villain committed were actually all about (dogmatism?), I was dazzled to see one of his first victim killed and his clothing vaporized (except for underwear!). The hotplate full of brains which the monster dips into ever-so-discretely with a spoon was positively captivating! So was the creature's 24-inch forked tongue. It was a privilege to see this crazy, unforgettable movie! C (AIP Television, b/w)

07/17 *Attack of the Mayan Mummy* (1963) Nina Knight, Bruno VeSota, Ramon Gay. Hypnosis reveals that a young woman was an Aztec princess in a previous life. That's a better description than the movie deserved. *Newsday* gave it one star and warned "Not to be confused with the attacks of the 'Puppet People,' 'Mushroom People,' or 'Giant Leeches.' Quit while you're ahead." I wouldn't have missed seeing this atrocity for the world, but it was positively painful to sit through. Producer Jerry Warren mixed long-winded, incredibly talky U.S.–filmed sequences with scenes lifted from a dubbed Mexican mummy flick and the whole thing made absolutely no sense. Of course, in all fairness, I did sleep through half of it. A truly wretched movie. The fact that it was so completely unwatchable made it an event. C (Medallion/Warren, b/w)

07/31 *Creature with the Atom Brain* (1955) Richard Denning, Angela Stevens, S. John Launer. A deported gangster returns to the U.S. with a scientist who can turn dead men into zombies. Any movie that could boast a theme that even hinted at elements of *Night of the Living Dead* was a winner for me. Even though it was a big stretch to compare the two, this Columbia quickie was a serviceable, brisk, typical '50s gangster-horror yarn. The opening scene featuring a zombie walking down a dark street put me in the right mood. A no-frills hour of old-fashioned B-movie fun. Channel 9 played it to death for years. C (Columbia, b/w)

08/07 Looks like *Fright Night* was pre-empted.

08/14 *I Walked with a Zombie* (1943) Frances Dee, James Ellison, Tom Conway. A nurse's experiences with a zombie patient on a remote West Indian isle result in unusual, terrifying intrigue. The wonderful atmosphere and a low-key sense of dread helped balance the poetic and somewhat dreamy pacing of this tale of doomed romance and voodoo from producer Val Lewton and RKO. The nighttime journey through the sugar cane fields was extremely tense, even if nothing really happened. My introduction to Lewton's subtle horror style was a bit challenging to stay awake through in the wee hours, but I knew I was watching something special. Actor Darby

Jones' rather subdued zombie was a bit disconcerting (I was more accustomed to the flesh-eaters of *Night of the Living Dead*), but this was obviously something much different. C (RKO, b/w)

08/24 *The Body Snatcher* (1945) Boris Karloff, Bela Lugosi, Henry Daniell. A 19th century Edinburgh doctor is blackmailed by the villainous coachman who secures bodies for medical research. More sophisticated chills from Val Lewton and RKO that built to a frenzied, horrific conclusion. This had a harder horror edge than the previous week's film, and was nearly as engaging as the zombie classic. Good, old-fashioned period chills. C (RKO, b/w)

09/04 *The Dark Eyes of London* (1940) Bela Lugosi, Greta Gynt, Hugh Williams. A Scotland Yard inspector investigates several murders near the Thames, all linked to an institute for the blind. Although this movie was commonly shown on TV under its U.S. title *The Human Monster*, *Fright Night* gave fans the rare chance to see the film under its British title — albeit in a faded, dirt-speckled print. It was a pretty good Edgar Wallace murder thriller with a cool Rondo Hatton–esque character who complimented Lugosi's villainy very well. C (Anglo Amalgamated, b/w)

09/11 *The Werewolf* (1956) Steven Ritch, Don Megowan, Joyce Holden. A man, once the unwilling subject of scientific experimentation, becomes a monster. "Great transformation scene, not much else" and "Nothing to bark about" said a local newspaper TV critic, who gave the film an embarrassingly dismal one and a half stars. While the man-into-wolf scene is extremely effective, the movie had a whole lot more going for it. Wonderful use of locations, an interesting story that emphasized the destruction of one innocent man's family life and an evocative, convincing performance by Ritch made for a balanced, intriguing and scary chapter in *Fright Night*'s history. I had previously only seen this film in a three-minute Columbia 8mm home movie version, and seeing the full-length feature was a thrill. The exciting, wild-looking werewolf makeup was similar to the work done for *I Was a Teenage Werewolf* (1957). *Newsday* joined the critical bashing: "A werewolf leaves a trail of blood and gives an affirmative answer to the question: Can lycanthropy be dull?" C (Columbia, b/w)

09/18 *The Black Cat* (1934) Boris Karloff, Bela Lugosi, David Manners. A newlywed couple find themselves trapped in the mountaintop home of a Satanist and his followers. The ultimate golden age dynamic duo played well off each other in this bizarre and very somber Universal classic. The Satan worship elements, art deco house of horrors, skin-stripping torture, dead bodies in glass coffins, and innocent couple accidentally caught up in all of it made for a highly memorable viewing experience, but I went to bed in a depressed funk. Like *The Raven* (1935), it was a nasty picture. C (Universal, b/w)

09/25 *Murders in the Rue Morgue*

10/02 *Fright Night* becomes *Mr. Moto's Casebook* through 11/13 with no introductory bumper for any of the films shown.

Mr. Moto in Danger Island (1939) Peter Lorre, Jean Hersholt.

10/09 *Mr. Moto Takes a Chance* (1938) Peter Lorre, Rochelle Hudson.

10/16 *Mr. Moto Takes a Vacation* (1939) Peter Lorre, Virginia Field.

10/23 *Thank You Mr. Moto* (1937) Peter Lorre, Sidney Blackmer.

10/30 *Mr. Moto's Gamble* (1938) Peter Lorre, Lynn Bari.

11/06 *Mr. Moto Takes a Chance* (1938) Peter Lorre, Rochelle Hudson.

11/13 *Mr. Moto's Last Warning* (1938) Peter Lorre, George Sanders.

11/20 *Mr. Moto's Casebook* is replaced by the TV sports series *The Champions* until 12/11.

12/11 *Fright Night* returns with *I Married a Monster from Outer Space* (1958) Tom Tryon, Gloria Talbott, Peter Baldwin. A young bride discovers that her husband's body has been taken over by a creature from a distant galaxy. While the Mr. Moto films were at least tolerable substitutes for *Fright Night*'s usual fare, seeing the show replaced by a sports program for over a month was unbearable. Not knowing if *Fright Night* would ever return, I was delighted when this diverting sci-fi horror movie marked its return and satisfied my hunger for monsters. The movie was presented without a bumper, but at least *Fright Night* was back and the creepy aliens enveloping human victims in a cloud of smoke kept a smile on my face the whole night. Memorable opening theme music too. C (Paramount, b/w)

12/18 Looks like *Fright Night* was pre-empted by another installment of *The Champions*. It was like Channel 9 was again teasing fans with their "now you see it, now you don't" programming changes.

12/25 *The Invisible Man* (1933) Claude Rains, Gloria Stuart, William Harrigan. A doctor is puzzled by the disappearance of his assistant, who has become an invisible man and terrorizes the English countryside. *Fright Night* was back ... at least for a little while. The *New York Times* gave this Universal classic its highest rating, saying, "Grand old thriller, one of the real champs. Best part: snowy fade-in, country tavern." That wintry introduction and the wonderful fantasy-horror overtones of this James Whale production did indeed convey the ideal atmosphere for a holiday telecast. The movie became a tradition of sorts, being broadcast again on the program the following Christmas. Interrupted with commercials for Ronco kitchen gadgets and K-Tel holiday music LPs "that make a great gift," this was a highly memorable, incredibly cozy Yuletide treat and became an annual event for me for a lifetime, much like *King Kong* on Thanksgiving. What you might call a historic *Fright Night* telecast. "And throw a rug in the car ... it's cold when you have to go about naked!" C (Universal, b/w)

1977

A new era in moviemaking and science fiction begins with the opening of George Lucas' *Star Wars*. It's a tough year for *Fright Night* as the show gets placed on the back burner for a time. When the show does return, it gets bumped a half hour later (to 1:30 A.M.) to make way for the new dance music show *Disco '77*.

01/01 *The Mad Magician* (1954) Vincent Price, Eva Gabor, Mary Murphy. A deranged magician has a bent for murder. More pseudo–3-D thrills from Price. A few good nail-biting Grand Guignol murder sequences gave the film a fun, campy feel, however unlikely the premise may have been. The local newspaper critic said it was just a "routine murder mystery yarn." (Columbia, b/w)

01/08 *Fright Night* is shelved for the next two months and replaced by the program *Steve Allen's Laughback* until 03/12. I must have again written two dozen letters to WOR, begging for *Fright Night*'s return.

03/12 *The Mummy's Curse* ... thank God, maybe my letter campaign helped bring the show back. The good news was that *Fright Night*, amazingly, would never again be pre-empted or replaced for more than one weekend at a time for the next nine years.

03/19 The bad news was the first such weekend came right away. *Fright Night* was pre-empted by a telethon.

03/26 *House of Horrors* (1946) Robert Lowery, Martin Kosleck, Virginia Grey. An insane artist saves a criminal fiend, the Creeper, from drowning and uses him in murderous schemes. The *New York Times* had just two words for this Universal chiller: "Perfectly lousy." Reviews like this were all the more reason to tune in. This vehicle for the talents of genre favorite Rondo Hatton was a perfectly entertaining B-picture, quite undeserving of such a harsh review. The print Channel 9 telecast had oddly clean, high-quality sound to it. C (Universal, b/w)

04/02 *White Zombie*

04/09 *Horror Island*

04/16 *The Raven*

04/23 *Cult of the Cobra* (1955) Faith Domergue, Marshall Thompson, Richard Long. **A group of GI's in an Asian city are the unwelcome observers of a cobra worshipper's ritual and later find themselves facing death at the hands of a woman who can change herself into a snake.** *Newsday* said "Buy the premise, buy the flick," a catch-all saying they used way too frequently, but in this case it was applicable. Good entertainment, certainly better than I thought it would be, if not all that memorable. It floated around to a variety of other Channel 9 movie programs. C (Universal-International, b/w)

04/30 *The Spider Woman Strikes Back* (1946) Gale Sondergaard, Rondo Hatton, Brenda Joyce. **A young girl, hired to nurse a blind woman, fears that her predecessors may be used to feed a strange plant.** That's what Sondergaard was up to, all right, but Brenda Joyce (of Tarzan film fame) as the young unsuspecting victim didn't catch on until after she had downed several nightly glasses of drugged milk (*a la She-Wolf of London*). The monsters in this rarely shown, often-maligned Universal quickie were the blood-drinking plant in the basement, and Hatton lumbering menacingly in the dark shadows of the menacing mansion. Sondergaard stole the show with her terrific knack for the sinister masked by artificial sweetness. Like the tainted milk, this movie wasn't great for fending off drowsiness, but it was still a fun thriller. "Would you like to read to me, Jean?" (Universal, b/w)

05/07 *Monster from the Ocean Floor* (1954) Anne Kimbell, Stuart Wade, Dick Pinner. **An American vacationing near a Mexican village hears strange stories of a sea monster rising from the Pacific.** One of producer Roger Corman's earliest works, I loved this tight little monster picture with its giant, blurry, one-eyed rubber octopus. It was one of the most embarrassingly low-budget creatures ever filmed; director Wyott Ordung kept the monster out of sight for as long as possible. The year before, Ordung wrote the incredible *Robot Monster* (1953) which would be seen in the not-too-distant-future on *Fright Night*. *Newsday* simply said "It works," and gave the film a fair two-star rating, but it seemed unlikely that the film's shortcomings would have escaped them had they actually seen it. The standard *Fright Night* bumper was dropped for this telecast due to technical difficulties; the optical slide (with the words *Fright Night* on a black, lightning-covered background), used between commercials, was substituted. The organ music from Channel 9's *Thriller Theatre* program warbled and played for a few moments before the film began. "Mother nature ... sometimes she knows not when to start and sometimes she knows not when to stop." C (Palo Alto, b/w)

05/14 *Man Beast* (1956) Rock Madison, Asa Maynor, George Wells Lewis. In the Himalayas, a group of American travelers encounter the legendary Abominable Snowman. Anything with the name of producer-director Jerry Warren attached to it usually got a deserved critical bashing, but this flick's eerie, wintry feel, formidable snow monsters and kooky guide with frozen eyebrows was pretty darn good and has earned a few kudos over time. The incorporation of the same public domain music used in *Night of the Living Dead* (1968) enhanced the spooky effect for me. Cheap as hell, but not bad at all. C (Warren, b/w)

05/21 *Beginning of the End* (1957) Peter Graves, Peggie Castle, Morris Ankrum. A small town is destroyed by grasshoppers over eight feet tall. Channel 9's trimmed-down *Fright Night* presentation of this film only lasted about an hour so it was a pretty easy flick to get through. Producer-director Bert I. Gordon's "special" effects included see-through giant locusts occasionally walking on the sky and were definitely amusing and endearing. I dug that opening theme song too. C (AB-PT Pictures, b/w)

05/28 *Ring of Terror* (1962) George Mather, Austin Green, Esther Furst. A young pre-med student at a Southern medical college must open a crypt and steal a dead man's ring as his fraternity initiation. I had never seen or heard of *Ring of Terror* at the time. It turned out to be an odd movie with a cemetery caretaker relating a story told through older footage (obviously from some other movie). Sort of what I imagined Jerry Warren would have done with the *Tales from the Crypt* (1972) formula. It was just offbeat enough to hold my interest and I did find the cemetery scenes kind of spooky. C (Playstar, b/w)

06/04 *The Creature Walks Among Us* (1956) Jeff Morrow, Rex Reason, Leigh Snowden. The Creature from the Black Lagoon, trapped in Florida waters, is transformed by surgeons into an air-breathing, nearly human animal. Post-transformation, the Creature was really kind of big and scary-looking. The ending left me feeling quite sad. Oddly, the two previous Creature films never made a *Fright Night* appearance. C (Universal-International, b/w)

06/11 *The Deadly Mantis* (1957) Craig Stevens, William Hopper, Alix Talton. A giant prehistoric insect is liberated from its North Pole ice prison and destroys everything in its path. Another movie that I was very familiar with in digest form thanks to a Castle Films 8mm version I had owned. The full version shown on *Fright Night* didn't seem to add all that much and I think I preferred the mini-version. Not the most exciting giant insect of all time, but I can still hear the creature's buzzing sound. C (Universal-International, b/w)

06/18 *Tarantula* (1955) **John Agar, Mara Corday, Leo G. Carroll. A scientist's experiments cause a spider to mutate to giant size. It roams the desert searching for victims.** More giant bugs. This film was notable not only as a *Fright Night* feature, but as the film selected to revive Channel 11's *Chiller* for one night in October of 2008. Pretty good special effects for the time and a generous dose of monsters made this picture a good deal of fun for both events. And, as everyone knows by now, Clint Eastwood managed to save the day in a cameo role! C (Universal-International, b/w)

06/25 *The Thing That Couldn't Die*

07/02 *Face of Fire* (1959) **Cameron Mitchell, James Whitmore, Bettye Ackerman. Life in a small rural community changes forever when a man, attempting to save a young boy from a house fire, is horribly disfigured.** Another rarely seen gem, this moving and intelligent movie was based on the Stephen Crane story "The Monster." Profound in its moral stand and extremely well-made on a low budget, this film took the viewer much deeper than its lurid title suggested and managed to get my young brain really thinking about its message. The film featured a fine performance by Whitmore. Bravo! (Allied Artists, b/w)

07/09 *Creature from the Haunted Sea* (1961) **Anthony Carbone, Betsy Jones-Moreland, Robert Towne. Traveling in the waters off Cuba with stolen money, a crook murders other members of his gang and blames the deaths on a sea monster.** If it had anything to do with a beach, my favorite place to be besides sitting in front of the tube, I was bound to love it. A crude and crusty comedy-horror mess from Roger Corman, but it was charming in its own ridiculous way. The monster had to be seen to be believed ... it rivaled the Monster from the Ocean Floor! Although Corman was spoofing with this creature, I doubt it would have looked much better had the approach been serious. C (Filmgroup, b/w)

07/16 *Creature with the Blue Hand*

07/23 *The Disembodied* (1957) **Paul Burke, Allison Hayes, John Wengraf. American adventurers in the jungle are bewitched by voodoo into carrying out the commands of the beautiful wife of a missionary doctor.** A local newspaper critic astonishingly gave this dull and sweaty film a three-star rating, but its leaden pace made me suspect they never viewed it. Allison (*Attack of the 50 Foot Woman*) Hayes was sure a beauty and she was always at her best when she played a vixen motivated by greed, but even she had trouble making this picture click. I was bored. (Allied Artists, b/w)

07/30 *The Wasp Woman* (1959) **Susan Cabot, Anthony Eisley, Barboura**

Original theatrical lobby card for the rarely seen *Face of Fire* (1959).

Morris. **The aging owner of a cosmetics company discovers a formula derived from the jelly of queen wasps that can bring back youth.** This would have been a great movie for Allison Hayes. Funny how watching this flick over thirty years ago, I had no appreciation for the stress of aging that lead character Janice Starlin experienced. Some of the offices I have worked in over the years were scarier than anything that I saw going on at Janice Starlin Enterprises and I would have welcomed some of the violent interruptions shown in this movie. It took a bit of time to reach the stinging climax, but it wasn't a bad picture. Viewed now in the era of Botox, it seems especially relevant. C (Filmgroup, b/w)

08/06 *Track of the Vampire*

08/13 *The Cat Creature* (1973) **Meredith Baxter, Stuart Whitman, John Carradine. A mysterious cat is linked to the theft of an ancient Egyptian amulet.** A great cast that also featured Gale Sondergaard, Kent Smith and Keye Luke added to the fun of this feline fright flick originally made for ABC-TV by director Curtis Harrington (*What's the Matter with Helen?*, *Devil Dog*). It had a real spooky feel in that TV-movie kind of way, with suspense touches and a style distantly reminiscent of the television classic *The Night Stalker.* It was a nice, unusual touch to have beautiful young rising star Baxter in a chiller like this. The unusual casting was reminiscent of Elizabeth Montgomery raising eyebrows in her post–*Bewitched* shocker *The Legend of Lizzie Borden.* A very good flick. (Columbia/Screen Gems, color)

08/20 *Creature with the Atom Brain*

08/27 *Mad Magician*

09/03 *The Curse of Nostradamus* (1960) German Robles, Julio Aleman, Domingo Soler. A vampire swears to destroy the family of a man who killed one of his ancestors. This K. Gordon Murray import kicked off a month's worth of Mexican monster movies on *Fright Night* and provided a rare opportunity to see some oddball pictures that were truly unlike anything else on Earth. Two years before, Channel 9 had a Mexican Monster festival on its weeknight *Showcase 9* program, and this would be the subgenre's last big go-round at the station. As was usually the case with these films, the plot was a bit mixed up but the visuals were intriguing. German Robles in formal dinner wear was always a cause for celebration. (AIP Television, b/w)

09/11 *The Vampire's Coffin* (1960) Abel Salazar, German Robles, Ariadna Welter. A servant removes the stake from a vampire's body after a doctor has disinterred him. What stood out for me most about this very low-budget sequel to the classic Mexican chiller *The Vampire* (1957) was the grating, unbearably annoying voice of the little girl character (clearly dubbed by an adult). Even without that distraction, it was a bit of a letdown when compared to the film's predecessor. However, there is no such thing as a crummy K. Gordon Murray import in my book, and despite its dull proceedings it was a thrill to see this rarity late on a Saturday night. C (AIP Television, b/w)

09/18 *Swamp of the Lost Souls* (1957 aka *Swamp of the Lost Monsters*) Gaston Santos, Sara Cabrera, Manola Saavedra. A murder investigation leads a detective and his sidekick to a swamp where a horrible creature lurks. There was more comedy than horror in this K. Gordon Murray western-themed monster movie, similar in spirit to *The Living Coffin.* Kind of juvenile fun and the rubber-suit monster was undeniably a very poor man's nod to *Creature from the Black Lagoon* (1954), but it was serviceable Mexican nonsense. It was always fascinating to see those hand-painted title cards that resembled the bad artwork of comic books like *Tales from the Tomb, Witches' Tales,* etc. *Fright Night* utilized a very scratchy print with a decidedly pink hue as I recall, but I knew I was watching something I wasn't going to see every day. (AIP Television, color)

09/24 *World of the Vampires*

10/01 *Frankenstein* (1931) **Boris Karloff, Mae Clarke, Edward Van Sloan.** **A medical student creates "life" in a fabricated human being.** *Fright Night* began another thematic festival and kicked off with a run of groundbreaking golden era classics from Universal. The *New York Times* called this iconic chiller "[a] highly artistic shocker, truly. Look closely. And run, Mae! At 'em Boris!" A local newspaper said "[H]e still holds together pretty well." This film was shown uncharacteristically out of sequential order considering Channel 9's usual attention to detail, but who cared? Clive's orgasmic cries of "It's alive!" are probably still echoing in my old family den at this very moment. C (Universal, b/w)

10/08 *Dracula* (1931) **Bela Lugosi, Helen Chandler, David Manners. Count Dracula, a vampire who has lived for 300 years in the Carpathian mountains, forsakes his castle for London in search of fresh blood.** The *New York Times* got a bit verbose when it said "the film progresses steadily and unhurriedly, with visual artistry and restraint that render the horror even more bloodcurdling." *Newsday* took a more pedestrian approach saying, "Welcome back, you old bat." The opening 15 minutes of this legendary Universal classic were probably among the best and most evocative of any horror movie ever made. It did slow down considerably thereafter, but I loved every single second of it. C (Universal, b/w)

10/15 *The Mummy* (1932) **Boris Karloff, Zita Johann, David Manners. An archaeological expedition finds the mummy of an Egyptian prince, which comes to life seeking its mate.** *Newsday* gave it four stars and said it was the "[f]irst and best of its kind ... dated but go with it." The *New York Times* said it was a "[s]uspense antique that creaks exotically and becomingly." Once again, the opening 15 minutes of this Universal granddaddy were probably the most exciting of the whole picture, but despite its pace that dragged nearly as slowly as Imhotep's mummified wrappings, it deserved to be showcased among *Fright Night*'s finest. C (Universal, b/w)

10/22 *The Wolf Man*

10/29 *The Man Who Reclaimed His Head* (1934) **Claude Rains, Joan Bennett, Lionel Atwill. A struggling anti-war writer goes to work for a scheming publisher.** Universal's alluring title and a cast that included Atwill suggested a perfect movie candidate for *Fright Night*, but this film was far more of a human drama about profiteering and the horrors of war. Still, its great story and the dramatic conclusion left me with no regrets for giving it a chance. Admittedly borderline material for *Fright Night*, but it was rarely seen and one could easily forgive the marketing deception of the title. (Universal, b/w)

11/05 *Mermaids of Tiburon* (1962) **Diane Webber, George Rowe, Gaby Martone. An adventurer on a South Pacific island discovers that there is a race of women underwater.** There are two versions of this movie, a color print with ample nudity and this one, in glorious black and white and devoid of just about all such titillation. Channel 9 used the latter. Though mermaids were not exactly the subject matter I was accustomed to seeing on *Fright Night*, it wasn't half as bad as I thought it would be. The mermaids were actually pretty convincing and it was all fairly painless fun with a decent storyline. C (Filmgroup, b/w)

11/12 *The Bride and the Beast* (1958) **Charlotte Austin, Lance Fuller, Johnny Roth. Hypnosis reveals that a young bride was a gorilla in a previous life.** This film had the distinction of being legendary schlockmeister Ed (*Plan 9 from Outer Space*) Wood's sole contribution to *Fright Night*, if only as an author of this story. Unsurprisingly very lowbrow in its approach, it once again illustrated how much of a challenge it was to make a gorilla movie scary. But as camp entertainment, it was a scream. Especially viewing the amorous facial gestures of young Charlotte in response to her hairy friend. It made for a twisted evening. C (Allied Artists, b/w)

11/19 *Equinox*

11/26 *The Astro Zombies* (1968) **Wendell Corey, John Carradine, Tom Pace. A doctor creates a zombie robot that attracts the attention of an international spy ring.** Probably the only real reason to watch this was a chance to see *Faster Pussycat, Kill! Kill!*'s Tura Satana in action, but at the time even that wasn't enough to keep my eyes open. Though campy and crazy, it still was an incoherent mess from notorious moviemaker Ted (*Blood Orgy of the She Devils*) V. Mikels, and was very, very hard to watch ... unless you were something short of sober. C (Jack H. Harris Entertainment, color)

12/03 *Dungeons of Harrow* (1962) **Russ Harvey, Helen Hogan, William McNulty. A man is shipwrecked on an uncharted island where a mad count and his servant reside in a castle of horrors.** All the *New York Times* cared to say was "And hooey!" Well, I guess I couldn't blame them on this one, but I loved this crazy tale of leprosy and insanity in a madman's castle on a lost island. I found the sets intriguing and effective, the color and lighting creepy, and the surprise in the dungeon quite shuddery. This low-budget effort (see the shipwreck effects and you'll see I *do* mean very *low*-budget) kept me thoroughly engaged from start to finish. Not in the same edge-of-the-seat way *Psycho* or other high-end films had, but in a cozy way — like curling up with an old-fashioned ghost story on a stormy night. The acting, however, was painfully wooden as if the cast were auditioning for a high school play. C (MPS, color)

12/10 *Dorian Gray* (1970 aka *Secret of Dorian Gray*) Helmut Berger, Herbert Lom, Richard Todd. **An aristocratic young man begins a dissolute life, which is reflected only in the portrait of him rapidly aging in a secret room.** A rarely seen European version of the Oscar Wilde story, this film was one of the racier and hipper features shown on *Fright Night* at that time. It really had just about everything: a great-looking cast, intriguing plot, high fashion (for the time), straight sex, gay sex (at least implied) and a nice horrific pay-off at the end. The aging portrait artwork was handled magnificently! The film's original movie poster is a beauty and a much sought-after piece of memorabilia in part because of that striking artwork. A solid early '70s horror spectacle. C (Republic, color)

12/17 *Grave of the Vampire* (1972) William Smith, Michael Pataki, Lyn Peters. **Two generations of a family of vampires clash in a quiet university town.** This is one of those *Fright Night* features that even the most casual viewer remembers seeing. It had that modern '70s drive-in movie

Original theatrical lobby card featuring the striking artwork for Dorian Gray (1970).

flair, blood, violence, and in-your-face horror that were extremely memorable. The opening scene where a young girl is raped by a vampire in a cemetery was genuinely jolting. The rest of the picture was less so and a bit anticlimactic, but it was still a great horror show. *Newsday* did not agree and their one-star rating was followed by a harsh commentary: "Pish-tish and pox upon this pale tale of a son's strange memories of dear old dad." C (Millennium Entertainment/Pyramid, color)

12/24 *The Invisible Man*
12/31 *The Body Snatcher*

1978

The Hillside Strangler claims his last victim on the West Coast and film director Roman Polanski (*The Fearless Vampire Killers*) takes refuge in France after pleading guilty to charges of sex with a minor. Meanwhile, a few telethons slow the pace of *Fright Night, Disco '77* bites the dust and is replaced by another dance show (*Soap Factory Disco*), but the horror movies keep a-comin'.

01/07 *Horror Hotel* (1960—aka *The City of the Dead*) Christopher Lee, Betta St. John, Patricia Jessel. A woman who was burned as a witch makes a pact with the devil for eternal life. In exchange she provides him with human sacrifices obtained from the hotel she runs. This suspenseful, imaginative and widely seen low-budget chiller migrated its way from a long run on Channel 5's *Creature Feature* and was an ideal addition to *Fright Night*'s line-up. The film's director, John Llewellyn Moxey, brilliantly created a mood of foreboding that lingered throughout the whole movie. He was also responsible for the equally riveting TV-movie classic *The Night Stalker* (1972). From its fog-saturated creepy sets, eerie photography and haunting Gregorian-style chanting to stellar performances by most of the cast (the English ones try to feign New England–American accents), this movie was a downright scary pleasure. It also had the kind of lines you loved repeating with friends who shared an enthusiasm for the film. I started marking Candlemas Eve on my calendar shortly after watching this. "You might find the church interesting. Unfortunately, it no longer has a congregation." C (Vulcan/Trans-Lux, b/w)

01/14 *Night Caller from Outer Space* (1965 aka *Blood Beast from Outer Space*) John Saxon, Patricia Haines, Maurice Denham. A mutant from another world captures Earth people in order to re-populate his dying planet. Despite a wonderfully campy opening theme song, this eerie British thriller (and another *Creature Feature* leftover) was extremely suspenseful and tense in much the same way *Horror Hotel* had been the previous week. The not-so-subtly disguised alien arriving at the home of a young girl and standing in the shadows at the front door or the nasty goings-on inside a sleazy book store provided some truly unnerving scenes. Intelligently approached (but often criticized for its rather anticlimactic unveiling of the alien's face), this movie left me quite edgy when it was time to walk the dark hallway to my bedroom. C (New Art/Armitage, b/w)

01/21 *Beginning of the End*

01/28 *The Unearthly* (1957) **John Carradine, Allison Hayes, Myron Healey. A mad scientist performs operations on prisoners that will guarantee eternal life.** Migrating over to Channel 9 from a long run on Channel 11's *Chiller*, this entertainingly dreary low-grade picture was a great opportunity to see Tor Johnson in a meaty role (I guess he made all of his roles "meaty") and, unfortunately, Allison Hayes with a contagiously bad set of the blues. Her moping really got me down, but the movie was still a lot of unsophisticated fun. Hereafter, the film was re-run often on *Nine All Night* and various other Channel 9 movie shows. C (AB-PT Pictures/Republic, b/w)

02/04 Looks like *Fright Night* was pre-empted for a telethon.

02/11 *Curse of the Swamp Creature* (1968) **John Agar, Francine York, Jeff Alexander. Three men and a beautiful woman, searching for oil in the deadly swamplands, meet an insane doctor who is working on an experiment to create a half-reptile creature.** I knew I was in for a treat when the opening scene featured a hammy mad doctor channeling Colin Clive and imploring a rubber hand emerging from a tub of dry ice to "Live! Breathe!" From the maker of *In the Year 2889* (1967) and *Mars Needs Women* (1967), Larry Buchanan, this movie had exactly the same astonishingly pitiful low-budget quality and irresistible charm. Again, its inclusion on *The Monster Times'* list of all-time bad movies made me ecstatic to finally have an opportunity to see it. Its backyard amateur feel was truly intoxicating. The swampland environment was much less crucial to the plot than the mad doctor's swimming pool which, through bad editing, we were to believe was a tank filled with hungry crocodiles. And what was up with that kooky doc's giant-sized Jackie O. sunglasses? I felt like I needed a pair of those to hide my shame after watching this! A wonderful classic of bad cinema and I truly loved it. C (Azeala/AIP Television)

02/18 *Yog, Monster from Space* (1971) **Akira Kubo, Etsuko Takohashi, Yukiki Kobayashi. "A militant astro-quaser" as the station described it, bent on world domination takes possession of a Jupiter-bound rocket and lands on a Pacific island.** And when it did, all hell broke loose.

One of the rare Japanese horror–sci-fi epics to make an appearance on *Fright Night*, but it was unquestionably one of the best possible choices. Often listed in TV guides sans the *Yog*, this was a fun chiller with the alien life force mutating ordinary sea creatures into gigantic monsters at a breakneck pace. Best of all was the hysterical, yet somehow mildly intimidating, walking octopus. This was really enjoyable kiddie matinee-level garbage, so I can't really blame a local newspaper for feeling it was only worthy of just one star and calling it a "monster miss-mash!" The movie had played theatrically in the New York area with *The Abominable Dr. Phibes* (1971). (American International, color)

02/25 *Octaman*

03/04 *House of the Black Death* **(1965 aka** *Blood of the Man Devil***) John Carradine, Lon Chaney, Jr., Andrea King A Satanic curse plagues a family of devil worshippers as a werewolf prowls the grounds of their estate.** A promised werewolf that never materialized was only one of the many disappointments that plagued this film. It's a very low-budget, tedious and slow-moving affair from budget-conscious producer Jerry Warren, whose only real highlight was Lon Chaney's hoofs. A rare treat for bad movie lovers, but wicked to stay awake through in the late night hours. This film kicked off a mini–Jerry Warren festival on *Fright Night*. (Warren, b/w)

03/11 *Invasion of the Animal People* **(1962) John Carradine, Barbara Wilson, Sten Gester. Ice-age giants controlled by alien brains begin a reign of terror on Earth.** Chilly thrills for a cold March night. The huge, hairy monsters featured in this Lapland film were photo favorites in *Famous Monsters of Filmland* magazine, so it was again a thrill to finally see the movie. Another Jerry Warren cut-and-paste job, but a good deal more interesting than some of his other movies that were similarly handled. Deserving of an Oscar compared to next week's feature. C (Unger, b/w)

03/18 *Curse of the Stone Hand* **(1964) John Carradine, Ernest Walch, Chela Bon. A lurid secret lies behind a hidden door in an old mansion.** The Jerry Warren fear-festival finally came to a brutal, torturous close with yet another reworking of some incoherent foreign footage and U.S.–filmed filler. While the movie remains very vivid in my recollection, especially the sets and strange stone hands from the foreign portions, I had absolutely no idea what was going on. It was truly grand in its awfulness, but I was happy to have witnessed it. The *New York Times* was spot on when they said it was "for stone heads." (Warren, ADP, b/w)

03/25 *Man with the Synthetic Brain* **(1972 aka** *Blood of Ghastly Horror***) John Carradine, Kent Taylor, Tommy Kirk. A mad scientist implants an electrical device into the brain of a man and turns him into a killer**

zombie. According to Sam Sherman, a writer once referred to this movie as *Man with the Sympathetic Brain*, which might have fit just as well. The legendary cult movie director Al Adamson and producer Sherman followed in the footsteps of Jerry Warren when they punched up the director's earlier film, *Psycho-A-Go-Go* (1965), with some newly filmed scenes and ended up with this impossibly incoherent yarn. The newer, distinctly horror-minded portions, such as Regina Carrol's transformation into a hideous, mummified woman, were a lot of fun though. Undeniably crude and confusing, but it still felt very satisfying to watch. C (Independent-International, color)

04/01 *The Black Cat* (1934)

04/08 *The Strange Door* (1951) Charles Laughton, Boris Karloff, Sally Forrest. A cruel tyrant, subject to fits of insanity, keeps his brother prisoner in a castle dungeon. Having only seen Laughton in *Island of Lost Souls* (1932) on Channel 5's *Creature Feature* and, as a very young child, *The Canterville Ghost* (1944), I relished another opportunity to watch this delightfully hammy actor in action. He did not disappoint, and this tale of medieval menace, much like *The Black Castle*, was diverting to watch. I recall that the scene where Laughton throws a giant half-eaten chicken leg at Michael (*Curse of the Undead*) Pate made me very hungry. A movie with a swashbuckler feel, it remains engaging thanks to Laughton. C (Universal-International, b/w)

04/15 *Black Friday* (1940) Boris Karloff, Bela Lugosi, Anne Nagel. A partial brain transplant turns a kindly professor into a criminal killer. Universal's merging of the gangster and horror genres, favoring the former, had some decent *film noir* touches and a great cast, but just didn't deliver the punch one might have hoped for. Lugosi's cries of terror when he was locked in a closet were so damn whiny. Equally annoying was the frequent spinning of the calendar and blaring musical accompaniment. It seemed like a film I should have liked, but I just couldn't get into this one. C (Universal, b/w)

04/22 *Were Wolf of London* (1935) Henry Hull, Warner Oland, Valerie Hobson. While traveling in Tibet, a botanist discovers a strange plant that only blooms in moonlight. Universal's first splash into Lake Lycanthropy was a highly effective, absorbing thriller. Hull's makeup (by the legendary Jack Pierce) seemed, to me, far more evil-looking than Lon Chaney's and the opening scenes in the mountains of Tibet felt quite eerie and atmospheric. Even the comic relief between Mrs. Whack and Mrs. Moncaster was amusing in this entertaining, tight production. A local newspaper's review was both annoyingly useless and a feeble attempt at their own brand of humor: They warned "keep away, this werewolf has rabies." C (Universal, b/w)

04/29 *The Cat Creeps* (1946) Noah Beery, Jr., Paul Kelly, Lois Collier. A

strange band of people gather in a crumbling house in the middle of New York Bay, trying to solve a ten-year-old murder and ward off a killer's attacks. Not sure why Channel 9 thought this film took place in New York, as the island was covered in tropical flora and palm trees ... and there's certainly nothing like that up in these toxic waters! It was another rarely seen Universal mystery thriller, and one of the last genre films the studio produced in the '40s. The movie seemed to be a bit influenced by the atmosphere and style found in Val Lewton's *Cat People* and *I Walked with a Zombie*, but there was only a very slight resemblance. A perfectly typical, adequate and entertaining oldie, but a local newspaper called it a "feline flop." (Universal, b/w)

05/06 Looks like *Fright Night* was pre-empted for a telethon.

05/13 ***Don't Look in the Basement*** **(1973) William McGhee, Jessie Lee Fulton, Robert Dracup. A young nurse goes to work at a violent mental institution where patients are treated with bizarre therapies.** "Keep repeating ... it's only a movie ... only a movie ... only a movie" was an intriguing advertising catchphrase that had been used to market movies like this one on the drive-in circuit for years following the success of *Last House on the Left* (1972). Expecting this to be the wild experience I envisioned that notorious film to have been, I was a bit disappointed by this extremely low-budget, poorly acted, somewhat dull horror flick. For one thing, there wasn't much in the basement. The boiler room in my house was scarier than this. Though I found it more depressing than frightening, I did, however, enjoy its almost 8mm amateur movie style (poorly superimposed title credits gave it a real backyard feel) and that crazy judge with an axe to grind. This must have been like an opportunity to perform Shakespeare for this actor and, frankly, he was a bit unsettling. The producers recommended this movie not be seen by those over 30. Now that I am way over 30, I agree ... but for different reasons. C (Hallmark, color)

05/20 ***Island Monster*** **(1957) Boris Karloff, Franca Marzi, Patrizia Remiddi. A ring of drug smugglers terrorizes an island and kidnaps the daughter of an agent assigned to stop them.** Look no further, you have reached the *worst* film ever shown on *Fright Night*! And if you've seen films like *Attack of the Mayan Mummy* or *Curse of the Stone Hand*, you'll know that's no small accomplishment. The station televised a lot of dreck on *Fright Night* during its 14-year history, but this had to be the lowest they had ever sunk. Except for the deceptive title and the presence of Karloff, whose voice was terribly dubbed by another actor, this absolutely miserable, torturous and boring non-drama had no place on *Fright Night*. If Channel 9 paid more than a buck and half to show this film, they were robbed. Maybe I was just in a bad mood at the time, but it was absolute beg-for-death torture to sit through. I became very annoyed watching this picture and though I made it through to the bitter end, I never saw the film again for over thirty years. Upon watching the movie recently, it proved every bit as unbearably dead-ass dull as it was the first time 'round. I forgave *Fright Night* for this ghastly lapse in judgment, but I never forgot it. There was a tortured-looking graphic on the movie's title card that should have served as a warning. C (Romana, b/w)

05/27 *Touch of Satan* (1971 aka *Touch of Melissa*) Michael Berry, Lee Amber, Emby Mellay. A man stumbles upon a farmhouse, scene of violent murders and home of a family haunted by a witch's curse. The local newspaper gave this movie a one-star rating and described it as "dark deeds in dullsville." After a dimly lit pitchfork killing at a walnut farm in the opening minutes, it took nearly 50 more minutes for anything to really start happening. A crazy old woman in a fright wig (who looked like Lionel Atwill in *Mystery of the Wax Museum*) finally got the action going. The film crackled with that faded, dirty print and low-budget drive-in feel. Though it mostly missed the mark, it was still kind of likable in a let's-not-watch-that-again-too-soon kind of way. C (Dundee, color)

06/03 *Mesa of Lost Women* was scheduled, but replaced by *Rendezvous at Midnight* (1935) Ralph Bellamy, Valerie Hobson, Catherine Doucet. Police attempt to solve the murder of a commissioner. *Mesa*, featuring Jackie "Uncle Fester" Coogan, would have certainly been the more quirky, enjoyable genre movie to show but obviously something went wrong and this rarely seen mystery quickie from the Carl Laemmle, Jr., days of Universal was pulled out of Channel 9's vault and filled the time slot. A weak whodunit, but as a dusty obscurity from the old days with a nice vintage cast, it was an unusual and significant telecast. (Universal, b/w)

06/10 *The Vampire Bat* (1933) Fay Wray, Lionel Atwill, Melvyn Douglas. A European village is terrorized by blood-sucking bats. This film had been popping up for years before *Fright Night* on other Channel 9 movie shows, and was one of the first genre films I ever saw. It was a harmless mystery thriller filmed on Universal's back lot; the presence of Dwight Frye as the mad Herman Gleib (looking as if he was still wearing his Renfield suit from *Dracula*) was an added bonus. It had the same nice, creepy atmosphere that permeates many of these dusty golden oldies and was a nifty time-killer. The film became a regular late night telecast on public television stations that frequently showed public domain movies during the '80s and '90s. C (Majestic, b/w)

06/17 *Creature with the Blue Hand*
06/24 *Nylon Noose*

07/01 *The Brighton Strangler* (1945) John Loder, June Duprez, Michael St. Angel. An actor in war-torn London, brain-injured when his theater is bombed, begins to take on the personality of a homicidal maniac, a character he had mastered on the stage. An interesting, well-produced melodramatic thriller dusted off from the vault and something of a rarity, proving RKO was almost as prolific in the horror genre as Universal. The British atmosphere of the period was nicely captured. While Loder was no Laird Cregar, an actor for whom this movie seemed ideally suited, the picture was a lot of fun, sophisticated and highly entertaining. (RKO, b/w)

07/08 *Dungeons of Harrow*

07/15 *The Land Unknown* (1957) Jock Mahoney, Shawn Smith, William Reynolds. A U.S. Navy expedition, forced down in an Antarctic storm, finds itself several thousand miles down and several million years in the past. This was kind of a U.S. precursor to the forthcoming wave of Japanese-made monster flicks in that it featured a guy in a rubber dinosaur costume. The movie had a good adventure feel to it and enough amusing effects to make for a worthy *Fright Night* experience. But Mahoney's sleepy, emotionless acting style was better suited to his portrayals of Tarzan and, once again, was magnified in dullness by the late hour. C (Universal-International, b/w)

07/22 *Mystery of Marie Roget* (1942) Patric Knowles, Maria Montez, John Litel. The disappearance of a Parisian actress leads to a murder trial. Another modest Universal quickie B-picture that was a very loose adaptation of an Edgar Allan Poe short story. A good B-movie cast tried hard and it managed to lightly entertain, but it was nothing you'd remember for very long. Maria Ouspenskaya was a real stand-out for being one seriously cranky old broad! Another quickie televised pre-baseball games on weekends. (Universal, b/w)

07/29 *Crime of Dr. Hallet* (1938) Ralph Bellamy, Josephine Hutchinson, William Gargan. A young doctor's life is unexpectedly changed by a strange turn of events as he seeks a cure to a deadly disease in the jungle. Another of those "fringe" mystery drama movies that really did not the fit the *Fright Night* mold too well, but as a Universal rarity with a solid cast, it was a worthwhile, well-made drama quickie. A young Bellamy gives it his all trying to cure jungle fever. (Universal, b/w)

08/05 *Dungeons of Harrow*

08/12 *Dr. Jekyll & Sister Hyde* (1971) Ralph Bates, Martine Beswick, Gerald Sim. A young doctor changes himself into a woman who becomes a killer. The local newspaper felt it was only a "passable thriller," but when this was shown on *Fright Night*, I was already a huge fan having caught it on a memorable premiere telecast on *The CBS Late Movie* some time before.

Its controversial transformation premise and nudity made the film off-limits to me as a young child, but it had been worth the wait to see it, even in a censored version. Bates was less hammy than usual and Martine was simply brilliant as his sinister alter ego. This was the first Hammer film to make an appearance on the show, and every frame of this clever retelling of the classic story was fascinating to watch. While the special effects at the end were a bit unsatisfying, this film magnificently captured the feel of Victorian England and cleverly incorporated the Jack the Ripper atrocities of the era. A brilliant title theme and music score by David Whitaker added tremendously to the feeling of period and class with which this picture pulsated. A great night at the movies! C (EMI/Hammer, color)

08/19 *The Sorcerers* (1967) Boris Karloff, Catherine Lacey, Elizabeth Ercy. A poor old couple concocts a machine that places other people under their control. Pictures like this sure made a kid afraid to get old. An interesting plot, wherein a couple in their golden years was able to feel the sensations experienced by their younger victims, and an earnest performance by Karloff made for a worthwhile viewing experience. The *Wasp Woman* formula didn't halt the aging process and neither did this scheme. *Fright Night* would show more senior citizen shenanigans (the macabre oddity *Homebodies*) a few years later, but one always came to the same conclusion with movies like this: Old age really sucks! (Tigon, color)

08/25 *Fright* (1971) Susan George, Honor Blackman, Ian Bannen. A young girl is stalked by a homicidal maniac while babysitting in an isolated country house. Talk about bad timing ... the one night Ms. Blackman got up the courage to go out to dinner and look what happened! The somber tones of the opening theme "Ladybird" immediately set an uneasy mood for this tense and scary British *Halloween*-esque import. Scream queen Susan gave a sincere performance reacting to the psychotic stalker lurking outside and the picture had a great "real feel" style, enhanced by what appeared to be ad-libbed dialogue. The terrorized babysitter formula would become a genre unto itself as the years would go by, but this jolter was one of the groundbreakers and, at times, a genuine nail-biter. C (British Lion, color)

09/02 *Decoy for Terror*

09/16 *House of the Seven Corpses* (1974) John Ireland, Faith Domergue, Carole Wells. Disaster hovers over a group of filmmakers who use a deserted mansion with a gory history. It was a treat to see some old veterans of the horror genre (including John Carradine) assembled for this movie in what was a kind of combination haunted house — where-are-they-now show. But you had to wonder if the bitter has been persona each star paraded throughout the movie was just acting or were they really *that* cranky. It was also rough watching Ireland berate poor Faith. This picture moved a bit slowly (right through to its deadly finale) but it definitely had a consistently macabre, somber atmosphere of dread. C (Television Corp. of America, color)

09/23 ***Terror House*** **(1972 aka** ***Folks at Red Wolf Inn, Terror at Red Wolf Inn*)**. **Linda Gillen, John Neilson, Arthur Space. A young college student wins a trip to a remote inn where students have disappeared in the past.** Packed tighter than a sardine can with cannibalism innuendos, some of this movie's dialogue started to feel a wee bit redundant. The most disturbing thing about it was watching the innkeepers' deplorable table manners at meal time. Two parts dark humor and a dash of the macabre, it was a recipe for good fun ... if in bad taste. Not so much scary as it was amusing. C (Red Wolf, color)

09/30 ***The Baby*** **(1973) Ruth Roman, Michael Pataki, Anjanette Comer. A social worker investigates a strange family who treats a fully grown man as an infant.** Wow, talk about bizarre! This one got the prize as one of the freakiest stories ever told on *Fright Night*. No doubt viewers walked away from this one feeling like the victim of a Mickey Finn. You had to wonder how the producers pitched the premise of this weird psycho-drama to investors to even get this project off the ground. But we're lucky they did. Roman delivered a bang-up performance as Mrs. Wadsworth, a cougar mom you didn't want to mess with. In fact, the whole cast seemed very comfortable with the strange subject matter. In a twisted way, this was a must-see ... but you definitely needed a shower afterward. C (Quintet Films, color)

10/07 ***Murders in the Rue Morgue***

10/14 ***She-Wolf of London***

10/21 ***Captive Wild Woman***

10/28 ***The Frozen Ghost***

11/04 Looks like *Fright Night* was pre-empted.

11/11 ***Calling Dr. Death***

11/18 ***The Cat Creeps***

11/25 ***House of Horrors***

12/02 ***The Black Raven*** **(1943) George Zucco, Wanda McKay, Noel Madison. An eloping couple arrives at a hostelry that, unknown to them, plays host to murderers, embezzlers and escaped convicts.** It sounded like the Motel 6 in Fort Lauderdale to me. *Fright Night* finally got around to airing this PRC quickie, an atmospheric mystery vehicle that paired Zucco with future Frankenstein's Monster Glenn Strange. All the elements were here: murder, thunder and lightning, a creepy hotel and a dark cellar. And if one's expectations weren't too high, it worked pretty well. C (PRC, b/w)

12/09 ***Invisible Ghost*** **(1941) Bela Lugosi, Polly Ann Young, John**

McGuire. A man is tormented by the nocturnal reappearance of his dead wife. You had to hand it to Lugosi. Even as a kid I recognized that his role in this movie, and most of the others he made at the time, was a far cry from his glory days in *Dracula*, yet he took his part quite seriously and did his job well. I felt quite bad for his character suffering so deeply from the loss of his wife. The movie really creaked, but it had an eerie charm about it and was a neat and quick little ghost story that was enhanced by the late night hour. C (Monogram, b/w)

12/16 *Voodoo Man* (1944) Bela Lugosi, George Zucco, Wanda McKay. A doctor kidnaps young women to use in voodoo rituals that he believes will revive his dead wife. Like the week before, we were served up another dedicated husband gone mad! A long-time favorite shown on the Saturday horror movie programs over at Channel 11, this picture, a terrific example of corny C-level '40s horror, made its way over to Channel 9. Kooky John Carradine seemed to be on crack playing his mentally unhinged character Toby to the hilt, but it's possible that Zucco's relentless and irritating voodoo chanting may have been the cause of his insanity. A relic from the good old days and a fan favorite. (Monogram, b/w)

12/23 *The House of Fear* (1939) William Gargan, Irene Hervey, Dorothy Arnold. A stage actor is murdered during his performance and rumors spread that his ghost haunts the theater. Not to be confused with the Sherlock Holmes *The House of Fear* (1945) that was shown over at Channel 5. This was a much rarer Universal murder mystery thriller with a nice New York City feel and a few spooky touches, the best of which was a ghostly facial apparition materializing in a desolate theater. Irene Hervey (*Night Monster*) was a very attractive woman with a very direct and honest acting style and any movie she appeared in was made better by her presence. (Universal, b/w)

12/30 Looks like *Fright Night* was pre-empted for a telethon.

1979

The horrors of man's meddling with nuclear energy make real-life headlines when an accident occurs at Three Mile Island, Pennsylvania. *Fright Night* ignores the fallout by continuing to present a wide range of fictional horror films and introduces a short-lived Sunday night edition.

01/06 *Dead Man's Eyes* (1944) Lon Chaney, Jr., Jean Parker, Paul Kelly. A man wills a blind friend his eyes, but when the donor is found dead, the blind man is accused of murder. *Newsday* said, "Chaney struggles with the load." He seemed to manage okay to me, but again it was just another one of those *Inner Sanctum* mysteries that left you feeling a bit indifferent. The eye makeup was kind of creepy. Beautiful but wooden co-star Acquanetta made an appearance and would return in two weeks for an appearance in *Jungle Woman* (1944). C (Universal, b/w)

01/07 (Sunday Edition) ***The Ghost of Frankenstein*** **(1942) Lon Chaney, Jr. Evelyn Ankers, Ralph Bellamy. The monster nursed by Dr. Frankenstein rises up to destroy his creator.** The local newspaper gave it just one and a half stars, saying the film was just "[a] mere shadow of the original." Perhaps in some ways it was, but Universal had still managed to generate some great atmosphere in it and assembled a fine cast to carry off this movie, the fourth in the franchise. Another local TV guide seemed to believe "you can see through this one," but *Newsday* came to the rescue, giving the movie a solid three-star rating. "Your father was Frankenstein, but your mother was the lightning!" C (Universal, b/w)

01/13 ***The Jungle Captive*** **(1945) Otto Kruger, Rondo Hatton, Vicky Lane. A scientist experimenting in glandular transplants steals the corpse of an ape woman from the morgue and proceeds to restore life to her.** *Newsday* gave it a passable two star rating, which was probably more generous than what it might have received had the newspaper actually seen the film. This third movie in the Ape Woman trilogy (started by *Captive Wild Woman*) was shown out of sequence by Channel 9, but it didn't matter all that much. With any of these franchise films, you really didn't need to view them in order and the practice of using previously seen footage by Universal tended to make them feel rather interchangeable. Kind of a snoozer, but not the worst 60 minutes I ever spent. (Universal, b/w)

01/14 (Sunday Edition) ***The Black Cat*** **(1934)**

01/20 ***Jungle Woman*** **(1944) Evelyn Ankers, Lois Collier, Acquanetta. A lakeside sanitarium is terrorized by a ferocious gorilla that once was a beautiful woman, a scientific experiment gone awry.** A pretty accurate two-star rating from *Newsday* was about as generous as anyone could really be with this movie. This sequel to Universal's *Captive Wild Woman* appeared to have been such a rush job it's almost 50 percent flashbacks from the previous movie in the series. But it was still likable and nostalgic as a '40s quickie and it was always a pleasure to see Evelyn earning her paycheck. (Universal, b/w)

01/21 (Sunday Edition) ***Dracula's Daughter***

01/27 ***The Man Who Cried Wolf*** **(1937) Lewis Stone, Barbara Read, Tom Brown. An actor confesses to murders he did not commit in order to cover for his true plan to kill an old enemy.** The *New York Daily News* gave this rarely seen Universal mystery a solid three-star rating. It had a good, unique story, well-paced and intriguingly performed. Rather light crime fare, though, for a *Fright Night* installment; it fell a bit outside the show's preferred themes. Its unusual plot and strong performances made it worth waiting up for. (Universal, b/w)

01/28 (Sunday Edition) *The Man Who Reclaimed His Head*

02/03 Looks like *Fright Night* was pre-empted (and not shown on a Saturday night again until 02/24).

02/04 (Sunday Edition) *Beast of the Dead*

02/11 (Sunday Edition) *Island of Living Horror*

02/18 (Sunday Edition) The *Night Evelyn Came Out of the Grave* (1971) Erica Blanc, Anthony Steffan, Marina Malfatti. Recently released from a psychiatric clinic following the death of his wife, Lord Cunningham returns to his British estate intent on rebuilding his life. Unfortunately Lord Cunningham also has this thing for red-headed beauties and keeps murdering them along the way. I had originally seen this movie on a double bill with *Deep Red* (1975) a few years earlier, when my dad had failed to notice it had an R rating and I neglected to point it out. *Deep Red* left a far stronger impression on me than this confusing, dubbed import with another one of those deceptive titles. With most of its mild nudity and violence trimmed, the movie didn't hold up that well on TV, but it was still cool to see any Euro-trash picture on *Fright Night. Newsday* gave it one star. The title is the best thing about it ... and maybe Erica dancing and prancing. C (Phoenix, color)

02/25 (Sunday Edition) *Deathdream* (1974 aka *Dead of Night*) John Marley, Lynn Carlin, Richard Backus. A young man, believed killed in battle in Vietnam, returns to his family's home and exhibits bizarre behavior. Director Bob Clark had a real knack for great horror films, first with the zombie masterpiece *Children Shouldn't Play with Dead Things* (1973) and later with the USA Network's *Saturday Nightmares* holiday classic *Black Christmas* (1974 aka *Stranger in the House*). Not to mention his work in mainstream cinema with cult favorites *A Christmas Story* and, at the twilight of the drive-in era, *Porky's*. That's quite a résumé! This early effort, though often overlooked, was equally riveting and as chilling as his better known horror films. The slow build of its "Monkey's Paw"–derived story, along with great performances and subtle, disturbing makeup (courtesy of the Ormsbys, who had handled *Dead Things*), made for a truly frightening night! Sleep was not forthcoming that evening! C (Quadrant, color)

02/24 *Invaders from Mars* (1953) Arthur Franz, Jimmy Hunt, Helena Carter. A young boy witnesses a Martian spaceship landing but cannot convince anyone of the imminent danger. He should have teamed up with Bobby Driscoll in *The Window.* While this very theatrical production, kind of a variation on a *War of the Worlds* theme, looked and felt a bit like a Broadway show, it had some of the same innocent early charm of the pulp fiction novels and sci-fi comic books of its time. A great, dramatic music score and the chilling scenes of humans being sucked under the sand by the aliens were actually very creepy! C (National, color)

03/03 ***Hatchet for a Honeymoon*** **(1970) Stephen Forsyth, Laura Betti, Dagmar Lassander. The owner of a bridal shop brutally murders young women in an attempt to unleash a terrible childhood memory.** Along with *Blood and Black Lace*, this Mario Bava–directed movie turned up quite frequently on Channel 9's roster. I was never a fan of all the hoopla surrounding weddings, so in my own twisted way I found these honeymoon horror stories rather amusing. This one was a slow and confusing tale about childhood trauma and the deadly consequences. C (Mercury, color)

03/10 ***Night of the Sorcerers*** **(1973) Jack Taylor, Maria Kosty, Kali Hansa. A group of researches encounter a tribe of voodoo practitioners who turn women into bloodthirsty vampires.** Wow ... now *this* was really something! Twisted by anyone's standards, this was the kind of movie *Fright Night* became legendary for. It was like one of the covers of those grade-D Eerie Publications comic books (*Terror Tales, Weird,* etc.) come to life. Where else would you see a drive-in classic like this, where female victims' heads are chopped off in the African wilderness and the girls return to life as leopard-print bikini-wearing vampires? In its uncut form, this movie was quite violent and raunchy, so even liberal Channel 9 had to have used the scissors quite a bit. There must have been jump cuts a-plenty in the opening scene, which depicted a woman having her clothes literally whipped off, her rape and decapitation. The movie no doubt became a bit frustrating to watch with all these cuts. But still, wouldn't it be great today to check out what's on TV this coming Saturday night and see this movie listed? From Spanish director Armando de Ossorio, who went on to helm the *Blind Dead* series of chillers. (Profilmes/Hesperia, color)

03/17 ***Death Smiles on a Murderer*** **(1973 aka** ***Death Smiles at Murder***) **Klaus Kinski, Ewa Aulin, Angela Bo. An ancient formula for raising the dead allows a man to exact revenge upon his enemies.** This Italian gothic horror movie's sets, production and style were all above average, but it still seemed to have an air of cheapness about it anyway. However, put Kinski in a black top hat and tails and you had an instant horror film. This one had the bonus of a few Poe-inspired touches, suggestions of lesbianism and more than a few references to necrophilia. While all that may sound good, it was hard to follow and just didn't have much pizzazz. It came to

TV as part of a horror movie package of imports being circulated by Avco-Embassy. (DANY, color)

03/24 Looks like *Fright Night* was pre-empted.

04/07 *Wild Women of Wongo* (1958) Jean Hawkshaw, Ray Rotello, Mary Ann Webb. A Stone-Age tribe of beautiful women on the island of Wongo discover that another tribe of handsome men is interested in them. If one could survive *Untamed Women*, one could certainly endure this cute, tongue-in-cheek crap featuring a bevy of scantily clad beauties eager to dump their ugly male counterparts for the hot hunks on the other side of the island. But it would take quite a bit of caffeine and/or alcohol for the average viewer to make it all the way through this vapid specimen. It had the look of your grandpa's old 8mm beach movies, and the closest thing to genre elements in the whole effort were a few crocodiles and a stone "temple" borrowed from a Florida tourist attraction. C (Wolco/Tropical, color)

04/14 *Night Caller from Outer Space*

04/21 *Robot Monster* (1953) George Nader, Claudia Barrett, Gregory Moffett. After an atomic attack, the last humans on Earth must fight off a monster from Mars. *Newsday* was a bit easier on this movie than expected, giving it two stars. It was notorious even back in those broadcast days as a major turkey, even a non-discriminating kid like myself was embarrassed by the low-grade level of thrills that a gorilla suit, diving helmet and a bubble-making machine generated. I didn't know at the time that this picture was intended for 3-D, but can't imagine that would have helped much. Despite (or possibly because of) its undeniably atrocious production values, this woeful attempt at horror was completely enjoyable. I loved that furry alien shaking his fist at us humans! C (Three Dimensional, b/w)

04/28 *Slime People*

05/05 *Vampire Men of the Lost Planet* (1970 aka *Horror of the Blood Monsters*) John Carradine,

Al Adamson does his best Lugosi impression in *Vampire Men of the Lost Planet* (1970).

Robert Dix, Vicki Volante. Members of an expedition to another planet hopes to find the source of a plague of vampirism on Earth. This rag-tag SF adventure combined bizarre foreign film footage of big-fanged cavemen and director Al Adamson's poverty-stricken US-filmed scenes that look hopelessly amateurish. With crummy recycled and colorized *One Million B.C.* (1940) dinosaur footage and assorted low-budget creatures to contend with, the wonderful Adamson cast of regulars just carried the show like the troopers they were! It was easy to see everything that was wrong with this picture and so many of the bad films shown on *Fright Night*, but somehow these films still managed to entertain and amuse in some charmingly inexplicable way. From Sam Sherman's essential Independent-International Pictures package hand-picked for Channel 9, the film was a better fit for the station's Saturday morning horror movie shows. C (Independent-International, color)

05/12 *The Human Vapor* **(1960) Tatsuya Mihashi, Kaoru Yachigusa, Yoshio Tsuchiya. A scientific experiment gives a man the power to turn himself into a mysterious gas.** A sci-fi film from Japan devoid of giant monsters and miniature sets. It was a well-made film, mature and cerebral, but tended to be a bit talky (a problem for any dubbed picture) and favored drama over thrills ... a tough position for a movie to be in at this late hour. The special effects were on a par with *The Invisible Ray.* Well, they couldn't *all* be in-your-face horror fests, but this was at least something kind of different. (Toho, color)

05/19 *Equinox*

05/26 *The Eye Creatures* **(1965) John Ashley, Cynthia Hull, Warren Hammack. Multi-orbed aliens invade a lover's lane.** Horrifically corny comedy dominated this Larry Buchanan remake of *Invasion of the Saucer Men* (1957), which looked much older than its release date had suggested. Like all of Buchanan's strange but wonderful remakes of American International movies, minimal creativity or originality got added to the ultra-low-budget productions, but it would always be fascinating to see what kind of a mess he'd come up with. Compared to the ping-pong ball eyeballs, painted wet suits and dime-store fright mask creations in his other movies, these puffy, marshmallowy man-monsters weren't that bad at all. It was another *Monster Times* pick for its all-time bad movie list, so naturally I loved it, but frequent hard-to-view murky night scenes were another reason to keep the Visine close by. (AIP Television, color)

06/02 *The Vampire Bat*
06/09 *Creature with the Blue Hand*
06/16 *Invasion of the Animal People*
06/23 *Attack of the Mayan Mummy*

06/30 *Monster from the Ocean Floor*

07/07 *Step Down to Terror* **(1958) Rod Taylor, Colleen Miller, Charles Drake. After a six-year absence, a man returns to his home town to a family who does not suspect he has become a psychopathic killer.** A Universal-International murder story that was more drama than horror and had nearly the same feel and gloss of situation comedies being shown on TV at the same time. The neatly coiffed neighborhoods and almost perfect family situations seemed so artificial and manufactured that you almost welcomed the intrusion of a homicidal killer to shake things up. Though it was predictable and tame, it was a passable time-waster ... but its dull villain was a completely forgettable character. A remake of Alfred Hitchcock's *Shadow of a Doubt* (1943). (Universal-International, b/w)

07/14 *Tower of London* **(1939) Boris Karloff, Basil Rathbone, Vincent Price. A 15th century duke spares no one in his cruel and murderous rise to the throne.** Like they did with their Gothic thrillers *The Strange Door* and *The Black Castle*, Universal attempted to make this historical drama pass for a horror film with as many genre trappings as could be placed on its beautiful sets. A great cast under expert direction from Rowland V. Lee (*Son of Frankenstein*) did an admirable job of creating a sinister mood, but somehow the fun dungeon scenes (and a few touches like an ominous-looking Karloff sharpening his big axe blade with a raven on his shoulder) just weren't quite enough to make you truly relish the experience. One of those golden era *Fright Night* features you wanted to enjoy more than you actually did, but it still remained essential viewing in spite of the less than thrilling history lesson. C (Universal, b/w)

07/21 *The Disembodied*

07/28 *Die Monster Die* **(1965) Nick Adams, Boris Karloff, Freda Jackson. A man conceals a meteor that has crashed on his estate. It threatens to mutate any living thing that comes in contact with it.** The brash, gritty yet clean-cut American masculinity of Nick Adams was quite a contrast with the wet grass and country tea kettle flavor of an English estate. It was kind of the same feeling you got when Nick barged in uninvited on Tokyo for *Frankenstein Conquers the World* (1965) on Channel 7's *4:30 Movie* ... reluctant acceptance. But with deadly monsters on the loose, everyone probably felt a good deal safer with him around. Some spooky scenes on the fog-enshrouded estate and Karloff repeating his *Invisible Ray* glowing shtick made for a pleasing horror yarn. Based on an H. P. Lovecraft story. Not bad. C (American International, color)

08/04 *The Dark Eyes of London*

08/11 *Blood and Black Lace* **(1964) Cameron Mitchell, Eva Bartok, Mary**

Arden. **Fashion models become the victims of a brutal masked killer.**
Director Mario Bava's stylish direction, moody lighting and great color were
the high points of this acclaimed, though long-winded and somewhat dull
Italian slasher film. (Woolner, color)

08/18 *Fright*

08/25 *The Sorcerers*

09/01 *The Thing from Another World* **(1951) James Arness, Kenneth Tobey,
Margaret Sheridan. A group of scientists and a reporter discover the
remains of a flying saucer beneath the North Pole ice.** For a few seconds,
the Winchester Pictures logo and rousing theme at the movie's start almost
made you anticipate another Howard Hawks western drama. Instead, the
smoldering emergence of the film title from what looks like the blackness of
space and a magnificent backing score begin a brilliant, high-end, tremendously
suspenseful, heart-pounding thrill ride in the unlikely isolation of a North
Pole research station. The film was singled out in Steinbrunner's book *Cinema
of the Fantastic,* and its inclusion on *Fright Night* would seem both logical and
deserved. I recall being mildly irritated by the obnoxious cross chatter between
characters, typical in Hawks' films, but not at all bothered by the relatively
brief screen time given the humanoid carrot that wreaks havoc throughout the
picture. *Famous Monsters of Filmland* magazine was obsessed with publishing
elusive pictures of the creature, but after viewing this classic, I realized the sum
of this film's parts is far greater than any one single monstrous element. Once
again, less was more. Classic entertainment! Just wish that obnoxious news-
paperman Scotty had gotten a good beating from the Thing. C (RKO, b/w)

09/08 *Cat People*

09/15 *Curse of the Swamp Creature*

09/22 *Battle of the Worlds* **(1961) Claude Rains, Bill Carter, Maya Brent. A
hostile planet is on a collision course with Earth.** That wasn't precisely
what this picture was about, but it was close enough. The *New York Times*
called it "[a] bore ... Poof!" Space operas like this were never that interesting
to me either, but *Fright Night* often "forced" me to sit and actually watch
some movies closer (after investing so much effort to wait up for them), and
with this one, I was glad I did. It wasn't the fastest moving picture ever made,
but it had a certain intriguing charm that grew on me. Irritable Rains' explo-
ration of the interior of the rogue planet was somewhat exciting. This one was,
admittedly, an acquired taste that made its way over from Channel 11's *Chiller.*
The film's director, Antonio Margheriti, showed a much stronger flair for
gothic horror with *Horror Castle* (1963) and *Castle of Terror* (1964 aka *Castle
of Blood*), two regulars over on Channel 5's *Creature Feature.* C (Topaz, color)

09/29 *The Little Shop of Horrors* **(1960) Jonathan Haze, Mel Welles,**

Jackie Joseph. A man nurturing a plant with a bloodthirsty appetite is forced to kill innocent people. Renowned for its comical cameo by Jack Nicholson as a pain-craving dental patient, and as the basis for a smash Broadway show and movie musical remake, this original ultra-low budget effort was a Roger Corman quickie with much of the director's wry sense of humor. It was very cute and the scratchy print cheapness was wonderful to watch. Actor Welles would later be responsible for directing another *Fright Night* beauty, *Lady Frankenstein*. C (Santa Clara, b/w)

10/06 *Berserk* (1967) Joan Crawford, Michael Gough, Ty Hardin. The gruesome death of a worker causes crowds to mob a struggling circus where murder becomes the featured attraction. "Mommie Dearest" made her *Fright Night* debut, and seeing the aging actress give one of her typical hard-as-nails performances was a great treat. But when she would go into "cougar mode" and attempt to act and appear alluring and sexy, it made even a young kid like me wince. Needless to say, it was a very campy and wonderfully tacky movie. I was always one of those kids who found clowns scary, so mixing in a few murders wasn't going to make matters at this creepy circus any worse. C (Columbia, color)

10/13 *Theater of Death* (1965 aka *Blood Fiend*) Christopher Lee, Lelia Goldoni, Julian Glover. Police investigate a series of murders in which the victims are drained of blood, all near a theater specializing in the macabre. Hemisphere Pictures had picked this British import up for their *Chiller Carnival of Blood* promotions to drive-ins; it circulated on TV under its tamer UK title. While a well-made thriller with good production values, the pseudo-vampire killings and Grand Guignol theater trappings (reminiscent of 1935's *Mad Love*) failed to pick the pace up of this rather slick but somewhat boring mystery. Lee was really mean in this one, but the movie fell far short of its potential. C (Hemisphere, color)

10/20 *The 10th Victim* (1965) Marcello Mastroianni, Ursula Andress, Elsa Martinelli. In a world of the future, humans are hunted for sport. Another example of Channel 9's unique flair for finding uncommon, odd-ball pictures to fill the *Fright Night* time slot. Andress was strikingly beautiful, but this abstract Italian-made sci-fi yarn ended up being just weird and tedious. In its day, the film was hailed by some as an ahead-of-its-time shocker and it was a critical favorite, but in the '70s it looked more like a convoluted rerun of *The Prisoner* to me. Cool music, nice photography and undeniably quirky, but still a misfire. C (Champion/Concordia, color)

10/27 *The Crimson Cult* (1968 aka *Curse of the Crimson Altar*) Christopher Lee, Boris Karloff, Mark Eden. A man searches an isolated country estate for his missing brother and stumbles upon a sinister cult. With Barbara

Theatrical ad mat for *Theater of Death* (1965) under its less sophisticated *Blood Fiend* title from Hemisphere Pictures.

Steele and Michael Gough also in the mix, you were pretty much assured a very good time. It wasn't as blood-curdling as it could have been, but the cast, color and typically heavy British atmosphere made this witchcraft-themed movie highly watchable. Steele's green makeup and get-up, like something out of Broadway's *Wicked*, and her muscle-bound servant wearing just a leather g-string, got things off to a rather heated start. (Tigon, color)

11/03 *The Thing with Two Heads* (1972) Rosie Grier, Ray Milland, Don Marshall. A bigoted doctor's life can only be saved by transplanting his head onto the body of a black man wrongly serving time on Death Row. Truly amazing! In the early '70s, American International Pictures began making a new line of contemporary horror films and this group of movies often rivaled the classic drive-in horror flicks they were renowned for in the '50s. This was a perfect example. With its sharp sense of warped humor and finger firmly on the hip pulse of the racial tensions of the day, this was a wonderfully berserk horror film and an absurd piece of solid entertainment. Milland and Grier could not have been better matched. Great stuff for *Fright Night*; it must have been ideal for those looking for some goofy humor with their horror that night. C (American International, color)

11/10 *Deathdream*

11/17 *Man with the Icy Eyes* (1971) Victor Buono, Faith Domergue, Barbara Bouchet. A Senator is murdered outside his home and a man with strange eyes is charged with the crime. The movie had the look of an Italian import but was filmed in the U.S. (Albuquerque, New Mexico to be precise) with redubbed English dialogue handled by people other than the original actors. It also was nothing more than an ordinary reporter-solves-a-murder mystery story and, despite some genre cast members, was a very weak and completely uninteresting choice for *Fright Night*. Another one of those movies with an intriguing title that failed to deliver the goods. (Cinegal, color)

11/24 *The Strange Door*

12/08 *Dear Dead Delilah* (1972) Agnes Moorehead, Will Geer, Michael Ansara. A murderer stalks an old Southern mansion seeking a fortune believed to be hidden there. Any kid watching this on *Fright Night* was no doubt startled to see *Bewitched's* Endora and *The Walton's* Grandpa in the middle of this demented and gory tale of Southern-fried loopiness. Something about Southern accents in movies like this always seemed to guarantee an abundance of violence and depraved secrets. Maybe it was the heat. A good, disposable horror cheapie and ideal for the late hour. (JMI/Southern Star, color)

12/15 *The Mind of Mr. Soames* (1970) Terence Stamp, Robert Vaughn, Nigel Davenport. A man who has been in a coma since infancy is revived and escapes from the institution that has been caring for him. Having literally required weeks to shake off *Fright Night's* presentation of *The Baby*, perhaps I wasn't in the mood for another tale of an infantile man at odds with his environment. It was undeniably well-acted and possibly, under the right conditions, it could have been viewed as an intriguing drama, but as a *Fright Night* feature, this film instead fell completely flat. Enough with the men in diapers! (Columbia, color)

12/22 *Kiss the Blood Off My Hands* (1948) Burt Lancaster, Joan Fontaine, Robert Newton. A man takes refuge in the apartment of a lonely woman

after committing a murder. Once in a while, it seemed evident that Channel 9 programmers Steinbrunner and Casey must have had a very small pool of films to pick from and this questionable *Fright Night* choice was another fringe one that didn't quite fit the bill. The foggy London atmosphere was there, as was the lurid title, but the type of thrills one might be hoping for were not. This was more of a crime melodrama and a tale of ill-fated romance laced with a few touches of noir. (Universal, b/w)

12/29 *Fury of the Wolfman* (1972) Paul Naschy, Perla Cristal, Mark Stevens. A man who is cursed and becomes a werewolf when the moon is full is made the prisoner of a mad female scientist. My only experience with Naschy at the time had come from seeing him in Sam Sherman's drive-in favorite *Frankenstein's Bloody Terror*, with which this film was said to be linked in some convoluted way. However, in some circles, the actor was better associated with the Wolfman character than even Chaney, Jr. While this very low-budget film borrowed many themes from the Universal formula (trading wolfbane for the "Heliotrope" plant), it also plunged head-first into that gory, over-the-top world of Euro-horror that *Fright Night* became such a great showcase for. The transformation footage was quite poor, but the throat-ripping, castle-stomping antics were a lot of fun. The best part of the picture: After all the madness, the surviving cast members practically skip out the front door as if nothing had happened. You have to love endings like that. Relax, nothing can really spoil this movie. From Avco-Embassy's dependable horror movie package. C (Avco Embassy, color)

1980

As the nation asks "Who shot J.R.?" while Mt. Saint Helens erupts, Channel 9 becomes focused on color and *Fright Night* takes on a real bloody drive-in feel. It kicks off with a lot of red!

01/05 *Silent Night Bloody Night* (1973) Patrick O'Neal, John Carradine, Mary Woronov. Residents of a small New England town live in the shadow of a dark secret that threatens its way of life. This little record-breaker was one of the most-often shown movies on *Fright Night* and rivaled *The Invisible Man* for being the most memorable of Channel 9's Yuletide season not-so-traditional telecasts. Leave it to WOR to abandon the more socially acceptable movies usually shown for this violent tale of a revenge-seeking madman stalking victims in an abandoned insane asylum around the holidays. The ominous wintry mood was set right from the startling opening minutes and never let up. From scary calls in the house to grisly, blood-dripping bedtime axe murders to an unnervingly somber rendition of the "Silent Night" theme, it was a magnificent low-budget bone-chiller. And that broken champagne glass ... watch out! I can't believe I sat alone in a darkened room after midnight watching this! The spooky Butler House was reportedly located on Long Island, not all that far from Channel 9's NYC operations. A *Fright Night* classic. "Tess ... I'm so lonely...." C (Cannon, color)

01/12 Looks like *Fright Night* was pre-empted for a telethon.

01/19 *The Crawling Eye* (1958) Forrest Tucker, Janet Munro, Jennifer Jayne. Alien creatures lurk within a radioactive cloud atop a mountain. A great winter monster movie that was perfect for a cold January Saturday night. There were plenty of snowbound chills in this tight and creepy thriller that made its way over from Channel 11's *Chiller*. The slimy, tentacled creatures, not fully revealed until the end, were really neat in their own (very) cheap way and the opening decapitation scene set a great tone for the suspense that followed. Good fun with a nice sinister quality to it. C (Tempean, b/w)

01/26 *Warlock Moon* (1975) Laurie Walters, Joe Spano, Edna MacAfee. A young couple traveling in the country discover an abandoned spa that is haunted by a witch. And an axe-wielding maniac! Walters' incredibly irritating mug (looking perpetually perplexed in that amateurish, overacting way) and the cliched goofiness of a script that insisted she be the only one who notices strange things going on tended to get irritating quickly. The film wanted to be a big shocker, but it simply wasn't. Still, it was really trying hard to jolt its audience and its low-budget "you'll-never-likely-to-see-this-movie-again" charm was welcome. You *would* see it again ... on *Fright Night* of course. C (Sweet Blindness, color)

02/02 *Thirsty Dead* (1974) John Considine, Jennifer Billingsley, Judith McConnell. Women are abducted and taken to a strange island to become slaves of a vampire cult. Some movies are so bad they are just end up being great fun to watch. Unfortunately, this wasn't one of them. The premise (sexy women being kidnapped and taken to a remote jungle compound by half-naked male warriors to be used as blood donors for a clan of mod-looking vampires) seemed promising, but it was a chore to get through this extremely dated movie. It had the look of a corny, made-for-television film and the astonishingly juvenile feel of a Saturday morning kid show. A nearly impossible *Fright Night* presentation to endure through the closing credits without lapsing into dreamland. C (International Amusements, color)

02/09 *Midnight Lace* **(1960) Doris Day, Rex Harrison, John Gavin. The wife of a wealthy businessman travels to London with her husband and begins receiving threatening phone calls.** What were the chances that Doris Day and Rex Harrison, of all people, would find themselves on *Fright Night?* Turns out ... pretty good! And it wasn't even a stretch to include them thanks to this sophisticated little thriller that delicately touched on the "obscene phone calls from a killer theme." And nobody was more surprised than I to have actually gotten moderately creeped-out by the stalker's falsetto voice. A crisp, fast-moving and unexpected chiller with Doris's star shining so bright she was almost out of focus. It looks like half the movie's budget went to her stylish wardrobe, making this film almost a *Sex and the City* of its time. (Universal-International, color)

02/16 Looks like *Fright Night* **was pre-empted for a telethon.**

02/23 *What's the Matter with Helen?* **(1971) Debbie Reynolds, Shelley Winters, Dennis Weaver. Two Depression-era mothers whose sons committed violent murders relocate to Hollywood and open a children's dance school.** This twisted movie had great atmosphere and style and the combination of these two dependable actresses handling such bizarre material actually worked well on a campy thrill level. Director Curtis Harrington, well known for his TV work (*The Cat Creature, The Dead Don't Die*), definitely kept things suspenseful and scary, but an unbearable children's recital scene was probably the most disturbing part of the whole picture. Reynolds and Winters had great chemistry and worked so well off each other, the implausible became downright believable. My mom took me to see this at a Saturday matinee when it was first released and I felt messed up for the rest of the day. "If you've got it, you don't have to show it off." C (Filmways, color)

03/01 *Tower of Terror* **(see** *In the Devil's Garden***)**

03/08 *Black Cobra* **(1963) Adrian Hoven, Wolfgang Preiss, Peter Vogel. An innocent man gets caught up in a crime spree orchestrated by a master criminal and his gang.** This is not to be confused with a raunchy Jack Palance movie about a crazy snake woman with the same title, which surely would have been a lot more interesting. The only scene that made this film seem even remotely appropriate for a *Fright Night* telecast involved a few escaped snakes threatening to bite some people. Otherwise, this obscure German crime drama import had absolutely nothing to offer except a remedy for insomnia. Just awful! C (Roberts & Barry Television, b/w)

03/15 *Blood Mania* **(1970) Peter Carpenter, Maria De Aragon, Vicki Peters. A young doctor is trapped in a nightmare of terror at the hands of a demented woman.** A local newspaper said it "[n]eeds a transfusion."

Original theatrical lobby card for *What's the Matter with Helen?* (1971).

I had to agree. Marketed to theaters by Crown International as a spine-tingling horror film (the poster featured a nude girl carrying a skeleton and bloody fingers spelling out the title), the movie was instead a talky blackmail soap opera that seemed very, very long. The payoff at the end was hardly worth the wait. Though I enjoyed the nice late '60s feel, I kept waiting for something to happen that never did. C (Crown International, color)

03/22 *Deadly Strangers* (1974) Hayley Mills, Simon Ward, Sterling Hayden. A young woman accepts a ride from a man who may be an escapee from an insane asylum. A quiet little British thriller with a curious plot. It had good performances and a decent surprise ending, despite some implausible turns along the road. It wasn't a nail-biter, but it kept the tension simmering. Mills and Ward had an interesting chemistry. C (Silhouette, color)

03/29 *So Sad About Gloria* (1975 aka *Visions of Doom*) Lori Saunders, Dean Jagger, Robert Ginnaven. A woman returns home after a nervous breakdown and begins having terrifying visions of axe murders. This unusual movie was listed in a local TV guide as a "low-budget melodrama," but this psychological horror story packed a lot more punch than that review suggested. Gloria's first major encounter with a maniac swinging a huge axe (his face was covered and distorted by a stocking) was pretty hair-raising. A solid scare show with a couple of good genuine jolts to keep the viewer on his toes. (Centronics, color)

04/05 *The Strange Door*

04/12 *Trauma* **(1963) John Conte, Lynn Bari, Lorrie Richards. When a teenager witnesses the horrifying murder of her aunt, the shock obliterates the incident from her memory.** This teenager looked to be at least 25 years old and if she had just moved to investigate her aunt's frantic and relentless screams a little quicker, she might have avoided all this trouble. The film's opening drowning scene took a disturbing long time to end and was quite unsettling to watch. So was a trip to the basement and the killer's face when he sets his sights on our heroine. Pretty well done for a rather obscure, low-budget quickie. C (Artists XVI, b/w)

04/19 *The Unsuspected* **(1947) Claude Rains, Constance Bennett, Joan Caulfield. A radio mystery show host becomes embroiled in a real-life murder.** A well-crafted Warner Bros. film by director Michael Curtiz (whose horror films *Doctor X* and *Mystery of the Wax Museum* were televised regularly over on Channel 11's *Chiller*). It had a rich '40s noir style and percolated with atmosphere and striking photography. While it may have fallen into that gray area as far as genre elements were concerned, it had enough mood and menace to merit the *Fright Night* seal of approval. A nasty opening murder sequence and Claude's understated performance made for an engaging evening. C (Warner, b/w)

04/26 *The Witchmaker* **(1969 aka** *Legend of Witch Hollow***) Alvy Moore, Thordis Brandt, Anthony Eisley. A group of psychic researchers enter a remote bayou to investigate a series of murders and encounter a cult of witches.** This very bizarre movie was kind of a cross between *The Blair Witch Project* (1999) and Roger Corman's *The Undead* (1957). Though it was a bit surreal to see Alvy Moore (Hank Kimball from TV's *Green Acres*) in a serious role, it added another kooky element to this odd story of medieval-style witches operating a coven in the middle of a modern-day swampland. Produced by L.Q. Jones, who took similar satanic elements and many of the same cast members and upped the ante with the riveting *Brotherhood of Satan*. This film played on Channel 9 endlessly. (Excelsior, color)

05/03 *The Day of the Triffids* **(1962) Howard Keel, Janette Scott, Nicole Maurey. A meteor shower causes the Earth's population to go blind and unleashes an invasion of killer plant creatures.** A local newspaper accurately summed the picture up by saying "Trees terrorize a community — convincingly." A well-done sci-fi drama that was both exciting and suspenseful. It also sported some unusually nasty and menacing flora. The added anxiety created by having humans deal with this engaging situation while being blind was a great touch, making this alien invasion seem even scarier. A nice mix of stories ran parallel to each other to keep things interesting. This picture was in constant rotation at various TV stations in the New York area for years. C (Allied Artists, color)

05/10 Looks like *Fright Night* was pre-empted.

05/17 *Doomwatch* **(1972) Ian Bannen, Judy Geeson, John Paul. A scientist investigates strange mutations on an isolated British island and discovers that its inhabitants are slowly being poisoned.** After his disturbing performance as a psychopathic killer in *Fright*, I had expected Bannen to start twitching again in this ecological horror yarn (and several times it looked like he might). The movie was fairly interesting, suspenseful, and credibly acted, with a palpable sense of menace early on, but a lackluster and boringly optimistic ending was a bit of a letdown. C (Tigon, color)

05/24 *Why Would Anyone Want to Kill a Nice Girl Like You?* **(1968 aka** *A Taste of Excitement***) Eva Rienzi, Paul Buck, Peter Vaughan. A young woman traveling in the south of France suspects she is being stalked after a number of attempts are made on her life.** Beautiful Eva made for a fetching victim, but it seemed like her own stupidity was to blame for her troubles (spontaneously running in front of cars, driving on harrowingly dangerous roads, etc.). Her panic one moment/total calm the next was both odd and a bit annoying, though it may have been the director's attempt to keep us guessing about her competency. Breathtaking scenery added to some nice European atmosphere and suspense, but the whole mystery ended up being a bit dull and silly. Today, it's a hard-to-find film in any format. (Group W, color)

05/31 *Night Evelyn Came Out of the Grave*

06/07 *Decoy for Terror*

06/14 *Blood and Lace*

06/21 *Deathdream*

06/28 *Student Connection* **(1974 aka** *Witness to Murder***) Ray Milland, Sylva Koscina, Ramiro Oliveros. The principal of a boy's school commits murder and discovers one of the students has witnessed his crime.** Kudos to Channel 9 for uncovering this very rarely seen, dubbed, Italian-Spanish thriller. It was always a pleasure to see Milland raise his eyebrows and look menacing and he was in fine form here as he intimidated the young boys of the boarding school he oversees. There were a few tense moments and eerie nighttime thrills, but unfortunately this film dissolved into just one long chase scene through prominent European locations. Today, it's another hard-to-find film in any format. (Lotus, color)

07/05 *Touch of Satan*

07/12 *The Thing from Another World*

07/26 *Woman in Hiding* (1950) **Ida Lupino, Howard Duff, Stephen McNally. A woman falls for the charms of a con man but realizes her mistake when she suspects he has killed her father.** Told in flashback, this suspense drama was another passable fringe *Fright Night* entry with a good enough story and effective noir style to make the time pass by quickly. Very much in the same vein as *Step Down to Terror*, but a bit darker and with a few more pleasingly frantic moments. It wasn't a nail-biter, but it delivered. Stars Lupino and Duff were married in real life. (Universal-International, b/w)

08/02 *Dr. Jekyll & Sister Hyde*

08/09 *The Man Who Could Work Miracles* (1936) **Roland Young, Ralph Richardson, Edward Chapman. A man who denies the power of miracles suddenly discovers he has the ability to create them.** Based on an H.G. Wells story and featuring screen dialogue written by the author, this film took a big step back to the creaky golden days of cinema and featured a cast of notable genre players. A very lightweight fantasy in the *Here Comes Mr. Jordan* mold that was perhaps more appropriate for a holiday telecast, but it was modestly engaging and a momentarily diverting departure from the colorful and bloody usual fare *Fright Night* was serving up. C (Film Classics, b/w)

08/16 *Blood & Black Lace*

08/23 *Horror Hotel*

08/30 *Fright*

09/06 *Silent Night Bloody Night*

09/20 *What's the Matter with Helen?*

09/27 *Homebodies* (1984) **Peter Brocco, Frances Fuller, William Hansen. A group of senior citizens, threatened with eviction from their apartment building, take matters into their own hands.** Like *The Sorcerers*, this film did not paint a pretty picture of the trials and tribulations of those living in their so-called "Golden Years." It was also, however, a surprisingly adept attempt at dark humor (with a strong underlying message) and it cleverly turned these frail, vulnerable retirees into a band of formidable killers. One could never tell which direction the film would go next, demanding the viewer's constant attention and holding it right through to its bizarre ending. A highly untraditional and diverting horror film and one which left the viewer less indifferent to the plight of the elderly. (Cinema Entertainment, color)

10/04 ***The Crimson Cult***

10/11 ***Thirsty Dead***

10/18 *So Sad About Gloria*

10/25 *Torture Chamber of Dr. Sadism*

11/01 *Brotherhood of Satan*

11/08 *Grave of the Vampire*

11/15 *House of the Seven Corpses*

11/22 *Secret of Dorian Gray*

12/06 ***Count Yorga, Vampire*** **(1970) Robert Quarry, Roger Perry, Michael Murphy. A group of young couples unknowingly participates in a séance with a vampire.** I had seen this intriguing movie written up in *Castle of Frankenstein* magazine and found its cool advertising artwork (a bevy of scantily clad vampire beauties attacking a male victim) captivating. The movie proved to be equally so. Quarry was magnificent as a unique and formidable modern Dracula-type, suavely charming, sharply intellectual and a little bit hammy.

A terrific scene featured Yorga straining to keep his cool when some scheming vampire hunters relentlessly chatted him up as daylight approached. The *New York Times* gave it a strong recommendation: "Effective California ambiance ... sophisticated and clever." C (American International, color)

12/13 *The Creature's Revenge*

12/20 ***Baron Blood*** **(1972) Joseph Cotten, Elke Sommer, Massimo Girotti. A vampire baron's descendants restore his old castle, making it a tourist attraction and reviving the baron himself.** Sommer was something of a

Robert Quarry as the distinguished *Count Yorga, Vampire* (1970).

major crossover Euro-star at the time and her good looks and heavy accent added nicely to the feel of this atmospheric maniac-loose-in-a-castle production from Mario Bava, who helmed the classic *Black Sabbath* (1963). It had a kind of old-fashioned monster movie flavor to it and a few jittery moments. C (American International, color)

12/27 *Curse of the Vampires*

1981

While many young people begin watching the new phenomenon of MTV and its music videos, *Fright Night* is still the primary destination for fans seeking a wide assortment of domestic and imported modern horror.

01/03 *Horror Express* (1972) Christopher Lee, Peter Cushing, Silvia Tortosa. An expedition in a remote region of Manchuria uncovers a frozen beast and transports it by train, unleashing a monster among the passengers. This fine pairing of Cushing and Lee was an exciting and engaging slice of Euro-horror. Unlike some entries in this genre, it was easy to follow, often chilling and solidly entertaining. The effect of eyes becoming white orbs after the monster absorbed the memories of its victims was clever and unsettling. And a neat cameo by Telly Savalas added to the surprises. This film was shown countless times on Channel 9. *Newsday* gave it two stars. C (Benmar, color)

01/10 *The Devil's Nightmare* (1972) Erica Blanc, Daniel Emilfork, Jean Servais. A priest struggles to save the souls of tourists stranded in a European castle where the Devil hovers. Hemisphere Pictures released this film theatrically in the U.S. shortly after the huge success of *The Exorcist* on a double feature with *In the Devil's Garden*, playing up the aging movies as if they were exorcism-themed. "This time the devil wins!" proclaimed the ads. While the guests of Baron Von Rhoneberg were embroiled in a sinister plot involving Satan utilizing the seven deadly sins to snare his victims, the devilish fun that unfolded did not include vomit (well, just a little), spinning heads or demonic possession. Blanc was hypnotic as a beautiful succubus and the little bald devil guy was creepy as hell. Watching the fat bus driver devour a huge and delicious looking (but deadly) banquet may have brought on a bad case of the munchies ... or nausea. USA's *Saturday Nightmares* picked the film up later for a number of telecasts. C (Hemisphere, color)

01/17 Looks like *Fright Night* was pre-empted.

Erika Blanc goes to pieces after waking in *The Devil's Nightmare* (1972).

01/24 *The Mole People* (1956) John Agar, Hugh Beaumont, Cynthia Patrick. An archaeological team discovers a strange civilization living deep inside a remote mountain. I had been familiar with the mole creatures thanks largely to the Don Post Studios mask offered in the back pages of *Famous Monsters of Filmland* magazine. Seeing the movie they came from was an interesting experience and provided typical Universal-International '50s style sci-fi adventure thrills. C (Universal-International, b/w)

01/31 *Psychomania* (1973 aka *Death Wheelers*) George Sanders, Beryl Reid, Mary Larkin. A motorcycle gang learns the secret to eternal life and wreaks havoc on an unsuspecting English town. There haven't been too many biker horror films made, so this one, which was a late night favorite at the time, gained a bit of a following. Some eerie moments and menacing looking choppers made for an entertaining British chiller with wonderfully in-your-face '70s flavor. The movie marked veteran star George Sanders' last role before committing suicide. C (Benmar, color)

02/07 *Deathdream*

02/14 *Fangs of the Living Dead* (1969 aka *Malenka*) Anita Ekberg, Gianni Medici, Diana Lorys. When a woman inherits a castle, she finds it inhabited by a strange man and several women whom she suspects may be vampires. This film made the drive-in rounds in the early '70s as part of a package called *Orgy of the Living Dead*. Despite wonderfully atmospheric sets and the ambience of a dubbed Euro-thriller, it unfortunately moved slowly and lacked the kick other, similar movies had. *Newsday* said, "Anita, not looking one day older and as 'statuesque' as ever, inherits a castle along with an especially annoying set of ancestors...." C (Ben Barry & Associate Television/Europix, color)

02/21 *Psycho*

02/28 *Psychic Killer* (1975) Jim Hutton, Julie Adams, Paul Burke. A man, falsely imprisoned, develops psychic powers that allow him to take revenge on those who wronged him. Very good performances by Hutton and Adams (*Creature from the Black Lagoon*) highlighted this film, and the actors performed their roles with a believable seriousness that kept a somewhat over-the-top plot grounded in plausibility and moved it along at a nice clip. A few inventive killings gave the movie a kind of cool, contemporary thriller feel. The ending didn't come as a much of a surprise but it was a diverting experience getting there. C (Avco Embassy, color)

03/07 Looks like *Fright Night* was pre-empted for a telethon.

03/14 *Don't Look In the Basement*

03/21 *Children Shouldn't Play with Dead Things* (1973) Alan Ormsby, Anya Ormsby, Valerie Mamches. An acting company goes to a lonely burial island to shoot a movie and finds strange and ghoulish creatures which the "director" decides to use in his film. Channel 9's description was filled with inaccuracies, but you got the idea. Obviously inspired by *Night of the Living Dead,* this was a *Fright Night* bar-setter everyone remembers seeing. It was a totally macabre, scary (in a fun, dark comedic way) and offbeat horror yarn with more than a few warped quirks. Not the least of which was Alan's necrophilia tendencies, which (even as a kid) had me thinking "What's up with That?" Like the character who actually did pee his pants, I nearly had an accident myself after one particular graveyard jolt early in the show. The resurrection of the corpses was brilliantly orchestrated. A *Fright Night* classic! C (Genini/Brandywine/Motionarts, color)

03/28 *Children of the Damned* (1964) Ian Hendry, Alan Badel, Barbara Ferris. Scientists attempt to study a group of children from across the globe, all of whom have displayed unique and extraordinary powers of intellect. A local newspaper said, "Sequel takes up where *Village of the Damned* stopped — and goes too far," yet gave the film a surprisingly good three-star rating. While it was not quite as captivating as its predecessor, it created an engaging, somber mood and the children were modestly menacing. A few familiar British genre film performers also popped up along the way. C (MGM, b/w)

04/04 *Why Would Anyone Want to Kill a Nice Girl Like You?*

04/11 *The House That Screamed* (1971) Lilli Palmer, John Moulder-Brown, Mary Maude. **Young teenage girls attempting to escape from a strict boarding school are brutally murdered.** A haunting and memorable chiller that rose far above the pack thanks to extremely competent performances (especially Palmer as the headmistress and domineering mother). The film featured great photography, magnificent, moody lighting and well-decorated sets. Surprisingly, there was relatively little gore in this evocative and tense period piece, but it overflowed with rich atmosphere, style and intelligence in nearly every scene. The menace was palpable and Palmer displayed remarkable acting depth as a vigorous disciplinarian who may actually love the wayward girls she both cares for and torments. The *New York Times* said it was a "well-handled chiller from Spain" and *Newsday* said it had "[a] shocker or two." C (American International, color)

04/18 *The Night Evelyn Came Out of the Grave*

04/25 *Fear No Evil* (1969) Louis Jourdan, Bradford Dillman, Lynda Day George. **A man becomes possessed by a spirit inhabiting a strange antique mirror.** An NBC made-for-TV movie that had a lot of trouble getting going; I recall dozing about a third of the way in. But the supernatural material was approached subtly and intelligently as it tried hard to please its more mature target audience. It was interesting to see performers like Carroll O'Connor early in their careers and performing in genre material. Still a miss, but you could do worse. (Universal, color)

05/02 *Assignment: Terror* (1970 aka *Dracula vs. Frankenstein*) Michael Rennie, Karin Dor, Craig Hill. **Aliens resurrect Earth's most fearsome monsters in order to conquer the planet.** What sounded like it would be a great monster bash featuring sci-fi legend Rennie from 1951's immortal *The Day the Earth Stood Still,* turned out to be an extremely low-budget slice of European cheese. The film also featured Paul Naschy (the movie was yet another spin-off in his endless family of werewolf films) and, like many of his other movies, had that cartoonish horror feel that could be fun ... *if* you were in the right mood. The carnival setting and the separate fights between the poorly made-up monsters sort of channeled the spirit of Universal but, of course, it was a very, very different experience. It was nothing more than goofy lowbrow fun made better by the cast taking it all quite seriously. (Jaguar, color)

05/09 *Gorath* (1973) Akira Kubo, Kumi Mizuno, Yumi Shirakawa. **In the year 1980, space patrol ships discover a flaming meteor 6000 times our mass heading towards Earth on a collision course.** A precursor to *Meteor* (1979) and *Deep Impact* (1998) and kind of a Toho Studios retread of *When Worlds Collide*. The film circulated theatrically on the kiddie matinee circuit for years and was one of the more intelligent Japanese sci-fi extravaganzas to be shown on *Fright Night*. It was pretty well-done and the special effects, though still that time-worn old-school use of miniatures, were entertaining. It always got the adrenaline pumping to see disaster strike Tokyo, this time via massive flooding. But when a real-life magnitude 9.0 earthquake and tsunami devastated Japan in early 2011, the reality was bitterly sobering and horrific, far more frightening and infinitely more dramatic than any studio could ever have imagined on film. (Toho, color)

05/16 *The Companion* (1972 aka *Die, Sister, Die*) Jack Ging, Kent Smith, Edith Atwater. A man hopes to convince his ailing sister's nurse to join him in a plot to kill her. Films with bland, ambiguous titles like this often proved to be surprisingly delectable *Fright Night* treats. This movie featured good performances, a nicely macabre murder story and more than a few good plot twists. Certainly enough thrills to hold one's attention for 90 minutes. "Go ahead and scream, Amanda ... it can't help you now!" C (Cinema Shares, color)

05/30 *No Survivors Please* (1964) Maria Perschy, Robert Cunnigham, Uwe Friedrichsen. Aliens take control of newly dead bodies in a plot to conquer the Earth. This was a somewhat talky and mundane German sci-fi thriller despite its intriguing title, but also another rarely televised oddity. Viewing it at a late hour depreciated the film's cerebral qualities and left you wanting more ... or just to hit the sack. I'm not sure many viewers survived to the end of this picture. C (Albin, b/w)

06/05 *The Sorcerers*

06/13 *Invisible Terror* (1963) Hannes Schmidhauser, Ellen Schwiers, Herbert Stass. A criminal sets his sights on a formula for invisibility that a young scientist has created. With its grain, crackle and scratches, this dirty-print German import picked up by Channel 9 was the type of movie you either loved and relished or hated and snoozed through. Actually, it was possible to experience both. Like other sci-fi–fused thrillers that came out of Deutschland, this rarely shown oddity was hard to follow, sometimes dull and tedious, but somehow just felt strangely satisfying to watch and doze through. And if you missed parts, it really didn't matter. Those looking for cool special effects were sorely disappointed. (Aero Films, b/w)

06/20 *They Came from Beyond Space* (1967) Robert Hutton, Michael Gough, Jennifer Jayne. Scientists investigating a meteor shower become possessed by an alien intelligence. A local newspaper said, "They should have stayed there." Director Freddie Francis (*Dracula Has Risen from the Grave, Tales from the Crypt*) certainly had an impressive résumé, but this film was not one of his better efforts. Even for those with a taste for British sci-fi, this slow-moving movie must have felt like a bore. The film was often shown on local Long Island station WSNL-TV's Saturday afternoon *Shock Theater* and it fared no better in daylight. C (Amicus, color)

06/27 *The Incredible Two-Headed Transplant*

07/04 *Deathmaster*

07/11 *Death Smiles on a Murderer*

07/18 *Blood and Lace*

07/25 *Fury of the Wolfman*

08/01 *The Baby*

08/08 *The Thing from Another World*

08/15 *In the Devil's Garden*

08/22 *So Sad About Gloria*

08/29 *Baron Blood*

09/05 *Night Fiend* **(1973 aka** *Violent Blood Bath***) Fernando Rey, Elisa Laguna, Marisa Mell. Authorities search for a murderer stalking beautiful young women.** Licensed in the U.S. by Independent-International Pictures, this visually attractive Italian-Spanish production was actually nothing more than an exceedingly dull crime drama under either of its annoyingly misleading titles. Though the nicely photographed Spanish locations made for an atmospheric backdrop, the film just seemed like one endless (dubbed) chatter scene after another. Most of the murders are revealed after the fact in the edited television version, making for a decidedly non-violent picture. *Night Fiend* sounded like it might be a fun, obscure type of shocker, but was, in fact, a long distance dud. It may have fared better in its uncut format. (Independent-International, color)

09/12 *Mr. Sardonicus* **(1961) Ronald Lewis, Audrey Dalton, Guy Rolfe. The sight of his father's corpse causes a man's face to freeze in a horrible grimace.** William Castle's gothic chiller lacked the bizarre punch of his previous release (*Homicidal*, the producer's cash-in on *Psycho*), but was a serviceable, old-world horror story. Co-star Oscar Homolka was well-cast as a horrible henchman with a thing for leeches. Castle's films (*13 Ghosts*, *House on Haunted Hill*) usually had a campy feel, but the master showman always delivered a good time and rarely disappointed. This one was no exception. C (Columbia, b/w)

09/19 *Piranha* **(1972 aka** *Piranha! Piranha!***) Peter Brown, William Smith, Ahna Capri. A young photographer, her brother and a guide set out by motorcycle to photograph the jungle wildlife of the Amazon River area and encounter a cold-blooded hunter.** Despite the title, most records indicate that the film shown was this Bill Gibson–produced adventure drama often seen on Channel 9, not the Roger Corman release from 1978. The flesh-eating fish hardly deserved top-billing in this extremely low-budget jungle thriller. Though the plot is loose and the acting very amateurish and improvised, it was a really fun romp. The picture was very sweaty and gritty, with an almost western feel to it, and Smith did a great job being not-so-subtly sinister as a hunter of *everything* (in a kind of mod variation on 1932's *The Most Dangerous Game*). Nicely faded Eastman color added to the mood. C (Magellan-Bolivar, color)

09/26 *Night of the Blood Monster*

10/03 *Psychomania*

10/10 *Crucible of Terror* (1971) Mike Raven, James Bolam, Mary Maude. A mad sculptor dabbles in the occult in his quest to create the perfect female statue. Raven served up a formidably weird and surly womanizing sculptor character, but this slow-moving English horror drama languished in confusing plot elements and overall dull proceedings. There was enough to casually hold your interest, but you wouldn't be scared by any of it and you wouldn't be in a rush to see it again. C (Filmways, color)

10/17 *Theater of Death*

10/24 *Witchmaker*

10/31 *The Thirsty Dead*

11/07 *Invasion of the Bee Girls* (1973) William Smith, Victoria Vetri, Cliff Osmond. An alien life force transforms women into human queen bees who drain the life from men. They accomplished this by essentially having lethal sex with unsuspecting guys, in this campy tale of the horrible consequences of promiscuous relations. Even at this late hour, Channel 9 must have had to splice the hell out of this raunchy and bizarre movie, as uncut prints are loaded with nudity and sexual references. While the girls didn't exactly sprout wings and a stinger, they did get sufficiently weird and the eyeball effects were cool. A really strange movie to stumble onto, especially for the casual viewer simply looking for something fun to watch on Saturday night. Sexy starlet Beverly Hills (*Island of Living Horror*) made a welcome appearance. C (Sequoia/Centaur, color)

11/14 *When Worlds Collide* (1951) Barbara Rush, Richard Derr, Peter Hansen. As a giant asteroid threatens to crash into the Earth, scientists rush to build a spacecraft that will allow some people to escape the impending destruction. The *New York Times* described this George Pal production as "[b]etter than average, with some striking effects." It was an engaging sci-fi drama and the effects, including a clever depiction of the flooding of New York City, were entertaining for their time. The depiction of humans taking on an "every man for himself" attitude once things started getting dicey was spot on, but the logic-defying three-minute journey to a K. Gordon Murray–painted planet felt like a weak wrap-up. All considered though, a very solid, enjoyable film. C (Paramount, color)

11/21 *Psychomania*

11/28 *Terror House*

12/05 *Warlock Moon*

12/12 *The Witch* (1966) Richard Johnson, Rosanna Schiaffino, Ivan Rassimov. While researching ancient erotic literature, a young historian uncovers a connection to witchcraft and supernatural forces. Another stellar example of Channel 9 unearthing a real obscurity for telecast on *Fright Night.* Where did they find these things? This strange but intelligent little Italian import was sometimes a challenge to follow and dipped heavily into a moody European psychological horror vein, but the results were undeniably interesting. Kind of what you might call a supernatural art film. (Interfilm/Arco, b/w)

12/19 *Psychomania*

12/26 *Tomb of the Living Dead*

1982

You won't see too many Academy Award winners like this year's Best Picture, *Chariots of Fire,* on *Fright Night* but you will see great chillers like *Brotherhood of Satan* and a few oddball items like *B ... Must Die.* New York's other iconic horror movie showcase on Channel 11, *Chiller,* would bite the dust later this year.

01/01 *House of Doom* (1973 aka *House of Psychotic Women, Blue Eyes of the Broken Doll*) Paul Naschy, Diana Lory, Eduardo Calvo. A drifter takes a job as a caretaker at the estate belonging to a family of strange sisters. *Fright Night* started the year off with another Naschy movie, and though no werewolves were in sight, there was eye-popping gore to be seen. Uncut prints of this film depict plenty of nudity and violence; Sam Sherman readily admitted he had to pull out the big scissors out for this one. A weird movie and a bit more cerebral than usual for a Naschy showcase. C (Independent-International, color)

01/08 *Swamp Water* (1941) Dana Andrews, John Carradine, Walter Brennan. A trapper hunting in dangerous swamp country encounters a fugitive and his daughter. The murky, menacing swamp, with its dark shadows and eerie landscapes that set the backdrop for this drama, was extremely

Psychotic women and bloody violence abound in *House of Doom* (1973).

atmospheric and well photographed. But being just a routine, rather stiff melodrama, the movie was not a great fit for *Fright Night*. When you were expecting a scare flick, movies like this were a big letdown. (Fox, b/w)

01/06 Looks like *Fright Night* was pre-empted for a telethon.

01/23 *The House That Screamed*

01/30 *Horror Express*

02/06 *Destination Nightmare* (1958) Boris Karloff, Tod Andrews, Denise Alexander. Four chilling tales of the supernatural. Culled from episodes of an unsold television series called *The Veil*, each story was hosted by and often featured Karloff. Unfortunately the film had that kind of bland '50s TV show style and the stories, ranging from tales of ghosts and reincarnation to bizarre chance encounters, were all pretty generic. The remaining *Veil* episodes were turned into two additional TV movies, *Jack the Ripper* and *The Veil*. C (Medallion, b/w)

02/13 *When Michael Calls* (1972 aka *Shattered Silence*) Michael Douglas, Elizabeth Ashley, Ben Gazzara. A woman begins receiving phone calls from a young child who died 15 years earlier. Like *The Night Stalker* and

Helter Skelter (1976), this ABC movie's first telecast caused quite a stir in my classroom the following day. There was always something chilling about strange or threatening phone calls and the sound of the phone ringing could always be counted on to put a viewer on edge. A good cast and believable performances helped make this movie suspenseful. (Palomar, color)

02/20 *Murder Mansion* (1972) Evelin Stewart, Analia Gade, Ida Galli. Inclement weather forces a group of people to take refuge in a mansion next to a cemetery. The familiar haunted house plot is given a nice eerie treatment in this Spanish-Italian production. The movie drips with mood, creepy sets and intense color ... not to mention truckloads of fog. Though relatively tame compared to other films of its kind, it was a fun, old-fashioned chiller. C (Mundial, color)

02/27 *The Thing with Two Heads*

03/06 *Dear Dead Delilah*

03/13 *In the Devil's Garden*

03/20 *Children Shouldn't Play with Dead Things*

03/27 *Don't Look in the Basement*

04/03 *Witches' Mountain* (1972) Patty Sheppard, Ana Farra, Monica Randall. A couple traveling in a remote mountainous region stays at a castle that is home to a coven of witches. While this movie immediately had that pleasingly dubbed air of heavy atmosphere the Europeans were renowned for, it droned on with precious little action and a convoluted plot that was impossible to follow. I kept waiting ... but nothing. Some nice music and scenery, but otherwise a very tame movie. Channel 9 continued to get more mileage out of their Avco-Embassy horror film package. C (Azor, color)

04/10 *Equinox*

04/17 *House of the Seven Corpses*

04/24 *Demons of the Dead* (1972 aka *All the Colors of the Dark, They're Coming to Get You*) Edwige Fenech, George Hilton, Ivan Rassimov. A coven of devil worshippers stalk a young woman recovering from a car accident that caused her to lose her baby. Well-made thriller bounces back and forth between scary, nightmare-like sequences and reality like a hellish tennis match. A scene featuring an intruder lunging to stab Fenech in her apartment was particularly hair-raising. The picture had kind of a *Rosemary's Baby* (1968) feel about it, but far less subtle. Imported by Sam Sherman. (Independent-International/LEA Film/C.C. Astro, color)

05/01 *Dr. Jekyll & Sister Hyde*

05/08 *Horror Rises from the Tomb* (1973) Paul Naschy, Emma Cohen, Helga Line. Tourists staying at a medieval castle discover the head of

a warlock executed hundreds of years before. Naschy enthusiasts certainly had reason to thank *Fright Night,* as the actor turned up in numerous movies throughout the show's lengthy history, and this was one of the best. His films were an acquired taste, much like the over-the-top Mexican movies of K. Gordon Murray. I enjoyed this installment more than some of his others as it featured a neat little *Night of the Living Dead*–esque zombie attack. Plenty of gore and nudity were likely trimmed, but it still must have been a bloody good show that night. Another dip into the Avco-Embassy TV horror movie package. C (Cabri, color)

05/15 *The Night Evelyn Came Out of the Grave*

05/22 *Psychomania*

05/29 *The Incredible Two-Headed Transplant* (1971) **Bruce Dern, Pat Priest, Casey Kasem. A successful cranial transplant creates a two-headed monster which escapes and leaves a trail of death and terror.** A few years ago, MGM creatively placed this movie on a double feature DVD with *The Thing with Two Heads,* and the duo made a brilliant pair! This had a lower brow, less wryly comic drive-in feel but was equally over-the-top. I couldn't help but think that lovely Pat Priest's training with *The Munsters* should have prepared her for these horrific events. And what a year this was for big John Bloom. Ah, they don't make 'em like this any more! The local newspaper gave it two stars —"one for each head." C (American International, color)

06/05 *Summertime Killer* (1972) **Karl Malden, Olivia Hussey, Christopher Mitchum. A private detective is hired to track down a serial killer who has been hunting men connected with the mob.** Hussey (*Black Christmas*) could always be depended upon to deliver a great performance, and she does so here along with a very solid cast. However, despite an engaging vigilante plot that takes a few unexpected turns, a revenge motive alone did not necessarily make for ideal *Fright Night* material. This was just an okay drama reminiscent of a *Streets of San Francisco* episode, but a film that could have easily been missed without much regret. (Vicuna/Isasi, color)

06/12 *Crucible of Terror*

06/19 *The Crawling Eye*

06/26 *Blood Mania*

07/03 *Why Would Anyone Want to Kill a Nice Girl Like You?*

07/10 *Inn of the Frightened People*

07/16 *B ... Must Die* (1975) **Darren McGavin, Patricia Neal, Walter Coy. A down-on-his-luck trucker in a tumultuous Latin American country becomes caught up in a scheme of deception and murder.** An ultra-

obscure movie that I missed on this telecast and had a heck of a time locat-
ing to watch today. While the brilliant performances were completely captivating (including Burgess Meredith — who at one point actually cackles
like his Penguin character from *Batman*), and the unfolding drama was an
unusual and intriguing story, this partially dubbed European drama could
not evenly remotely be deemed as appropriate genre fare for *Fright Night*.
(El Iman/Taurean, color)

**07/24 *Massacre in the Black Forest* (1967) Cameron Mitchell, Dieter
Eppler, Antonella Lualdi. Warriors battle against the tyranny of the
Roman Empire.** Channel 9 continued to dip deep into a well of obscure
European features but unfortunately came up with still another that was
not well-suited to fit the *Fright Night* criteria. This was a routine gladiator
movie with some violent battle sequences and an intriguing title, but little
else to hold one's attention. Hard to believe this was the only film they
could come up with to fill the time slot. (Ergas, color)

**07/31 *Cursed Medallion* (1975 aka *Night Child*) Richard Johnson, Joanna
Cassidy, Ida Galli. After receiving a strange medallion, a young girl
becomes possessed by a murderous demon.** Capitalizing on the popularity
of exorcism and possession themes of the time, this Italian film was actually
a well-made, nicely photographed and sophisticated production. Even the
odd-looking child star (Nicoletta Elmi) managed to generate a pretty genuine face of fear in some scenes. But its overall pace was very slow and the
big finale wasn't quite worth the wait. (IIF, color)

**08/07 *Bell from Hell* (1973) Viveca Lindfors, Renaud Verley, Alfredo
Mayo. A young man returns home from a mental institution, seeking
revenge on the family members who placed him there.** *Fright Night*
dipped back into Avco-Embassy's TV horror package for another highly
confusing but moderately suspenseful and offbeat psycho-sexual horror
movie with a few shocks and surprises. Kind of a slow-mover for the first
third, but it had a decent pay-off. If you were becoming bored, a great eye-
gouging sequence at the midpoint perked things right up. One always went
to bed feeling his soul had been slightly soiled after watching the erotic
overtones and nastiness some of these movies served up. C (Avco Embassy,
color)

08/14 *Deadly Strangers*
08/21 *Fright*
08/28 *Beast of the Dead*

Opposite page: **Original pressbook art for the theatrical release of *The Incredible
Two-Headed Transplant* (1971)**

09/04 *Beast of Morocco* (1968) William Sylvester, Diane Clare, Aliza Gur. A man traveling in the desert encounters a strange castle and a beautiful vampire woman. This film was a regular on late, late shows for many years and finally turned up on *Fright Night*. Despite some cool exotic filming locations, it was a very sleepy movie, more fantasy than horror, and lacked meaty vampire thrills. More talk than scares. (Associated British Pathe, color)

09/11 *Crypt of Horror* (1963 aka *Terror in the Crypt, Crypt of the Vampire*) Christopher Lee, Ursula Davis, Adriana Ambesi. A strange nobleman, troubled by an ancient legend that threatens his daughter's life, invites a young scientist to his castle to see if he can rid her of the curse. Confusing history surrounded this film: Not only did the title belong to more than one movie (another Christopher Lee movie called *Castle of the Living Dead* also goes by the name *Crypt of Horror*), it turned out there was more than one version of the same movie that Channel 9 actually showed. *Fright Night* seems to have shown the original UK version, while the U.S. version (sometimes titled *Terror in the Crypt*) ran on Channel 11's *Chiller*. That issue somewhat settled, the movie was a wonderfully atmospheric Italian-Spanish production with chillingly authentic castle settings that created a macabre Poe-like mood. Pure gothic! The presence of the formidable Lee (in a rare good guy role) didn't hurt. C (AIP Television, b/w)

09/18 *Brotherhood of Satan* (1971) Strother Martin, L.Q. Jones, Ahna Capri. During the day, witches look like everyone else, but at night they hold a whole town in the grip of terror. Said *Newsday* at the time: "The weird perpetuation of satanic endeavors is the central theme of this small effort, which stars a few decent supporting players in lead roles. Passable." In other words, great acting, great story and a great *Fright Night!* This was a major step up in professionalism and quality from the production team behind *The Witchmaker*, with some of the same cast members. It was realistic and plausible in a creepy, fantastic, better-hope-it's-not-true way. Martin was brilliant as the cult leader. A terrifically scary movie with a nicely disturbing and downbeat finale. Lucky movie theater patrons were given a free packet of "Satan's Soul Seeds" when this movie was released ... what the heck sprouted from *those* things? C (Four Star/Excelsior, color)

09/25 *Exorcism at Midnight* (1973) Basil Dignam, Suzanne Neve, Anthony Ainley. A voodoo practitioner places a curse on a man which kills him and causes his vengeful spirit to return. The amount of trouble Sam Sherman experienced in order to include this film in his company's movie package for Channel 9 would indicate this movie may well have been cursed. But the end result, an older British film called *Naked Evil* augmented with some newly produced scenes to create a disjointed but reasonable voodoo and murder tale, wasn't half-bad. It was a bit of a mash-up with a title that was more enticing than the actual movie, but it had its moments. C (Independent-International, color)

10/02 *The Resurrection of Zachary Wheeler* (1971) Leslie Nielsen, Bradford Dillman, Angie Dickinson. A reporter uncovers a fantastic scheme to keep an injured Senator from dying. Acting jobs must have been hard to come by when this film was made, because it seems like every television B-star from the early '70s auditioned for this politically adventurous (and slightly ahead-of-its-time) but painfully low-budget sci-fi movie ... and they all seem to have gotten hired. However, anyone expecting Senator Wheeler to crawl out of the grave for his resurrection would have been sorely disappointed. Instead it's just a government corruption yarn with weird activities taking place in an Albuquerque hangar. The dated ending was kind of funny. "Death is embarrassing enough as it is!" C (Goldkey, color)

10/09 *The Man Who Could Cheat Death* (1959) Anton Diffring, Christopher Lee, Hazel Court. A London doctor becomes ageless by stealing the vital fluids of young girls. A remake of *The Man in Half Moon Street* (1944), this thoroughly enjoyable Hammer period chiller was an ideal selection for *Fright Night* with its beautiful sets, rich color, fine performances and well-staged scares. It was a great little British horror show with a kind of Jack the Ripper feel (even though it takes place in Paris) and was fun to watch. C (Hammer, color)

10/16 *The Omegans* (1968) Ingrid Pitt, Keith Larsen, Lucien Pan. An artist discovers that his unfaithful wife is plotting his murder and decides to turn the tables. He did this by luring her to a river poisoned with radioactivity which accelerated her aging. Fans of Pitt would surely have noticed the film's foreshadowing of her magnificent role as *Countess Dracula* (1971) later in her career. But unlike that great horror movie, this obscure sci-fi thriller was somewhat tedious and dull. The final pay-off was greatly hindered by very low-budget effects, but Ingrid made most any film worth viewing. (Wilder, color)

10/23 *The Witch*

10/30 *Count Yorga, Vampire*

11/06 *The Thing with Two Heads*

11/13 *The Sorcerers*

11/20 *Peeping Tom* (1960 aka *Face of Fear*) Carl Boehm, Moira Shearer, Brenda Bruce. A young photographer's obsession with women leads to a series of bizarre murders. Psycho-sexual killers would eventually become a dime a dozen, but at the time this was made (the same year *Psycho* was released), perversions and voyeurism mixed with murder were something new and shocking. This was a groundbreaking, fast-paced thriller that still held up in the '80s with its slick British flair for stylized drama and its intriguing focus on a maniac who possessed just enough depth and humor to actually generate some sympathy. Michael Powell's crisp direction was critically acclaimed and deservedly so. C (Anglo Amalgamated, color)

11/27 *Thirst* (1979) David Hemmings, Henry Silva, Shirley Cameron. A cult of blood-drinkers attempt to recruit a young woman into their ranks. Mostly because she was a descendent of Countess (Dracula) Bathory. Like the film *Thirsty Dead,* with which this low-budget Australian film is sometimes confused, this modern-day vampire tale was flat and boring, despite its attempt to be unique in its approach to vampirism. By abandoning traditional vampire themes and failing to replace them with anything better, it became a silly and tedious over-the-top drama. It just didn't work well and was remarkably unsatisfying. C (New South Wales Films, color)

12/04 *Baron Blood*

12/11 *In the Devil's Garden*

12/18 *Silent Night Bloody Night*

12/25 *Four Clowns* (1970) Documentary featuring the work of Laurel & Hardy, Charley Chase, Buster Keaton. Having shown the blood-curdling *Silent Night Bloody Night* the week before, Channel 9 opted for a more wholesome G-rated Yuletide movie (*A Christmas Carol* must have been booked by other stations). It's safe to say this was probably not shown with the *Fright Night* bumper, but rather a *Holiday Movie Special* tag. A charming salute to some amazing performers of the pre-sound era, but if you had been looking for a fright flick you'd have had to hunt for the Scrooge movie on another channel. (Young, b/w)

1983

Thanks to the national sensation Michael Jackson's *Thriller* album stirs up, monsters and zombies crawling out of their graves were never more in vogue. *Fright Night* is the perfect showcase for all kinds of ghouls, broadcasting everything from classics like *Phantom of the Opera* to stunners like *The Wicker Man,* but oddly not a single real zombie stumbled across the screen the entire year.

01/01 *Count Dracula* **(1970) Christopher Lee, Herbert Lom, Klaus Kinski. A young man travels to the wilds of Transylvania and stays in the castle of a vampire nobleman.** Like many horror movie fans back in the day, I had read endlessly in the pages of *Famous Monsters of Filmland* magazine how this was the definitive version of Bram Stoker's novel and how enthusiastic editor Forry Ackerman and star Lee were about it. Upon finally seeing it, I was a bit disappointed. Like the 1931 Lugosi version, the eerie first quarter of this low-budget Jess Franco production was the most entertaining, but it all went downhill thereafter. Ignoring the artificial hype surrounding this movie and reducing one's expectations considerably was the best way to approach it. Then it was just your average piece of Euro-horror but, as such, a good *Fright Night* installment. C (Corona, color)

01/08 *Don't Look in the Basement*

01/15 *Murder Clinic* **(1966 aka** *Revenge of the Living Dead***) William Berger, Mary Young, Barbara Wilson. A mysterious hooded killer stalks the halls of a Victorian-era mental institution.** The gothic setting and the reliable black-cloaked maniac stalking the shadowy hallways plot made this a terrific and welcome dubbed Euro-fright flick, even if it was nothing really new. It was similar in style to *Creature with the Blue Hand*, though the movie was far more serious and had none of the tongue-in-cheek flavor of the former. The nighttime exterior shots of the clinic were quite creepy and the glimmer of the all-too-sharp razor induced some uneasiness. The U.S. movie poster for this film was printed on a thick poster stock and simply showed the title and cast ... no alluring artwork, no catchy taglines, nothing — which seemed to foreshadow the fate of this flick. It would all but vanish in later years and become a very difficult film to get hold of in any reasonable quality. When it played on a triple horror bill as *Revenge of the Living Dead, Newsday* was quite harsh in its review: "Lord save us from this one. It's one of those doctor and the asylum pix, which offers the movie's makers the opportunity to indulge in especially unpleasant psycho-gore." (Leone, color)

01/22 Looks like *Fright Night* was pre-empted for a telethon.

01/29 through 02/05 Looks like *Fright Night* was pre-empted.

02/12 *Blacula* **(1972) William Marshall, Denise Nicholas, Vonetta McGee. An African prince is cursed by Dracula to be one of the living dead and begins a rampage in modern-day Los Angeles.** Unlike the sharply savvy *The Thing with Two Heads*, American International's infamous, budget-minded blaxploitation horror groundbreaker *Blacula* had a nasty edge. Marshall did a bang-up job as Prince Mamuwalde and it was a solid movie for its time, but there was plenty of material in it to offend a variety of people if it was taken too seriously. It was quite a little time capsule too with R&B band The Hues Corporation ("Rock the Boat") making a pre-disco era appearance. I thought Dracula was going to drool right through his fake fangs onto Marshall's face when he slurped the line: "You will never know the sweet taste of blood ... which will become your only desire!" One of those movies everybody remembers. C (American International, color)

02/19 *Stone Cold Dead* (1979) Richard Crenna, Paul Williams, Linda Sorenson. A deranged sniper on a murder spree photographs his prostitute targets. A sleazy Canadian crime drama with some disturbing murders (a young hooker gets shot in the middle of a job and flops unglamorously on the bed, for example) with a nasty enough edge to fit the *Fright Night* mold. I never thought I'd think it, but I had to wonder if films like this, *Who Killed Teddy Bear*, *Scalpel*, *Sniper*, etc., were putting ideas into any potential serial killer's head. (Ko-Zak, color)

02/26 *The Monster Club* (1980) Vincent Price, John Carradine, Donald Pleasence. Three tales of the supernatural are told in a mysterious club. Campy and somewhat juvenile British comedy-horror anthology melded bad rock music with monster mayhem. It would later become a staple on Joe Bob Briggs' *Monstervision* over at TNT in the early '90s. It was fun to see a stellar cast of horror favorites including Price, Carradine, Pleasance, Simon Ward and Britt Ekland mixing it up with monsters but embarrassing that the creatures looked no better than guys in 99-cent store rubber masks. But you couldn't be too hard on it ... it was really just a cheap, lightweight homage to a genre and its stars and, therefore, harmless entertainment. (Chips, color)

03/05 *Phantom of the Opera* (1943) Claude Rains, Nelson Eddy, Susanna Foster. A horribly disfigured violinist lurks in the shadows of the Paris Opera House and seeks to mentor a young vocalist. It had been some time since *Fright Night* had placed a Universal golden oldie on the projector, so this momentary departure from more modern horror was most welcome and met Channel 9's policy requirement for showing color films. While really a showcase for the musical talents of Eddy and Foster, the horror angle was well-handled (if a bit understated for the studio). It was worth enduring some long-winded opera scenes for the pivotal chandelier and unmasking scenes. Not an all-out classic, but *Fright Night* would have seemed incomplete without it. When advertising it for Channel 9's *Million Dollar Movie*, the station said, "Classic horror flick pulsates with terror, shocks and surprises. Brace yourself." C (Universal, color)

03/12 *Scalpel* (1977) Robert Lansing, Judith Chapman, Sandy Martin. After a young woman sustains a vicious attack that leaves her dis-

figured, a plastic surgeon makes her face resemble that of his missing daughter. "He lost the face of the woman he loved so he gave it to someone else," read the confusing advertising for this unpleasant but attention-getting little drama. It kicked off with a violent wallop (literally) and spiraled into a twisted tale of plastic surgery gone horribly wrong. Another slice of delicious Southern-fried decadence. (Avco Embassy, color)

03/19 *Lemora the Lady Dracula* (1973 aka *Lemora—A Child's Tale of the Supernatural*) Cheryl Smith, Lesley Taplin, William Whitton. A young girl travels to a mysterious house to visit her dying father and discovers that he lives in a world of witchcraft and vampires. This was one wacky, cheapo movie about various creatures of evil attempting to corrupt and/or kill a little girl and transform her into a vampire ... I think. It definitely had a disturbing fairy tale–like quality. It took some time to get with the program, but once I settled in and got caught up in its tangled web, I became hooked. The bus ride through the woods filled with zombies, werewolves and vampires was actually a little scary. Blood-sucking Lemora seemed like a cross between Elvira and Morticia Addams. To say this film was "different" was an understatement. C (Blackfern, color)

03/26 *Mind of Mr. Soames*

04/02 *Assignment Terror*

04/09 *Children Shouldn't Play with Dead Things*

04/16 *Don't Look in the Basement*

04/23 *Murder Clinic*

04/30 *Island of Living Horror*

05/07 *Beast of Morocco*

05/14 *Night of Dark Shadows* (1971) David Selby, Kate Jackson, Grayson Hall. A young couple moves into a mansion haunted by a witch. A sequel to the 1970 movie smash *House of Dark Shadows* (based on the popular TV series), it was slightly shorter on the overt scares delivered so well in the first film, but nevertheless had an eerie modern-gothic quality. Collinwood Manor would have been unsettling if all they ever showed was the hedge being trimmed. Props to MGM for not simply churning out another vampire clone of *House* and instead delivering a really good, sinister ghost story that sneaked up on you. That music score created instant goosebumps. (MGM, color)

05/21 *Stranger in Our House* (1978 aka *Summer of Fear*) Linda Blair, Jeremy Slate, Lee Purcell. When her cousin shares her home for a summer, a teenage girl begins to suspect she is involved in witchcraft. This made-for-television movie by *Scream* (1996) and *Nightmare on Elm Street*'s (1984) Wes Craven showed little of the flair for the shock he would later be known for. The upscale desert community setting, bright, colorful daylight scenes and abundance of hair perms were very distracting and evaporated any potential for scares the film might have been striving for. It was also difficult to shake *Exorcist* images of Blair (a problem she would have her entire career), who struggled to be a convincing heroine in this one. Look for a funny cameo by a young Fran Drescher acting like a 16-year-old version of her sitcom Nanny self. C (Finnegan, color)

05/28 Looks like *Fright Night* was pre-empted.

06/04 *Bell from Hell*

06/11 *The Last Man on Earth* (1964) Vincent Price, Franca Bettoia, Emma Danieli. A scientist struggles to survive in a world dominated by plague victims who have become the walking dead, bent on destroying him. Often credited as the inspiration for *Night of the Living Dead* (and it's easy to hypothesize that George Romero viewed this flick along with *The Killer Shrews* when developing his own movie idea), Price's zombie apocalypse and the first film version of Richard Matheson's novel *I Am Legend* was a completely engaging Italian-American co-production that dripped with a depressing, disease-filled mood of dread. The eerie black-and-white photography and Price's convincing and understated performance made for a very creepy viewing experience. While it lacked the brutal punch of *Night of the Living Dead*, it stood on the same solid ground as its cinematic cousin, and its nightmarish vision of the undead was genuinely scary. A deserved cult classic. C (AIP Television)

06/18 *The Sorcerers*

06/29 *Blood and Lace*

07/02 *Deathdream*

07/09 *Castle of Fu Manchu* (1969) Christopher Lee, Richard Greene, Rosalba Neri. A sinister Oriental madman devises a method to freeze the Earth's oceans and threatens to dominate the world. Jess (*Count Dracula*) Franco's take on the evil warlord and his Bond-like plot to take over the planet was moderately interesting thanks primarily to Lee's performance, but the kung fu and espionage-heavy film had little else to recommend it. It looked very choppy and rushed and yet it felt very, very long. "She fights like a man!" C (Balcazar, color)

07/16 *Dr. Jekyll & Sister Hyde*

07/23 *Murder Mansion*

07/30 *Corruption* (1968 aka *Laser Killer, Carnage*) Peter Cushing, Sue Lloyd, Noel Trevarthen. A surgeon discovers that the fluids contained in the human pituitary gland can restore the beauty of his disfigured girlfriend, sending him on a killing spree. While the plot may have sounded like a mod version of *The Man Who Could Cheat Death*, Cushing's excellent performance as a surgeon riddled with guilt and forced to commit violent and ghastly murders helped make this film a unique and highly satisfying experience. Well-paced and filled with sinister turns, this was a true hair-raiser (and remover!) Amusingly, the original advertising advised women to avoid this film. (Columbia, color)

08/06 *House of the Seven Corpses*

08/15 *Vampire People*

08/21 *Demons of the Dead*

08/28 *The Witchmaker*

09/03 *Horror House* (1969) Frankie Avalon, Jill Haworth, Dennis Price. **A group of bored young people decide to explore a haunted house one dark night and unearth the bloody secret of an old murder.** A good deal of creepy atmosphere hovered over this British haunted house where, once again, teenagers who look like 30-year-olds get violently stabbed to death by an unseen killer. If its bloody murders were substantially cut for television, the fun factor would have been seriously reduced. Someone should have told Avalon to gird his loins! Ouch! (Tigon, color)

09/10 *The Wicker Man* (1973) Christopher Lee, Ingrid Pitt, Edward Woodward. **A Christian policeman investigates the disappearance of a young girl on an isolated island where the villagers practice strange pagan rituals.** Over the years, this movie gained a substantial cult following thanks to a bizarre story, well-calculated levels of tension and suspense, strong performances and a wild finale. Engaging visuals and a relentless feeling of menace kept me feeling on edge from the very start of the hunt for Rowan Morrison. As the closing frames were broadcast, all I could say was "Wow!" A truly hypnotic, thought-provoking and absorbing movie masterpiece. "You have an appointment ... with the Wicker Man!" C (British Lion, color)

09/17 *The Incredible Two-Headed Transplant*

09/24 *Dear Dead Delilah*

10/01 *The Devil's Rain* (1975) William Shatner, Ida Lupino, Eddie Albert. **A man vows to destroy a cult of devil worshippers who have enslaved a desert community.** This movie was extremely popular on the drive-in circuit and played with nearly everything that was released in the late '70s. Ernest Borgnine was surprisingly effective as a demon with hooves and horns, and the isolation of the creepy desert town made for a decent scare movie in kind of the same sinister way as *Brotherhood of Satan*. The melting effects and messy finale were cool. John Travolta was seen in a minor role, his first feature film appearance. C (Bryanston, color)

10/08 *Grave of the Vampire*

10/15 *Baron Blood*

10/22 *Deep Red*

10/29 *peeping tom*

11/05 *The Cremators* (1972) Maria De Aragon, Marvin Howard, Eric Allison. **An alien life force takes the form of fireballs that consume human victims.** No great balls of fire out of this one. "From the sun come the fire-people, to incinerate all mankind," read the advertisements for this film from the makers of *Octaman*. Unfortunately, what sounded like a wild, over-the-top romp with a spark of originality was actually a dull movie with very cheap production values and some funny scenes of people being chased by fireballs that look like giant superimposed tumbleweeds. Only piles of ashes (in the shape of people and clearly no bigger than the palm of your hand) were left. Accepted as a cheese ball rather than a fireball, this low-budget goofy monster movie was still lovable. C (Arista, color)

11/12 Looks like *Fright Night* was pre-empted.

11/19 *Scream of the Demon Lover* (1970 aka *Blood Castle*) Carlos Quiney, Agostina Belli, Erna Schurer. **A young female scientist travels to the castle of a mysterious baron whose experiments have coincided with a serious of deaths.** Plenty of gothic atmosphere permeated this Italian-Spanish horror period flick, and viewers were even treated to a genuine monster instead of just supernatural goings-on. However, no doubt the scissors were applied to trim the graphic sexual situations (including a nasty rape scene) that films like this and others were notorious for. C (Prodimex/Hispamer, color)

11/26 *Death Moon* (1978) Robert Foxworth, Barbara Trentham, Joe Penny. **Traveling to Haiti on a vacation, a man discovers he has fallen under the curse of the werewolf.** I'm not sure the atmosphere of Haiti was captured too well in this made-for television movie, as it looked more like a Hawaiian luau. It was about on par with any average TV horror movie from the '70s and not terribly memorable. Foxworth went on to a starring role in TV's *Falcon Crest*, a prime-time soap. (EMI Television, color)

12/03 *Invasion of the Bee Girls*

12/10 *Seeds of Evil* (1975 aka *Garden of Evil, Garden of Death*) Joe Dallesandro, Katherine Houghton, Rita Gam. **A woman discovers that all the previous employers of her handsome gardener have died.** Warhol favorite Dallesandro (from *Andy Warhol's Frankenstein* [1973] among others) was easy on the eyes and well-cast as a muscled but not-terribly-sinister gardener, who provided 99 percent of the sex appeal in this rarely seen film oddity. His standard zoned-out performance actually worked quite well for this role, but he could have been a pool boy, telephone repair man ... just about anything. A strange movie that was somehow mildly absorbing despite the fact that nothing really happened. Seen at a late hour, it was bound to eventually induce drowsiness. C (Columbia, color)

12/17 *The Veil* (1958) Boris Karloff, Booth Colman, Leo Penn. A quartet of eerie stories linked to the supernatural. More quickie horror tales culled from Karloff's unsold television series of the same name, nearly identical to the other film versions (*Jack the Ripper* and *Destination Nightmare*) shown on *Fright Night*. It featured the modest horror episodes "The Crystal Ball," "The Doctor," "Summer Heat" and "Vision of Crime." (Medallion, b/w)

12/24 *Holiday Affair* (1949) Robert Mitchum, Janet Leigh, Wendell Corey. Christmas story about a war widow with a small child who must choose between two suitors. Like *Four Clowns*, this was probably shown as a holiday movie special *sans* the *Fright Night* bumper as its content seemed far removed from anything to do with horror. Another clue: The local newspaper said it was "well done" and gave it three and a half stars, which precious few *Fright Night* movies ever received. (RKO, b/w)

12/31 *In the Year 2889*

1 9 8 4

If Michael Jackson's hair catching fire and a nationwide crack epidemic don't scare you, *Fright Night* may do the trick with everything from stinkers like the so-bad-it's unbelievable *Curse of Bigfoot* and *They Saved Hitler's Brain,* to full-on chillers like *Lady Frankenstein, Eye of the Devil* and *Night Digger.*

01/07 *Deathmaster*

01/14 Looks like *Fright Night* was pre-empted for a telethon.

01/21 *Kiss of the Tarantula*

01/28 *The Night Evelyn Came Out of the Grave*

02/04 *Till Death Do Us Part* (1972 aka *Blood Spattered Bride*) Simon Andreu, Maribel Martin, Alexandra Bastedo. A young bride falls under the influence of Carmilla, a woman who has appeared in her nightmares. This gothic drama had some great moments of bloody mayhem, but many censored nude scenes may have made this a choppy affair at the time. The second half of the film was an explosion of man-hating lesbian horror. Unusual and intriguing. C (Morgana, color)

02/11 *Deep Red* (1975) David Hemmings, Daria Nicoldi, Gabriele Lavia.

At a conference for para-psychiatrists in Rome, a mentalist starts screaming when she gets strange thoughts from a twisted mind which later leads to her murder. *Newsday* once again suggested, "Buy the premise, buy the flick." Director Dario Argento caused quite a stir with this Italian-made slasher movie that I managed to see at a local drive-in on a double bill with *The Night Evelyn Came Out of the Grave*. The mood was scary and the murders were striking, with death by burning in a tub of hot water a particular standout. Highly unsettling in spots. Great, catchy theme music too. "You have killed ... and you will kill again!" The *New York Times* said, "From hunger, for all the wise talk." Whatever that means. C (Rizzoli, color)

02/18 *Silent Night Bloody Night*

02/25 *Revenge of the Stepford Wives* **(1980) Sharon Gless, Julie Kavner, Audra Lindley. A reporter arrives in the small town of Stepford, where ideal lifestyles mask a sinister undercurrent and a dark secret.** A made-for-television sequel to the unique and diverting original theatrical feature that held its own as a well-paced, sometimes sly and often humorous thriller. A good cast of competent period TV stars kept the story rolling, even if it was a more pedestrian retread. Julie (Marge Simpson) Kavner's robotic performance once she fell under the Stepford spell was, I suspect, unintentionally hysterical. (Avco Embassy, color)

03/03 *Witches Mountain*

03/10 *Island of Living Horror*

03/17 *Curse of Bigfoot* **(1978) Bill Simonsen, Jan Swihart, Bob Clymire. A group of archaeology students unearth the remains of a mummified creature in a small California town.** Pieces of an old '50s movie were used as flashbacks to pad out this no-budget mess that was truly so bad, it became essential viewing and an event to wallow in. Channel 9 showed this movie countless times (surprisingly, even in prime time when the film had no business airing any time before 3 A.M.) in a very scratchy, faded print version that made it seem even more astonishingly crude. As bad as this movie trip was, and it *was* a trip, it was a train wreck you couldn't take your eyes off. It sunk to lower depths than even the grade Z stuff churned out by Larry Buchanan and Jerry Warren. However, for all its countless, excruciating faults, the movie still wasn't as bad as *Island Monster*. Probably the best of the worst of Crap Playhouse's many candidates — but for all the wrong reasons! *Newsday* said, "He's big, but not good." C (Etiwanda, color)

03/24 *Beast of the Dead*

03/31 *They Saved Hitler's Brain* **(1968) Walter Stocker, Audrey Caire, Carlos Rivas. Two C.I.D. agents uncover a plot to activate the disem-**

bodied head of the infamous Nazi leader. This film started off with a miserably acted story of agents investigating the death of a scientist and then abruptly shifted gears and went into a Nazi story (which was actually footage from an older film called *Madmen of Mandoras* [1963]). Once Hitler's head shows up, rolling its eyes like a Charlie McCarthy dummy in a handy see-through carrying case, the film perked up. But it was still a grade D snoozer that ravaged one's senses. C (Crown International, b/w)

04/07 *Phantom of the Opera*

04/14 *Terror House*

04/21 *The Last Days of Pompeii* (1935) Preston Foster, Alan Hale, Basil Rathbone. In ancient Rome, a struggling blacksmith must take on the challenges of a gladiator in order to support his son. Though this oldie fell into the same bucket of ill-fitting movies as *Massacre in the Black Forest,* the film's selection as a *Fright Night* feature possibly came from the fact that it was produced by the same RKO team responsible for *King Kong.* The eruption of Vesuvius allowed for some striking special effects (for its day) to take center stage. As a relic of the old days it was unquestionably noteworthy, but missed the genre bull's eye by a mile. C (RKO, b/w)

04/28 *Touch of Satan*—replaced by *Zombies on Broadway* (1945) Wally Brown, Alan Carney, Bela Lugosi. A New York mobster forces two slow-witted press agents to find a genuine zombie for his Caribbean-themed nightclub. That's when the duo encounters Lugosi performing mad experiments on a tropical island. Channel 9 had to dig into its stash of old RKO features at the last minute to dust off this replacement film, but it wasn't a bad little comedy-horror thriller. The Brown & Carney team was obviously a poor man's Abbott & Costello, but this movie, with its Val Lewton–style voodoo flavor, was a harmless piece of good fun. The best player in the flick was an incredibly expressive and talented monkey. C (RKO, b/w)

05/05 *Piranha!*

05/12 *Dr. Who and the Daleks* (1965) Peter Cushing, Jennie Linden, Roy Castle. An eccentric inventor finds himself on a strange planet where he must battle an army of evil robots. As a British television series and movie franchise, Doctor Who developed a staunch following, but watching this extremely dated movie made me wonder what the appeal was. Cushing was always a great and entertaining actor but even he couldn't make this sci-fi fantasy intriguing for me. C (Regal, color)

05/19 *Night of the Cobra Woman* (1972) Joy Bang, Roger Garrett, Marlene Clark. A woman using venom to keep eternally young transforms into a snake. Unfortunately, a low special effects budget pretty much left most of the actual metamorphosis up to one's imagination. This Filipino import from Roger Corman's New World Pictures had the same sweaty appeal and many of the same cast members as the Blood Island movies (*Tomb of the Living Dead, Island of Living Horror*, etc.) and was a fun, lowbrow drive-in style jungle horror flick. Joy Bang? (Avco Embassy, color)

05/26 *Lady Frankenstein* (1971) Joseph Cotten, Rosalba Neri, Paul Muller. The daughter of Dr. Frankenstein continues her father's experiments and creates a monster who terrorizes the countryside. The doctor seemed like an angel of mercy compared to his horny, manipulative and deliciously evil daughter. A great piece of Euro-horror cake into which I sank my teeth unapologetically. With its great period flavor, raunch and reliable monster movie recipe, it was a *Fright Night* feast to be devoured. Director Mel Welles, who had starred in *The Little Shop of Horrors* for Roger Corman, brought countless tried-and-true horror film elements (bats, castles, lab equipment, grave-robbers, etc.) together seamlessly and the result was a thoroughly entertaining chiller with kind of a Hammer Films look. Technical problems at Channel 9 caused the *Fright Night* bumper to be dropped at the movie's start that night. Am I the only pervert who noticed the monster had a hard-on in the movie poster? *Newsday* called it "an Italian bomb...." C (New World, color)

06/02 *Night Digger* (1971 aka *Road Builder*) Patricia Neal, Nicholas Clay, Pamela Brown. A lonely middle-aged woman takes in a young drifter and begins a strange relationship with him. Patricia Neal passed away about the time I was seeking this film out for a refresh. She was one of those actresses who selected her roles carefully and anything she appeared in was pretty much guaranteed to be great. *Night Digger* was an eerie psychological thriller highlighted by mature, engaging performances from the Academy Award winner and her co-star Clay. The absence of any really graphic gore or violence actually heightened the chilling ambiance of this subtle, sophisticated horror drama. A well-done chiller from an MGM package picked up by the station. C (MGM, color)

06/09 *Touch of Satan*

06/15 *Curse of Bigfoot*

06/23 *Nightmare Honeymoon* (1973) Dack Rambo, Rebecca Dianna Smith, John Beck. A newly married couple witnesses a murder and is pursued by a group of killers. If you were expecting a low-grade guilty pleasure along the lines of *Honeymoon of Horror*, or the Italian atmosphere of *Hatchet for a Honeymoon*, this upscale MGM release may have been a disappointment. Despite good production values and Southern location filming, Smith's cries of "It's not enough! It's not enough!" rang so true. Does a wide-eyed thug with a pistol make for a sufficient *Fright Night* menace? Not really. It could have been a lot more interesting. (MGM, color)

06/30 Looks like *Fright Night* was pre-empted for a telethon.

07/07 *Dr. Jekyll & Sister Hyde*

07/14 *The Thing with Two Heads*

07/21 *Baron Blood*

07/28 *Eye of the Devil* (1966) David Niven, Deborah Kerr, Flora Robson. The owner of a struggling vineyard becomes immersed in pagan rituals to save his dying crops. A delightfully sinister atmosphere crept through this rarely seen British effort that featured a sophisticated cast including a beautiful Sharon Tate and Donald Pleasence. Kerr did a magnificent job of appearing increasing and convincingly alarmed at the sinister goings-on and the dialogue was crisp and believable. Spooky scenes abounded, including one when Kerr emerged from a crypt and was menaced by strange, hooded figures in the woods. Striking photography and locations added to the ominous feel. It was almost a cross between *The Wicker Man, Horror Hotel* and *The Omen* (1976) though far more subtle than any of them. An unusual, mature and really well-made thriller. C (MGM, color)

08/04 *Next Victim* (1971 aka *Next!, Blade of the Ripper, Strange Vice of Mrs. Wardh*) George Hilton, Edwige Fenech, Manuel Gil. The beautiful wife of an ambassador discovers that one of her lovers may be a black-mailer and serial killer. Hilton and Fenech paired up again for another grisly murder movie and one I had already been quite unnerved by when this chiller was shown on Channel 9 some time before in a Friday late night slot. The blood-spattered car window in the opening scene set a disturbing tone for what was really was a somewhat typical but fast-moving Italian slasher movie that managed to stir up a healthy dose of uneasiness. The film previously had a well-advertised midnight theatrical showing at New York's Forum on 47th Street and was played up as a foreign version of *Psycho.* "Heaven help whoever is next!" (Gemini/Maron, color)

08/11 *The House That Screamed*

08/18 *Corruption*

08/25 *The Mad Monster* (1942) George Zucco, Anne Nagel, Johnny Downs. A doctor transforms his simple-minded handyman into a were-wolf to exact a strange revenge scheme. Channel 9 pulled out this dusty old PRC quickie from the library in a rare departure from showing more modern, color horror films. Reliable Zucco had that despicable mad gleam in his eye and Glenn Strange, as the very big and manly werewolf in overalls, was menacing enough in a picture that tried hard to emulate the Universal monster movies of the time. Harmless fun; its old-fashioned flavor was a nice change of pace. C (PRC, b/w)

09/01 *Night of the Blood Monster*

09/08 *Dear Dead Delilah*

09/15 *Ship of the Zombies* (1974 aka *Horror of the Zombies, Ship of Zombies*) **Maria Perschy, Jack Taylor, Carlos Lemos. Two sexy models are sent out to sea on a publicity stunt and encounter a strange ship that appears to be abandoned.** But it was actually filled with a slow-moving crew of skinny, hooded zombies (aka the Knights of Templar)! Despite a painfully low budget (the quick shots of the toy boat galleon were amazingly bad) and almost comedic scenes of the skeletal crew "chasing" the beauties like a bunch of senior citizens, it was a really fun horror movie. There were even some nice, genuinely creepy moments when the corpses rose from their coffins in the ship's confines and out of the ocean onto the beach in wet robes. The film would later be a regular feature on USA's *Saturday Nightmares* program. C (Ancla Century/Independent-International, color)

09/22 *Stone Cold Dead*

09/29 *Tower of Terror*

10/06 *Dr. Who and the Daleks*

10/13 *Thirst*

10/20 *Inn of the Frightened People*

10/27 *Aliens Are Coming* (1980) **Max Gail, Tom Mason, Laurie Beach. Aliens circling Earth in a huge spacecraft take control of a young man's mind as part of their invasion plot.** Some decent UFO visuals highlighted this made-for-television movie, which borrowed more than a few sound cues from *Lost in Space*. The cast, acting and treatment are decidedly geared for a television audience still feeling left-over dazzle from *Close Encounters of the Third Kind* (1977) a few years before. The film liberally borrowed such elements as the face-burning effect when a spaceship passed overhead. Judging from the movie's conclusion, it looks like producers were hopeful for a series. None materialized. (Quinn Martin, color)

11/03 *Werewolf of Washington* (1973) **Dean Stockwell, Katalin Kallay, Henry Ferrentino. A man suffers an attack by a werewolf shortly before becoming press assistant to the president.** Political satire and horror mix about as well as oil and vinegar in this poorly acted cheapie that was often hard to view simply because of poor lighting and the crummy print Channel 9 broadcast. Stockwell's transformation was photographed in the same way as Chaney's some thirty years before and his dog-like mannerisms were kind of silly, but the effort was intentionally tongue-in-cheek. However, there was a particularly neat and unsettling scene that featured a sexy female trapped in an overturned phone booth during one of the werewolf attacks. C (Diplomat, color)

11/10 *The Uncanny* (1977) Peter Cushing, Samantha Eggar, Ray Milland. A writer discovers the supernatural powers of cats and tries to convince others by relating a series of horror stories. Capitalizing on the style and success of anthology movies like *Tales from the Crypt* (1972) and *Vault of Horror* (1973), this British feline fright show fell just a little flat in comparison. The stories and theme weaving through them failed to conjure up much in the way of chills. Passable entertainment, but it was a mostly unmemorable event. Cushing, an actor who could always rise above the material, was quite good as a frail and sympathetic old man with a knack for revenge. C (Rank, color)

11/17 *The Dark* (1979) William Devane, Cathy Lee Crosby, Richard Jaeckel. An alien creature stalks the city streets at night in search of victims. A few creepy opening scenes with a shadowy, big-clawed monster attacking people in isolated sections of a city showed promise, but the movie turned out to be just an average police hunt drama with a hyperactive (and disappointing) 10-minute climax. Pop music icon Dick Clark was a producer and *America's Top 40*'s famous host Casey Kasem had a small role. Not even big John Bloom (*The Creature's Revenge*) in platform shoes and bad makeup, shooting fire zaps out of his eyes, could perk this up. C (Film Ventures, color)

11/24 *Strange Vengeance of Rosalie* (1972) Ken Howard, Bonnie Bedelia, Anthony Zerbe. A traveling salesman is seduced by a young woman in the desert and becomes a prisoner when her biker boyfriend comes on the scene. How weird these movies must have been to watch in the wee hours that *Fright Night* was telecast! "Strange" doesn't begin to describe this kooky drama that left me wondering what the hell I had just seen. The bizarre relationships and behaviors depicted in this twisted story were well played in straight-up fashion by the cast and it had all the makings of a really nutty cult obscurity. This was the same unclassifiable league as the mentally draining *The Baby*. (Palomar, color)

12/01 *Cursed Medallion*

12/08 *Fear No Evil*

12/15 *Laserblast* (1978) Cheryl Smith, Roddy McDowall, Kim Milford. A teenager finds a futuristic weapon left behind by aliens in the desert and uses it for a murderous rampage. This sci-fi cult favorite had a comic book feel to it, right down to its aliens skulking around in the desert via stop motion animation. It also had a tongue-in-cheek flavor that really was the only practical approach to take on such a low-budget outing aimed at a youthful market. The frustrated teenager finding a fantastic means to exact revenge and transforming into a monster was a highly appealing theme to me at the time, but his makeup, limited to the neck up, was a bit clownish. It was a cheap, colorful time-waster, though, and another oddity of the sort that *Fright Night* was so great at unearthing. C (Yablans, color)

12/22 *Silent Night Bloody Night*
12/29 *Demons of the Dead*

1985

The sci-fi and fantasy genre is alive and well with *Back to the Future* becoming the highest grossing film of all time. Meanwhile, soda icon Coke changes its long-standing formula and debuts "New Coke." Also changing with the times, *Fright Night*'s bumper gets an update but Channel 9 keeps the formula intact and the show continues to deliver the best in late night horror.

01/05 *So Sad About Gloria*
01/12 Looks like *Fright Night* was pre-empted for a telethon.
01/13 *Exorcism at Midnight*
01/26 *Demons of the Dead*
02/02 *Lady Frankenstein*
02/09 *The Wicker Man*
02/16 *Tourist Trap* (1979) **Chuck Connors, Jocelyn Jones, Jon Van Ness. Young people stranded in a museum are stalked by a man with the power to animate mannequins.** *Rifleman* TV star Connors, though aging, was still a big, formidable man at the time this picture was made and his character, a stalking killer wearing bizarre masks, elicited a few scares with shades of *The Texas Chain Saw Massacre* (1974) lingering in the air. Otherwise, this movie was just a fair thriller with that '80s kind of cookie-cutter mass murder blandness that had become quite common. C (Compass, color)
02/23 *Scream of the Demon Lover*
03/02 *Kiss of the Tarantula* (1976) **Suzanna Ling, Eric Mason, Herman Wallner. A young girl exacts revenge on her abusers by sending her pet spiders to kill them.** There might have been a temptation to compare this film to *Carrie* (1976), but the revenge in this movie was achieved by another pretty young teenage girl gone bad via a more practical (if far-fetched) means than the supernatural. But hey, I had pet squirrels so who am I to judge? Seeing the thick spiders crawling all over a gang of obnoxious teens

making out in a car was a hoot. It was a decent little chiller and the macabre aftertaste lingered. C (Cinema-Vu, color)

03/09 *The Night Evelyn Came Out of the Grave*

03/16 *Island of Living Horror*

03/23 *Night of the Laughing Dead* (1973 aka *House in Nightmare Park*) **Frankie Howerd, Ray Milland, Hugh Burden. An actor is called to perform at a remote mansion where a sinister group of people plot his murder.** This wryly funny British comedy featured the often hysterical Howerd playing buffoon Foster Twelvetrees in a typical "old dark house" thriller. It worked well with Milland (who seems to be enjoying himself) also hamming it up. It wasn't the dopey slapstick of *Benny Hill* (popular on Channel 9 at the time after they began picking up BBC shows), but this Independent-International import (and favorite of Sam Sherman) was very amusing and I laughed out loud several times. Twelvetrees, nearly axed by a *Psycho*-like old lady, exclaimed to his rescuer, "If you hadn't come in here, it might have been Sixtrees!" It was that kind of humor. (Independent-International/EMI, color)

03/30 *The Fearless Vampire Killers* (1967) **Sharon Tate, Roman Polanski, Jack McGowran. Vampire hunters track down a family of bloodsuckers in the cold mountains of a remote country.** Most people either loved or hated this movie. I leaned towards feelings of warm affection. Admittedly it had a brutally long running time and strange sense of humor, but it was visually arresting and had a magnificent Hammer-like atmosphere. Trimmed by about 40 minutes, it would have been a minor classic. The movie ran for a time on *The CBS Late Movie* and then migrated over to Channel 9. It would later become a Christmas favorite over on Joe Bob Briggs' *Monstervision* at TNT; December was an ideal time to show the film with its snowy landscapes. C (MGM, color)

04/06 *Mystery of the Sacred Shroud* (1977) **Narrated by Richard Burton. The facts and history surrounding the ancient relic are examined.** Channel 9's selection of this film may have been a surprisingly on-target holiday (Easter) movie special presentation, rather than a *Fright Night* installment, but either way it worked. It was a well-made documentary that was biased towards supporting the cloth's authenticity (and it appears scientists still lean that way 30+ years later). Movies like this, *In Search of Noah's Ark* (1976), *Chariots of the Gods* (1970), etc. used to make the matinee rounds in the '70s and were undeniably intriguing ... but frustrating because you never really got definitive answers. I recall watching it as a *Fright Night* feature and irreverently thinking, "Well, this *is* a story of the dead coming to life." Was that wrong? (Andros, color)

Original theatrical ad mat for *Night of the Laughing Dead* (1973).

04/13 *Scalpel*

04/20 *The Next Victim*

04/27 *The Corpse Vanishes* (1942) Bela Lugosi, Luana Walters, Elizabeth
    Russell. A scientist murders young brides in order to obtain the glan-

dular fluid that will restore his wife's youth and beauty. Channel 9 must have kept a stash of these PRC and Monogram quickies on hand and once again pleasantly broke policy of showing more contemporary horror fare by serving up this oldie but goodie. These creakers from the beginning of Lugosi's career downturn were an awful lot of fun and you always knew what you'd get: bad acting, low-grade sets and cheap thrills. But that didn't mean the movie wouldn't be entertaining and this Grade C flick with plenty of familiar faces was completely serviceable. C (Monogram, b/w)

05/04 *Thirst*

05/11 *Ruby* (1977) **Piper Laurie, Stuart Whitman, Roger Davis. The daughter of a woman whose boyfriend was killed by gangsters years before begins to receive psychic warnings from the beyond.** This movie was supposed to be Laurie's big horror follow-up to *Carrie*. A campy chiller set in the '50s, it turned out to be just a so-so tale of revenge from beyond the grave. It quickly became mired in theatrics and suffered from slow pacing. Laurie was an excellent actress but even her skills failed to elevate this one from snoozer status. The film was a popular supporting feature on the drive-in circuit in New York and later turned up frequently on the local ABC affiliate's late show. C (Dimension, color)

05/18 *Peeping Tom*

05/25 *Torture Chamber of Dr. Sadism*

06/01 Looks like *Fright Night* was pre-empted for a telethon.

06/08 *Terror of Frankenstein* (1977) **Per Oscarsson, Leon Vitali, Nicholas Clay. A scientist manages to create a living man from the bodies of the dead in this adaptation of the Mary Shelley classic novel.** An unusual Swedish-Irish production imported by Sam Sherman's Independent-International Pictures and made by the same director, Calvin Floyd, who had handled the documentary *In Search of Dracula* the previous year. Despite a low budget, the movie was extremely faithful to the novel and effectively captured the period — probably better than just about any other Frankenstein movie until, perhaps, the DeNiro version years later. The monster was highly memorable: decidedly human, sympathetic and, occasionally and most importantly, scary. Genre fans with an appreciation for classic literature would have enjoyed this movie, but it largely (and unfairly) went unnoticed. C (Independent-International, color)

06/15 *Murder Mansion*

06/22 *Destination Nightmare*

06/28 Telethon.

07/06 *Bell from Hell*

07/13 *Beginning of the End*

07/20 *Homebodies*

07/27 *Don't Look in the Basement* replaced by *Nightmare Hotel* (1973 aka *It Happened at Nightmare Inn*) Judy Geeson, Aurora Bautista, Esperanza Roy. **Two sisters with strong moral views run a hotel in Spain from which young girls have disappeared.** Geeson's perky, unassuming nature was light and amusing at the beginning of the picture, but the sinister and grisly doings at her lodging house quickly sobered things up. Not as gory as one might expect, but a fast-moving, highly enjoyable Euro-horror that was a great deterrent for Spanish tourism. The two sisters running the hotel were well cast and largely responsible for making this movie as interesting as it was. Pair this movie up with *And Soon the Darkness* (1970) and you'd never have left the good old USA again. C (Ben Barry & Associates Television, color)

08/03 *Don't Look in the Basement*

08/10 *Zombie* (1964 aka *I Eat Your Skin, Zombies*) William Joyce, Heather Hewitt, Betty Hyatt. **The side effects of an experimental serum to cure cancer transform many natives into an army of zombies terrifying an island.** Any fame this film had was due largely to its positioning as the co-feature on an infamous double-bill with the immortal *I Drink Your Blood* (1970) from legendary drive-in movie producer-distributor Jerry Gross. But audiences who had just finished digesting the mayhem of that colorful chiller must have been sadly disappointed when this cheap and decidedly older black-and-white movie came up on the screen. Actually, it wasn't that bad, just very tame. A mild, run-of-the-mill '60s zombie thriller dogged by Joyce's hammy take on James Bond and loads of campy performances by other obscure cast members. The zombies were moderately intimidating. From the makers of the *Creature Feature* favorite, *The Horror of Party Beach* (1964). C (Gross/Iselin-Tenney, b/w)

08/17 *Deep Red*

08/24 *War of the Colossal Beast* (1958) Sally Fraser, Roger Pace. **A giant disfigured man, the result of atomic exposure, terrifies a Mexican town.** This sequel to *The Amazing Colossal Man* (1957) migrated over from Channel 11's *Chiller*, where it was a staple for many years. The gruesome half-human, half-skull facial makeup helped compensate for the shoddy Bert I. Gordon special effects, and it was a fun little monster movie. Though the film's long-time association with *Chiller* made it seem a little out of place on *Fright Night*, it was a nice throwback to the old days. C (American International, b/w)

08/31 *Thirsty Dead*

09/07 *Taste of Evil* (1971) Barbara Stanwyck, Roddy McDowall, Barbara

Parkins. **A young woman, brutally assaulted as a child on her family estate, returns to the scene of the crime.** ABC network regular Aaron Spelling produced this twisted tale of family secrets and, like most made-for-television films of that period, it featured a number of familiar small screen stars of the day. The opening scene of a dark figure approaching a little girl in her playhouse was highly unsettling, but the rest of the movie was pretty standard material. Directed by *Horror Hotel*'s John Llewellyn Moxey from a screenplay by Jimmy Sangster (screenwriter for *Horror of Dracula* [1958] and *The Curse of Frankenstein* [1957], among others). Fans might have expected stronger stuff, but it was still entertaining. Stanwyck sure knew how to be the boss. (Spelling, color)

09/14 *Graduation Day* **(1981) Christopher George, Michael Pataki, Patch Mackenzie. Members of a high school track team begin dying under mysterious circumstances.** Horror films from the '80s began to show radical signs of evolution, few of which were for the better. Novel ways of killing people, low-grade humor and irritating soundtracks began replacing monsters, mood and scares, and movies like this rarely left a good impression on me (despite the timeless appeal of knocking off annoying teenagers). It was corny and tiresome. C (IFI/Scope III, color)

09/21 *Blood Beach* **(1980) John Saxon, David Huffman, Marianna Hill. Police investigate the strange disappearance of beach-goers.** A great *Jaws*-like premise was dogged by a slow-moving script and shoddy monster visuals in the final reel. I still don't really know what the hell it was, though the logical guess was some type of giant crab. The sand siphoning downward as a precursor to monster activity was a neat little gimmick and created some suspense, but it was overplayed by the end of the movie. It wasn't bad, but it could have been so much better. The movie was later a frequent feature on USA's *Saturday Nightmares*. C (Gross/Shaw/Beckerman, color)

09/28 *The Attic* **(1980) Ray Milland, Carrie Snodgress, Ruth Cox. A woman, mourning the loss of her boyfriend many years before, is left to care for her cantankerous and domineering father.** I was a huge fan of Milland and anything he appeared in was always made the better for his presence. This movie, however, missed the mark quite a bit. The twisted relationship between a father and daughter culminated in a not-too-surprising revelation that failed to elicit much sympathy for either of the characters or make sitting through this long-winded psycho-drama all that worthwhile. Milland was certainly at his crankiest. C (Forum/Attic, color)

10/05 *Shock Waves* **(1977) Peter Cushing, Brooke Adams, Fred Buch. Vacationers traveling in strange waters encounter a derelict ship and an uncharted island where unstoppable Nazi zombie soldiers roam.**

Although the eerie, New Wave–looking zombies were more intimidating looking than actually threatening, this desert island horror drama was extremely creepy and suspenseful. *A la Ship of the Zombies*, the uniformed zombies rising from the ocean was a startling visual. Cushing, looking skinnier than usual, delivered another fine performance as an exiled Nazi officer. It was interesting to see maturing *Flipper* star Luke Halpin in a supporting role and John Carradine as a cranky skipper. A quality horror film and well done. C (Joseph Brenner, color)

10/12 *The Cremators*

10/19 *The Creature's Revenge*

10/26 *The Dark*

11/02 Looks like *Fright Night* was pre-empted.

11/09 *The Devil's Rain*

11/16 *Something Evil* (1972) Sandy Dennis, Darren McGavin, Johnny Whitaker. A young couple moves into a rural farmhouse where an evil force begins to manifest itself. A well-made TV movie directed by a young Steven Spielberg, originally shown on the CBS network. There were shades of *Rosemary's Baby* in Sandy Dennis' very convincing (and Mia Farrow–channeled) performance and the presence of stalwart Ralph Bellamy added to that inevitable comparison. However, the film was original in its approach, never got too over-the-top, hurried or silly, and managed to convey a very sinister tone of suggested malevolence. Much better than your average '70s TV filler. (Belford/CBS, color)

11/30 *Varan the Unbelievable* (1962) Myron Healey, Clifford Kawada, Ayumi Sonoda. Scientists experimenting on the waters of a mysterious lake in Japan accidentally awaken a huge prehistoric creature. This shorter, Americanized version of a Gamera-like Japanese giant monster movie wasn't half bad. Much like the original U.S. version of *Godzilla*, the inclusion of American actors and scenes did make the movie seem more accessible. The rubber suit effects and evocative b&w photography appeared more striking than usual. Western man's philosophy of sacrificing a few lives for the betterment of mankind once again backfired. C (Cory/Dallas, b/w)

12/07 *Maneaters Are Loose* (1978) Tom Skerritt, Steve Forrest, G.D. Spradin. Snarling carnivores are unleashed on a suburban community. To be truthful, all the chatty, long-winded mini-dramas going on within this small southwestern community made me wish the rather playful looking carnivores (aka tigers) would hurry up and start eating them. Lots of rising stars made appearances in this made-for-television movie, but that did little to ease the boredom. A decidedly tame romp and quite dated even in 1985. A Siegfried & Roy show had scarier moments. C (Finnegan/CBS, color)

12/14 *Fear No Evil*

12/21 *Jack the Ripper* **(1958) Boris Karloff, Morris Ankrum, Dorothy Alison. Four tales of the supernatural.** More stories culled from episodes of the ill-fated Karloff TV series, *The Veil.* The actual Jack the Ripper story shown in this set was a pretty good, subdued and compact horror yarn that featured the great Niall MacGinnis — from *Chiller* favorite *Curse of the Demon* (1957) — having accurate, detailed visions of the Whitechapel atrocities that skeptical authorities refused to acknowledge. Actually, all the stories were pretty decent in this compilation released by Hal Roach. C (Medallion, b/w)

12/28 Looks like *Fright Night* was pre-empted.

1986

After 35 years on the air, NBC's daytime drama *Search for Tomorrow* serves up its final telecast; it was television's longest running non-news program. *Fright Night*, however, continues its record-breaking run and serves up some big box office hits like *Beyond the Door* and *Grizzly.* The show also puts the spotlight on George Romero when it features two of his classics, *Night of the Living Dead* and *The Crazies.*

01/04 *The Mummy's Revenge* **(1973) Paul Naschy, Jack Taylor, Maria Silva. In Victorian England, an ancient Egyptian mummy returns to life seeking the blood of virgins to ensure his eternal life.** Sort of a colorful Spanish retread of the 1932 Universal *The Mummy*, but updated with big doses of violence and brutality. The movie dripped with low-budget Euro-flavor and had that now familiar Naschy horror comic book visual style that was guaranteed to hold your attention. I had to give the actor credit for amassing such a huge catalog of in-your-face scare flicks and *Fright Night* for showcasing so many of them. (Lotus Films, color)

01/11 *Murder Clinic*

01/18 Looks like *Fright Night* was pre-empted for a telethon.

01/25 *Fall of the House of Usher* **(1982) Martin Landau, Charlene Tilton, Ray Walston. A man and his wife travel to an isolated mansion where a family lives under a strange curse.** The American International-Roger Corman films based on Poe took up residence over at the local ABC affiliate in New York on *The 4:30 Movie* for the longest time, so it is far more likely that this feature was the rarely seen made-for television version that is extremely hard to find in any format today. Made by Sun Classics, an outfit that also specialized in releasing documentaries like *In Search of Noah's Ark* (1976), this $2 production featured unbelievably wooden country playhouse-style acting and cardboard sets that were literally ... cardboard. Yet, somehow, there *was* a spooky atmosphere and the cheapness was extremely endearing. (Sun Classics, color)

02/01 *House That Would Not Die* (1970) Barbara Stanwyck, Richard Egan, Kitty Winn. A house in Amish country where a woman and her niece have taken up residence attracts malevolent forces. Reviving another made-for-television film, *Fright Night* uncovered a movie laced with subtle occult themes and one that scored higher marks than the usual network fare. You could always count on Stanwyck to pick good film properties to appear in, even at this late stage of her career. A fairly fast-paced and suspenseful ghost story with a nice, moderately hair-raising climax. (Spelling, color)

02/08 *Kiss of the Tarantula*

02/15 *The Wicker Man*

02/22 *Companion*

03/01 *Great Alligator* (1979 aka *Big Alligator River*) Claudio Cassinelli, Barbara Bach, Mel Ferrer. An African tourist resort comes under attack by a huge crocodile that natives believe is the reincarnation of an angry god. Authentic-looking jungle locations added some steamy atmosphere to this dubbed, Italian-made variation on *Jaws*, but the no-budget special effects were a letdown. If expectations were kept to a bare minimum, it was kind of a fun drive-in flick, unlike the similarly themed *Up from the Depths*. The presence of Barbara Bach was an attractive plus. (Dania, color)

03/08 *Beast of Morocco*

03/15 *Next Victim*

03/22 *Night of the Laughing Dead*

03/29 *Mystery of the Sacred Shroud*

04/05 *Zombie*

04/12 *Phantom of the Opera*

04/19 *Bell from Hell*

04/26 *Night of the Sorcerers*

05/03 *Warlock Moon*

05/10 *The Crazies* (1973 aka *Code Name: Trixie*) Lane Carroll, Lloyd Hollar, Will MacMillan. The military seizes a small Pennsylvania town whose inhabitants have all become insane. The *New York Daily News* summarized the film by saying, "Biological warfare virus drives people mad — will drive you to bed." Not entirely true. George Romero's color follow-up to *Night of the Living Dead* wasn't nearly as jolting and bar-setting as the former, and did suffer from too much talk, political jabbing and long breaks in the action. But it was a decent film laced with a few scares, a palpable sense of paranoia and tension, and plenty of social commentary. As if Pennsylvania hadn't been through enough. C (Pittsburgh Films, color)

05/17 ***Silent Night Bloody Night***

05/24 ***Castle of Fu Manchu***

05/31 ***Doctor Franken*** **(1980) Robert Vaughn, David Selby, Robert Perault. A Manhattan doctor rebuilds a nameless patient with body parts of others under his care in a prestigious hospital.** Selby and Vaughn gave very strong performances in this well-made television movie, no doubt in the hopes of it becoming a series (which it did not). Although marred by comedic scoring when the hunky monster escaped the doc's brownstone lab and wandered through New York's financial district in surgery garb (plenty of perplexed New Yorkers looked on but, typically, nobody seemed too bothered), this otherwise intelligent updating of the Frankenstein story was quite compelling. Special thanks to Rob Craig for finding a copy of this elusive film. (Titus, color)

06/07 ***Island Claws*** **(1980) Robert Lansing, Barry Nelson, Steve Hanks. Scientific experiments result in the mutation of crabs, turning them into gigantic monsters.** Like *The Giant Spider Invasion*, they actually built a huge mechanical monster for this picture. The movie tried so hard to be suspenseful and shocking upon revealing the creature that you just had to love its earnest, if misguided, enthusiasm. It was a very old-fashioned horror movie whose style was dated even by 1980 standards, but if you checked your brain and went along for the ride, it was a whole lot of ultra-corny fun. (Island Claws Co., color)

06/14 ***Womaneater*** **(1958) George Coulouris, Vera Day, Peter Wayn. A scientist discovers a flesh-eating tree deep in the jungle and brings it back to London.** This odd British chiller had a undeniably retro-creepy atmosphere about it, but the gnarly, silly-looking low-budget tree (shaking its limbs and hugging its victims to death) kept it from being taken too seriously. It was great fodder for *Fright Night*. C (Columbia, b/w)

06/21 ***Chilling*** **(1974) Kevin O'Neill, David Blunt. A man who was abused as a child returns to his home town seeking revenge.** Like *The Nylon Noose*, this obscure British film is virtually impossible to find today. There's also precious little written about it in genre books or online sources. For now, a *Fright Night* "lost" film ... but it *sounds* like it might have been pretty good!

06/28 *Aliens Are Coming*

07/05 *Invisible Terror*

07/12 *Devil Dog—The Hound of Hell* (1978) Richard Crenna, Kim Richards, Victor Jory. **A family takes ownership of a puppy that was the result of Satanic breeding.** When I was a teen, the words "devil dog" immediately brought to mind a chocolate cake snack food with creamy vanilla filling. I'd have been better off just eating one of those and going to bed. A surprisingly awful made-for-television movie (considering it was directed by Curtis Harrington) and about as scary as a Sunday picnic. The climax, such as it was, featured a giant superimposed snarling dog, no doubt irritated by the black feather boa he appeared to be wearing. C (Zeitman/Landers/Roberts, color)

07/19 *Alice Sweet Alice* (1976 aka *Communion*) Paula Sheppard, Linda Miller, Mildred Clinton. **A strange and sinister girl becomes the prime suspect when her younger sister is murdered during her first communion.** This was one extremely chilling, suspenseful and cold-blooded thriller, whose story wrapped like a twisted pretzel around the confines of a small urban Catholic community. Eye-covering *Psycho*-esque violence punctuated a neat story filled with great performances. It seemed surreal to see an extremely young Brooke Shields in a very small role (though she is frequently top-billed in later VHS and DVD releases of the film) as a child victim. It was like seeing a child wearing a Brooke Shields face mask. Scary, disturbing stuff and it gave me ... *bad dreams*. You will never look at yellow rain slickers quite the same way again. (Sole, color)

07/26 *Werewolf of Washington*

08/02 *The Visitor* (1979 aka *Visitors*) Glenn Ford, Mel Ferrer, Sam Peckinpah. **A young girl with supernatural powers becomes the prize in a battle of good and evil.** Is that what this movie was about? With a theatrical release poster depicting a giant eyeball with claws hovering over a city, one might expect a pretty good sci-fi horror shocker. One would be exceedingly disappointed. I couldn't tell you what this long, confusing, disjointed movie was about if I tried, but it involved a young girl with unearthly powers and a strange being trying to reel her in. Made by the same people who went *Beyond the Door* (and it may have been part of a Film Ventures package picked up by Channel 9), but I think they were reaching too far with this one. How somewhat major stars like Ford, Ferrer, Shelley Winters and John Huston got involved in this, I have no idea. (Ovidio/Continental/International Picture Show, color)

08/09 *Tourist Trap*

08/16 *Beyond the Door* (1974) Juliet Mills, Richard Johnson, Gabriele

Lavia. **A pregnant woman begins to fall under the influence of Satanic forces.** After seeing numerous scary commercials for this movie on Channel 9, I got the chance to watch this notorious demonic possession import on the big drive-in screen when it was first released. While it was confusing as hell, the chilling sequences where Mills levitates upright, her eyes roll in two different directions, and she spews the obligatory pea soup were all quite memorable. A low-budget, very strange movie that for some even stranger reason had the ability to grab and hold. *Newsday,* however, took a dimmer view of the picture, calling it a "dumb and boring rip-off of *The Exorcist* and *Rosemary's Baby.* The amateurish acting matches the trite plot." I loved running around saying *"Who aaaaaarrrrreee yoooou?"* (Film Ventures, color)

08/23 *Grizzly* **(1976) Christopher George, Andrew Prine. A killer grizzly prowls for victims in a state park.** Everyone in my high school knew this was going to be a *Jaws* rip-off when it was theatrically released, but based on a recommendation from a classmate I went to see this in spite of my better judgment at the Smithtown All-Weather Indoor Theater. I did not take any recommendations from her seriously after that. Aside from the awesome landscapes that were brilliantly photographed for widescreen, this movie had more of a disaster flick feel and wasn't too suspenseful and engaging. The big bear wasn't really a great monster in the way that a huge eating machine shark had been and the whole thing came off flat and corny. C (Film Ventures, color)

08/30 *The Green Slime* **(1968) Robert Horton, Richard Jaeckel, Andrew Prine. A space station confronts a giant asteroid that harbors a deadly slime capable of generating monsters.** This movie made the cover of *Famous Monsters of Filmland* magazine and was a popular kiddie matinee feature on the theatrical circuit. With creatures that looked like escapees from an episode of *H.R. Pufnstuf,* the movie had a real Saturday morning feel. As a very cheesy sci-fi horror hybrid it was something of a must-see for bad movie experience lovers. Not one of producer Sam Sherman's favorite movies, as he felt the film was infringing on the green blood theme of Hemisphere Pictures' *Mad Doctor of Blood Island* back in the day. C (MGM, color)

09/06 *Prisoner of the Lost Universe* **(1983) Richard Hatch, John Saxon, Kay Lenz. Three diverse people are transported to a parallel universe where they encounter a brutal warlord bent on enslaving mankind.** Another low-budget sci-fi flick with a made-for-television look and a theme that embraced the fantasy superhero movement that had become popular at the time. It wasn't a crime that *Fright Night* showed films like this from time to time, as arguably they contain a number of genre elements, but it smelled like one of those *Star Wars* knock-offs and I wasn't that interested. C (Marall/Robertson, color)

09/13 *Screamers* (1979 aka *Island of the Fishmen*) Barbara Bach, Richard Johnson, Claudio Cassinelli. A group of prisoners escape to a Caribbean island where strange and deadly aquatic creatures protect a beautiful woman. I completely enjoyed this movie! It was an Italian horror film heavily inter-cut with American footage and while that's usually a Jerry Warren–style formula for disaster, in this case it worked quite well. The opening segments with treasure hunters wandering through eerie, fog-enshrouded beach caves and meeting with violent ends at the hands of scary monsters were as spooky as anything I ever saw on *Fright Night*. It wasn't completely coherent, but it was a whole lot of creepy fun. (Avco Embassy, color)

09/20 *She's Dressed to Kill* (1979) Jessica Walter, John Rubenstein, Connie Sellecca. A prestigious fashion design agency sponsors a weekend getaway where the models are being murdered, one by one. Cyanide lipstick, poisonous gas in a can of hairspray and assorted other model-unfriendly means of dispatch highlighted this made-for-television who-dunit. It was long, very dated, very campy but highly amusing as a product of the designer jeans era. (Barry Weitz Films, color)

09/27 *Shock Waves*

10/04 *Aliens Return* (1980 aka The Return) Jan Michael Vincent, Cybil Shepherd, Martin Landau. Two young children in a small New Mexico town encounter an alien spacecraft. Nice UFO effects and weird cow mutilations, but not much else in this dimly-lit sci-fi spooker (from the man who made *Satan's Cheerleaders* in '77) that wanted to be scary but fell several yards short. (Greydon Clark, color)

10/11 *Lady Frankenstein*

10/18 *Blood Mania*

10/25 *Night Gallery* (1970) Joan Crawford, Roddy McDowall. Three tales of the supernatural. A pilot movie for the famed television series, this was a very cool collection of horror stories woven together by legendary host Rod Serling. McDowall was, by now, an all-too-familiar ham in TV movies and Crawford helped add some credibility and fading star power to the production. Nothing really groundbreaking, but it was solid, atmospheric entertainment, especially in *Fright Night*'s late night time slot. The television series became something of a legend for '70s audiences looking for more up-to-date material to replace *Twilight Zone*. (Universal, color)

11/01 *Night of the Living Dead* (1968) Duane Jones, Judith O'Dea, Russell Steiner. Space experiments set off high-level radiation that activates the dead and transforms them into flesh-eating monsters. "Lights, camera, color!" Hal Roach Studios was taking a number of public domain movies and colorizing them for TV release and this all-time classic got painted up with the rather primitive technology of the time. But *Night of the Living Dead,* presented in "un-living color," was still a force to be reckoned with and, back in the day, the novelty effect was actually mildly diverting. Though some of the graphic gore was trimmed, Channel 9 still felt it necessary to include at the beginning of the show a warning carried over from an earlier *Million Dollar Movie* telecast advising parental discretion. In truth, George Romero's bar-setting zombie movie was far tamer than some of the gruesome flicks Channel 9 had shown in the past. *Fright Night* would not have been the all-encompassing program it was had this masterpiece of horror been bypassed. It was a spellbinding nail-biter even with awkwardly tinted pale green ghouls. *Newsday* gave the film four stars and described it as a "classic horror film with some of the most gruesome and grueling scenes on film." There's little room for argument that this was one of the best horror films ever made and it surely deserved to be called a *Fright Night* classic. The film was re-colorized far more effectively many years later for a DVD release by Sony. "Well, if there's *that* many of them, they'll probably get us wher*ever* we are." C (Hal Roach/Image Ten, color)

11/08 Looks like *Fright Night* was pre-empted.

11/15 *See No Evil* (1971) Mia Farrow, Robin Bailey, Dorothy Alison. A young blind woman unknowingly stays in a country house where all the occupants have been murdered. There was a slow, steady build-up in suspense in this well-handled thriller which made the viewer quickly grasp and absorb the dangerous and scary position this innocent young blind woman found herself in. Farrow was a true pro, allowing the viewer to forget she was an actress performing a role. Another nail-biter that made one genuinely thankful to have one's full set of senses! I loved the double-feature playing at the movie theater in the film's opening. C (Columbia, color)

11/22 *Rituals* (1978) Hal Holbrook, Lawrence Dane, Robin Gammell. A group of doctors on a camping trip in a remote Canadian woodland area are stalked by an unseen killer. When this movie played theatrically in my area, its advertising featured very amateurish artwork, parental warnings and hackneyed taglines like "[G]uaranteed to keep you on the edge of your seat ... or under it." I don't know why I failed to catch it, as it would have been right up my alley and really something to see on the big screen. Who would have dreamed the marketing claims for this obscure sleeper would actually prove true? Comparisons to John Boorman's *Deliverance* (1972) were understandably drawn, but this nerve-frying flick evolved into so much more with its frightening build-up of hopelessness and horrific twists and turns. Terrific performances, almost painful suspense and downright gruesome scares from start to brutal finish. I never looked at camping in the woods the same way again. The distant view of a decapitated head on a stick atop a cliff side was completely unnerving. A *Fright Night* classic. (Astral/Canart, color)

11/29 Looks like *Fright Night* was pre-empted.

12/06 *When Michael Calls*

12/13 *Curse of Bigfoot*

12/20 *Invasion Earth: 2150 AD* (1966 aka *Daleks' Invasion Earth: 2150 AD*) Peter Cushing, Andrew Keir, Bernard Cribbins. Doctor Who is transported to the future where he discovers that mankind has been enslaved by robots. If you were a fan of the British *Doctor Who* franchise, maybe this colorful follow-up to *Dr. Who and the Daleks* might have satisfied you, but as a horror fan looking for chills and thrills, sci-fi fantasy like this left me bored to death. The presence of Cushing, who handled the lead role with the same conviction as any of his portrayals of Dr. Frankenstein, was a plus, however. C (AARU, color)

12/27 *Fall of the House of Usher*

1987

Sixty-four years after it first opened, New York department store mainstay Ohrback's closes its doors for good. It's the homestretch for *Fright Night* too, but the program blissfully ignores its fate and serves up an eclectic mix of horror, sci-fi and fantasy movies as station executives begin to ponder the fate of all of Channel 9's programming.

01/03 *Thirst*

01/10 *Two Faces of Dr. Jekyll* (1960) Christopher Lee, Paul Massie, Dawn Addams. A doctor's experiment unleashes the dark side of his personality and creates a killer. Massie made for a very bland Dr. Jekyll and his interpretation of the role could best be described as awkward and wooden. There was no denying this movie was a treat as a rarely seen Hammer film, with the company's atmospheric sets and costuming creating the nice Victorian mood for which it was well-known. But as a horror flick, it was not the gripping tale of dual personality one would have hoped for. Hammer did a profoundly better job with *Dr. Jekyll & Sister Hyde*, whose sexuality gimmick was but one attention-getting element of a great horror story. C (Columbia/Hammer, color)

01/17 Looks like *Fright Night* was pre-empted for a telethon.

01/24 *Torture Garden* (1967) Burgess Meredith, Jack Palance, Beverly

Adams. A carnival sideshow hosted by the sinister Dr. Diablo allows patrons to see their futures. I don't recall any ordinary person getting his fortune told in a horror film that foretold of good things on the horizon. So it came as no surprise when this group of sideshow visitors had much to fear from Meredith's dire predictions. Meredith was always a fascinating actor to watch and he carried the picture well as a sinister carnie character. The stories (written by Robert *Psycho* Bloch) were a bit more cerebral than usual. I didn't really get the whole "look at the shears" gimmick, but it was still an absorbing movie. C (Columbia, color)

01/31 *The Night Evelyn Came Out of the Grave*

02/07 *Curse of the Fly* **(1965) Brian Donlevy, Carole Gray, George Baker. The son of a scientist whose attempts to conquer matter transfer ended with monstrous results carries on the experiments.** This was the third in a series of movies spawned by the original classic *The Fly* (1958), and while it didn't really cover any new ground, it was still a modestly entertaining sci-fi–horror hybrid. The moody lighting and photography and a few experiments gone horribly wrong gave the picture some pretty eerie atmosphere. It also sported a well-executed title sequence. C (Fox, b/w)

02/14 *Blood Beach*

02/21 *The Devil's Rain*

02/28 *Brotherhood of Satan*

03/07 *The Dark*

03/14 *Piranha*

03/21 *Circus of Horrors* **(1960) Anton Diffring, Jane Hylton, Erika Remberg. Escaping from a deformed patient threatening their lives, an unethical plastic surgeon and a nurse find shelter with a traveling circus.** Diffring as a mad doctor was, by now, nothing new, and neither were the circus confines in which this story took place. But it was a tight, enjoyable British thriller with a few good shocks and no matter how often the actor played the same role, it never got dull. Another film that had migrated over from a slot on Channel 11's *Chiller*. C (Anglo Amalgamated, color)

03/28 *Zombie*

04/04 *Great Alligator*

04/11 *Creature from Black Lake* **(1976) Jack Elam, Dub Taylor, Bill Thurman. Two college students trek into the Louisiana bayou to investigate reports of a huge hairy beast.** There was always something inherently creepy about bayou country, whether as a breeding ground for witches, murderers or even Bigfoot. However, after a promising start, the creepy factor quickly began to wane and the movie became mired in a swamp of dullness and uneventful searches for the creature. It could have been a fun cheapie, but the hard-to-see monster was relegated to a few flashbacks and a less than exciting finale. Co-star Dennis Fimple really got on my nerves with his over-acting. C (McCollough, color)

04/18 *Mystery of the Sacred Shroud*

04/25 *Hell Night* (1981) Linda Blair, Vincent Van Patten, Peter Barton. College students are stalked by a killer when they chose to spend the night in a mansion that was once the scene of a family massacre. A modestly suspenseful and atmospheric slasher flick that featured a cool Californian haunted house and a crazy monster hell-bent on murder. The house and tunnels beneath the mansion were extremely evocative and one immediately knew no good would come from this place. The premise may not have sounded original, but the delivery was surprisingly fun and it actually turned out to be something rare: a really good '80s horror flick with a wild finale. It reminded me of *Horror House*, but it was considerably more exciting. C (Compass, color)

05/02 *Happy Birthday to Me* (1981) Melissa Sue Anderson, Glenn Ford, Lawrence Dane. A young girl suffers blackouts and discovers that her friends are dying during each of her spells. This fairly ordinary slasher flick was pretty light on thrills and gore until a really nasty brain operation scene perked things up. A bit more thought-out than some of its competition. C (Columbia, color)

05/09 *What the Peeper Saw* (1972 aka *Night Child*) Mark Lester, Britt Ekland, Lilli Palmer. A disturbed young boy whose mother committed suicide starts a strange relationship with his stepmother, who begins to fear him. Channel 9 had to make do with a heavily censored version of this *Bad Seed* type of film which, in its original version, had plenty of nudity and uncomfortable sexual references. The movie was an interesting and obscure psychological thriller with lots of sleazy overtones that placed Lester far from the innocent trappings of his previous *Oliver!* fame. It was always great fun when a clean-cut star like Lester tried to break out and get in touch with his dark side and he gave his character a believably cold, evil edge. Britt was equally well-cast as the boy's fetching stepmother who had good reason to be afraid. A slow-building mood of subtle horror peaks with a neat, unexpected conclusion. (Leander/Leisure Media, color)

05/16 *Berserk*

05/22 *Up from the Depths* (1979) Sam Bottoms, Susanne Reed, Virgil Frye. A tropical resort is invaded by a huge shark-like creature that begins devouring tourists. The lush, Sandals resort-like locations of this Roger Corman–imported, Philippines-made *Jaws* cash-in were quite beautiful and, once again, a tropical paradise setting seemed like a good backdrop for a horror cheapie. But, a barely visible big rubber fish, some horrendous acting and goofy comedy chomped away at this silly thriller until nothing was left but bits of celluloid chum. Very, very bad in nearly every way imaginable, and a fine example of why *Fright Night* was sometimes referred to as "Crap Playhouse" by Channel 9 employees. C (New World, color)

05/30 Looks like *Fright Night* was pre-empted.

06/06 *The Visitor*

06/13 *Yeti* (1977 aka *Yeti — Giant of the 21st Century*) Jim Sullivan, Tony Kendall, Mimmo Craig. An enormous creature, half man and half beast, is unearthed from its tomb in an iceberg and brought to civilization, where it begins a rampage. An Italian-made exercise in total weirdness that was no doubt inspired by the Dino DeLaurentiis remake of *King Kong*. It had the look of a color Bert I. Gordon concoction. If you had the unique experience of seeing this movie, you had to wonder if they were really trying to make a serious scare flick or parodying the genre. Dubbed and very cheaply filmed, it was comparable to, but much blunter than, most Japanese giant monster films and was often extremely ludicrous to view. You really needed to be in the mood (or stoned) for something like this. (Stephano, color)

06/27 *Beast of Morocco*

07/04 *Grizzly*

07/11 *Island Claws*

07/18 *Dr. Strange* (1978) Peter Hooten, Clyde Kusatsu, Jessica Walter. A doctor with the powers of a sorcerer does battle with an evil enemy. Some occult overtones made this made-for-television superhero-style movie (based on a comic book) slightly more appropriate for *Fright Night* than, say, *Prisoner of the Lost Universe*. A big-screen, bigger-budget adaptation might have produced better results, but it wasn't really that bad. As the local newspaper would say, "Buy the premise, buy the flick." (Universal, color)

07/25 *Blood Mania*

08/01 *Ghoulies* (1985) Peter Liapis, Lisa Pelikan, Michael Des Barres. A young couple moves into a mansion that houses small, demonic creatures. It takes a whole different mindset to appreciate these slick but shallow '80s horror films. They seemed to lack the earnestness of their cheap predecessors and their calculated shocks quickly became familiar fare. Maybe I just couldn't get into the groove, but this corny, heavily overacted mess and its modestly animated, unsophisticated gremlins were just plain annoying. I'm sure I never made it to the end of this flick. C (Empire, color)

08/08 *Boy and His Dog* (1975) Don Johnson, Jason Robards, Susanne

Benton. **In a devastated post–World War IV world, a young man finds a strange companion in an intellectual dog.** *Newsday* said it was "a strange movie. And it is almost a good one." I agree. It's a bizarre, dark sci-fi comedy-drama with a young Johnson proving remarkably adept at handling an unusual man-dog relationship in a convincing manner. The film, sharply photographed and produced with a surprisingly slick look for an independent production, had a genuinely nasty edge to it too, with its premise of rape-driven males hunting for females. No doubt Channel 9 pushed the envelope a bit with this one. C (LQ/JAF, color)

08/12 *The Bees* **(1978) John Saxon, Angel Tompkins, Claudio Brook. A swarm of South American killer bees invades the United States, creating panic.** The black, smoke-like cloud of deadly bees darkening the skylines of various cities had a certain ominous look to it, but the movie was pretty flat on most other levels. Saxon carried his role with his usual authentic, controlled persona but miserable performances by other cast members and a campy, '70s porn-style music score wiped out most of the atmosphere. One of the most disturbing sights in the flick wasn't any bee sting victim, but rather aging co-star John Carradine's severely misshapen hands, the result of severe arthritis. But he was still the Carradine we knew and loved, and seeing him in anything was somehow reassuring. (Bee One/Zacharias, color)

08/22 *Deathdream*

09/05 Looks like *Fright Night* was pre-empted.

09/12 *Phantom of the Rue Morgue*

Channel 9 was about to completely change direction under MCA ownership, but the following two black-and-white drama films, perhaps a last gasp homage to days gone by, appeared in the *Fright Night* time slot and, by virtue of some of their genre elements, should probably be considered the final installments.

09/19 *Here Comes Mr. Jordan* **(1941) Robert Montgomery, Claude Rains, Evelyn Keyes. A prizefighter is killed before his time, so the powers from beyond permit him to return and inhabit a wealthy businessman's body.** Director Alexander Hall handled this lightweight fantasy with a subdued Rains and an often obnoxiously dense Montgomery making their way through an early adaptation of *Heaven Can Wait*. The after-death rules outlined in the movie seemed pretty simple but it took Montgomery and friends an annoyingly long time to get it. Nothing very special, and a rather big stretch to classify as a *Fright Night* feature, though it would have made a passable holiday special. Pleasant and harmless enough, but who wants pleasant and harmless on *Fright Night*? C (Columbia, b/w)

09/26 *Man of a Thousand Faces* (1957) **James Cagney, Dorothy Malone, Jane Greer. The story of silent film star Lon Chaney and his struggles both on and off the screen.** As a final bow for *Fright Night*, this homage to the man who really started it all in the early days of Universal seemed rather fitting. It was a tender, heart-tugging melodrama punctuated by a few quick makeup recreations of Chaney's most memorable film monsters (which, being markedly different looking from the classic Chaney versions, unfortunately failed to capture the power of the artist's original work). When the final credits rolled, viewers may not have realized it was truly the end of an era ... not just the silent era detailed in the picture, but the end of many, many wonderful years of late night movie madness on Channel 9. The show of a thousand faces, *Fright Night*, would be no more. C (Universal-International, b/w)

Index

205

Index